SYSTEMATIC PARENT TRAINING

PROCEDURES, CASES and ISSUES

WILLIAM HANSFORD MILLER

RESEARCH PRESS
2612 North Mattis Avenue
Champaign, Illinois 61820

Portions of the research cited in this book were supported in part by NIMH Grant 23275-01, 1R03
and Easter Seal Research grant N-7314.

Cover design / Steve McAdam

Dedicated to the well-adjusted and happy families in the community
who provide the standards for systematic parent training

CONTENTS

PREFACE

This manual is intended as a training text for professionals in the field of child mental health. As such, its fullest use will be possible for those readers who have some familiarity with social learning principles and procedures.

Readers who wish to refresh or develop their understanding of social learning concepts can readily do so by reviewing a number of excellent books in this area, such as *Elementary Principles of Behavior* by Whaley and Malott (1971) and *Behavior Therapy: Techniques and Empirical Findings* by Rimm and Masters (1974). The first book is an informally written, complete introduction to the scientific analysis of human behavior. The second book presents the current principles and procedures of behavior therapy in an extremely instructive and usable manner. Also, these and other basic texts can be utilized as reference resources as needed while the reader-practitioner begins to apply the interventions described in this manual.

The purpose and concern here is with *application,* not theory, although some readers may find evidence for an ideology of pragmatic procedures with mechanical means and relationship-minded goals. There has been an explicit attempt made to provide a coherent, step-wise framework for intervention procedures, and the guidelines are always based on demonstrated clinical utility.

This manual represents the accumulation of data and experiences from five years of clinical research in applying parent training procedures at the Neuropsychiatric Institute, UCLA. The original impetus for this research came from Dr. Martha Bernal, who was responsible for my "turn on" and early development in parent training. More recently, the presentation of this material in manual form is a result of the very responsive students at the University of Stockholm, who first suggested the idea of a training manual based on my lectures in Sweden in the summer of 1973.

In the production of this manual I owe a primary debt to Nancy Brown, whose typing, editing, support and endurance made the manuscript possible. Also, I wish to thank Drs. Stuart Greenberg, Fred Jones, Rolf Jacobs, and Susan Price for their valuable, constructive criticism and suggestions, and to many other colleagues and students who provided data, ideas and support throughout the years. Harriet Weiner, Maureen Duffy, Terry Fong and Sandra Moscovitch also provided much valuable support in data collection and reduction.

Finally, I am indebted to the referred families and the staff of the Children's Outpatient Department at the Neuropsychiatric Institute, UCLA, for making the family studies possible.

ONE / **INTRODUCTION**

Systematic parent training is one approach to the treatment of children with disturbing behavior. This book is intended for those who are presently utilizing social learning principles in intervening with families and children, and especially for clinicians and community agents of all backgrounds who seek efficient and effective alternatives to traditional modes of child therapy. Parent training is not for all families. However, when carefully applied in settings where the focus is on the therapeutic intervention with children and their families, the procedures and issues presented here can complement and enhance available clinical services. Furthermore, it is argued that, for many families who seek help for their children, systematic parent training is the treatment of choice.

PURPOSE

The purpose of this manual is to describe procedures that can provide effective child mental health care with a minimum of professional time and effort. The primary objective is the elaboration of a systematic method for parent-child assessment, intervention, and follow-up that can be utilized in child outpatient treatment facilities. As such, there is a constant emphasis on (a) a step-wise, flo-chart model of parent training; (b) the cost-efficient utilization of the available procedures; (c) the principle of accountability in the use of professional time; and (d) a widely applicable technology of parent training.

Sufficient experimental and clinical data are now available to organize and apply the methods currently used in parent training in ways that are *maximally effective* and *efficient*.

The flo-chart model structures the interventions according to their increasing complexity, professional expense and, to some extent, their impact on the family. However, the flo-chart is a guideline only, and does not limit the flexible and individualized use of parent training methods. The *cost-efficient* and *accountability* emphases also provide implicit guidelines for intervening in families, and help focus this manual on the application of systematic parent training as a low-cost treatment for large numbers of families with disturbing children.

A second objective is to present the principles and procedures in parent training in a way that will allow therapists to integrate these methods rapidly into their existing repertoires and conceptual frameworks. To facilitate the process, this manual contains many actual case examples of families viewed at different stages of the intervention sequences; they demonstrate both the successes and difficulties that all parent training therapists encounter. An additional advantage of the detailed case material is the demonstration of how the parent training therapist makes treatment decisions and judgments based on the family's week-to-week progress, which is not possible with the didactic material alone.

The third objective of this manual is the examination of practical issues found to be important in the application of systematic parent training. These issues, which will be represented throughout this manual, are examined in detail in Chapter 15. They are summarized below:

1. The assessment of deviant parent-child behavior.

2. The determination of goals in systematic parent training.

3. The determination of intervention outcome and the maintenance problem.

4. Individual differences in systematic parent training.

5. Future issues in systematic parent training.

TWO / BACKGROUND AND DEVELOPMENT OF PARENT TRAINING

THE NEED FOR SYSTEMATIC MENTAL HEALTH INTERVENTION

To date there have been few systematic efforts to develop effective mental health procedures. However, there is presently a growing conviction that relatively sophisticated *systems* approaches are required to understand and utilize the components of mental health care delivery programs (Rosenthal and Frank, 1956; Gottschalk, Mayerson and Gottlieb, 1967; Gelfand and Hartmann, 1968; Luborsky et al., 1971; Berkowitz and Graziano, 1972). It is generally agreed that the minimum components for such programs should include the following criteria:

1. Procedures to define and measure behavioral adjustment.

2. Procedures to produce desired behavior change.

3. Procedures to measure intervention outcomes.

4. Procedures to predict intervention outcomes for specific patient subgroups.

Each of these procedures has received attention recently from investigators attempting to develop more efficient means for intervening in families with problem children. A continuing difficulty, however, has been that, because of methodological problems, most research efforts in this field have not satisfactorily demonstrated the effectiveness of child intervention procedures (Gelfand and Hartmann, 1968; Pawlicki, 1970; Berkowitz and Graziano, 1972). There is some agreement that the minimal requirements of an adequate applied research design should provide for (expanded from Gelfand and Hartmann, 1968) each of the following steps:

1. Careful, objective pretreatment (baseline) measures of the focal symptom or behavior.

2. Systematic, independent variation of intervention procedures to demonstrate control over the patient's behavior.

3. Demonstration that observations of the patient's behavior are unbiased and valid.

4. Rigorous follow-up evaluation six months or more after the intervention is terminated.

The finding that none of the available published reports in family and child treatment met these requirements probably attests to the difficulties in using a "laboratory" model for studying families; but it may also indicate the need for intervention programs which specify the relevant treatment components in a systematic way.

ALTERNATIVES TO CHILD PSYCHOTHERAPY

Despite the methodological difficulties in family research, there are certain developments and trends which have been particularly important in the evolution of systematic parent training as an alternative to traditional child treatment. In recent years there has been a consensus that serious questions remain about the effectiveness of traditional child intervention and therapy practices (Levitt, 1957, 1963; Hood-Williams, 1960; Eisenberg and Gruenberg, 1961;

Creak, 1963; Eaton and Menolascino, 1967; Davids, Ryant, and Salvatore, 1968). Thus the original findings by Levitt (1957, 1963) that there is no scientific evidence to show that treated children improve more than untreated children continue to be reported in psychotherapy reviews (Rachman, 1971). As Hood-Williams (1960, p. 84) has noted, however, the available research as not *proven* that psychotherapy is ineffective (or effective), and these findings should be "a challenge to all workers in the field of child psychotherapy," indicating as they do that "present-day child guidance clinic practices are not highly effective in dealing with children's psychological malfunctionings" (p. 87).

At about the same time that child guidance practices were being critically studied several promising procedures, derived from social learning principles, were being utilized that suggested that effective interventions other than child psychotherapy were available (Ullmann and Krasner, 1965). These procedures, primarily contingency management and related techniques, have produced significant improvement in children with a variety of behavioral and emotional disturbances (Ferster and Simons, 1966; Werry and Wollersheim, 1967; Gelfand and Hartmann, 1968; Berkowitz and Graziano, 1972). Two unpublished studies comparing therapies have also shown that social learning procedures are at least as effective as, and perhaps more economical than, child psychotherapy in the treatment of such diverse clinical problems as extreme aggressiveness and mixed, "neurotic" disturbances (Humphreys, 1966; Link, 1968).

SOCIAL LEARNING
AND PARENT TRAINING

The initial controlled use of parent training was done by Hawkins, Peterson, Schweid, and Bijou in 1966. More recently, Bernal (1971, 1974) and Patterson and his associates (Patterson and Fagot, 1967; Patterson, 1969; Patterson, Ray, and Shaw, 1969; Patterson, Cobb, and Ray, 1973) have extended the application of social learning-based intervention procedures to the training of parents as therapeutic agents with considerable success. The training procedures usually have involved working with individuals and groups of families according to the following (from Miller and Gottlieb, 1974) steps and assumptions:

1. The documentation of appropriate and deviant child behavior before, during and after intervention, utilizing objective home, videotape, or clinic ratings by trained observers.

2. The application of intervention programs based on the assumptions that (a) appropriate and inappropriate child behavior is maintained by social agents (especially parents) who dispense important cues and consequences (reinforcers) for the child's behavior; (b) the family agents who dispense important reinforcers can be trained to alter the type and schedule of their reinforcement by using contingency management procedures. These procedures stress the contingent application of positive reinforcers by parents to produce positive parent-child interaction and to reduce disruptive behavior, and to produce consistency within and between parent functions; (c) this training may be generalized over time and stimulus setting so that the induced changes will be maintained.

3. The individualization of family programs based on week-to-week observations of family progress.

4. A team approach to intervention programs, i.e., each family's program is designed and engineered by professional and nonprofessional agents.

ADVANTAGES OF PARENT TRAINING

There are several reasons for conceptualizing the child's problem as a disturbance in the family social system and for training parents to produce the desired changes within the home setting. First, a number of studies have shown that normal and deviant child behaviors are largely under the control of reinforcements delivered by family members (Crandall, Good, and Crandall, 1964; O'Leary, O'Leary, and Becker, 1967; Patterson and Cobb, 1971; Shaw, 1971; Wahl et al., 1974). Therefore, in certain cases the most *direct* means of restructuring (treating) the child's disturbing behavior is through the parents. Second, the goal of all interventions is to induce desirable behavior which is *maintained after the treatment period is over.* Gelfand and Hartmann (1968, p. 210), reviewing recent developments in child behavior therapy, concluded:

It is likely that the best hope for permanent positive behavior change rests in modifying the client's social environment. In the case of children, it may prove more efficacious to modify the parent's child-rearing practices than to bring the child to the laboratory or clinic for direct interaction with the therapist. Parental education of this type may well have important preventive aspects also in that parents who are aware of the nature of their control of their children's behavior may be better able to prevent the occurrence of future problems and to promote appropriate interpersonal behavior.

Or, as Ferster and Simons (1966, p. 71) have put it: "Ultimately it is the parental environment which must maintain the child's behavior." Thus, following social learning principles, these investigators and others see the child's behaviors and attitudes, even when induced by treatment procedures in the clinic, as requiring *environmental* support for their maintenance.

A third reason for training parents as therapists is an economic one. Trained parents can reduce future child disturbances and mental health costs (Gelfand and Hartmann, 1968), and it has been found that advanced clinical skill is not required to effectively provide much of the necessary training. Technicians, trainees from various disciplines, and even parents themselves have taught child management skills to parents of disturbed or retarded children (Ryback and Staats, 1970; Bernal, 1971, 1974). This finding has potential significance for the improved utilization of professional time and effort and the less-than-fully-trained professionals in mental health delivery programs (Gendlin and Rychak, 1970).

TRAINING PARENTS IN GROUPS

Perhaps the most important development from efficiently providing child treatment through parent training has been the use of parent groups. Several studies have shown that parents trained in groups to produce desirable behavior in their problem children may do so as well as parents trained individually.

In the first group studies, Walder and his colleagues (Hirsch, 1968; Hirsch and Walder, 1969) initially taught parents the principles of contingency management. Then, when the parents learned how to apply the techniques to problems with their own children, they experienced almost uniform success, measured by videotape observations and parents' satisfaction reports. In the latter study (Hirsch and Walder, 1969), group size was studied, and equally effective child interventions were produced in nine weekly sessions in groups of ten and five families each as compared with "wait group" controls. Improvement in the referred child's behavior was reported in twenty-nine of the thirty families studied. More recently, Behrens (1970) compared individual and group parent methods to determine which procedure offered maximum benefit to the children treated.

Problem behaviors ranged from lack of self-help skills to sibling aggression. Using parent reports as well as pre- and posttests, the investigator found that both procedures produced significant improvement compared with an untreated group of parents with similar child problems. However, the individually trained parents required an average of twenty-four hours per parent to demonstrate competence (on the pre- and postmeasure) in using contingency management procedures, while the group-trained parents reached competence with only an average of *eight* hours per parent. Behrens (p. 32) concluded that "both training programs are equally successful in terms of gain scores," but "the amount of time saved by the group method is extremely significant." Also, it was noted that "by meeting as a group, the parents are given the opportunity to exchange ideas and to learn how other mothers deal with their children."

Other studies, although less well controlled, have also shown that parent group training is an efficacious method for improving the adjustment of retarded and emotionally disturbed children (Rose, 1969; Galloway and Galloway, 1971; Howard, 1970; Johnson, 1970; Peine, 1971). In each of these programs the group approach to training parents provided a low-cost, realistic means of producing therapeutic change.

Wiltz and Patterson (1974) reported the first investigation of the group parent training procedure that included direct observation of the child's behavior and functioning in the home. Studying two groups of aggressive boys (control and treatment groups), Wiltz measured changes in the proportion of observed deviant behavior of the child to his total social interaction in the observation period as a function of parents trained or not trained to use home contingency management programs. Intervention was found to produce significant decreases in deviant behavior in the treated group (assessed at five and nine weeks of treatment) as compared with baseline and untreated children's level of deviance. Similar excellent criterion measurement (via home observers) was used by Walker (1971) who compared aggressive and other deviant behaviors in children whose parents were group trained with a placebo group in which parents were given expectancies of success but not trained to use contingency management. Significant decreases in rates of targeted deviant behavior were observed only in the treatment condition. Also, contrary to the findings of previous reports (Levitt, 1957, 1963), both parent and home observer data showed *increases* in deviant behavior in the placebo condition.

The group parent training procedure studies cited here all support the utilization of this approach in settings where children are referred for the treatment of a broad spectrum of disturbances. With the development of direct home observation systems there is potent evidence from the home environment that improvements in a child's problem area can be actively induced by contingency management group intervention procedures. However, with few exceptions (Hawkins et al., 1966; Patterson, 1972), the studies found to date have failed to cite behavioral follow-up data indicating maintenance of induced change; success has usually been measured by improvements found at termination of treatment only.

SUMMARY

This overview of the development of parent training has emphasized the need for the systematic approach to the treatment of children who are disturbing to, and are disturbed by, their family environments. Also, although there are many limitations in existing parent-child intervention systems, there is clearly a major emphasis on the development of more *effective* and *efficient* procedures. This emphasis has resulted in new definitions for both these criteria. *Effectiveness* has come to mean not only a demonstration of intervention-induced higher levels of desirable interaction as compared with baseline assessment, but the autonomous maintenance of the desirable behaviors by family members at a time when the intervention agents are no longer present. Likewise, *efficiency* has been broadened to include the minimization of professional time and effort as well as the reduced cost to the family.

With this background in mind, the specific purpose of this manual may be restated as an attempt to provide a simplified, structured, and systematic organization of the available parent-child interventions so that effective procedures can have increased clinical, community, and research application.

THREE / GENERAL PARENT TRAINING CONSIDERATIONS

OVERVIEW

The procedures described are those which have been found to be effective for parents of outpatient children between the ages of two and thirteen years, and whose interaction disturbances are treatable by the parents in the home. Modifications of the interventions have also been successfully extended to inpatient and school settings.

All the assessment and intervention procedures described here for parent training were applied at the Neuropsychiatric Institute, University of California, Los Angeles. The clinical diagnoses varied from "severe adjustment reaction" to "schizoid," "minimally brain-damaged," and "delinquent," but all the children had very high rates of aversive behavior, especially aggression, destructiveness, and noncompliance. The children were usually referred by people in the local schools and by the parents who specified a number of disturbing behaviors they wanted decreased. However, as will be seen, both the presenting complaint *and* the interactional context of the child's problems within the family provided the focus of treatment.

PROVIDING EFFECTIVE PARENT TRAINING

Systematic parent training can be practiced by trained professionals and supervised paraprofessionals who work with children and families. In general, the procedures in this manual are effective even with the considerable individual differences in clinics, therapists and families. It may be useful, however, to enumerate some of the characteristics which can facilitate effective parent training.

Desirable clinic variables include staff openness to new approaches, and specifically openness to directive (as opposed to nondirective) treatment procedures. Systematic parent training requires active participation by the clinic staff. An atmosphere of free and constructive peer assessment, performance feedback and discussion is also important.

The methods used by a mental health clinic often reflect the attitudes of the community it serves. In settings where strong negative attitudes prevail about requesting help from mental health professionals any form of treatment may be difficult to apply. Parent training may be especially difficult unless representatives from the community, including previously successful clinic parents, are available to support and in some cases administer the actual training. If, of course, such direct community liaison can be established, then the procedures in this manual may have even greater value since more people will be available to provide the services.

Desirable therapist variables include all the characteristics usually associated with effective mental health treatment agents: empathy, a genuine desire to help others, and openness to constructive criticism. Systematic parent training is also facilitated by the therapists' personal motivation to constantly scrutinize and improve their work; to practice child and family treatment as a reeducative process requiring directive, active training methods; to seek and utilize community and paraprofessional help in parent training; and to provide some kind of documentation for their work in order to facilitate innovation and improvement.

An additional therapist characteristic of considerable importance in training parents is an awareness of *child development* principles. When developing optimally useful programs for children, the therapist is constantly required to help parents make decisions about *what behavior can be reasonably expected* of variously aged children. Experience and training in the accepted social, emotional and behavioral milestones of normal child development can greatly facilitate the therapist's application of parent training procedures.

Desirable family characteristics are the most difficult to specify. It is generally agreed, however, that the primary desirable family characteristic is *responsiveness to training* in at least one of the parents. Parental responsiveness includes the *presence* of parental characteristics such as a strong motivation to improve the family interaction, capability of functioning in a predictable manner, and sensitivity about other family members' needs. It also includes the *absence* of excessive rigidity about avoiding new methods of child rearing or maintaining negative, pessimistic attitudes about their children.

This manual, then, is for clinics, therapists and families who possess, at least in part, the desirable characteristics noted above. Strengths in one of these three categories can often offset weaknesses in another; parents with rigid negative attitudes can at times respond to intensive professional time and effort by very skilled therapists. Likewise, a rigid or confused clinic atmosphere can have a deleterious effect on many marginally motivated parents.

USING THIS MANUAL

The materials presented here are intended to provide *guidelines* for the intervention agent rather than a "cookbook" for parent training. Intervention agencies or agents usually already possess a practiced mode of operation and style of intervention and may be familiar with some of the parent training procedures. This manual of procedures attempts to help organize the services the agency provides to the community, and in some instances how the interventions are provided. Thus, because some intervention agents or agencies may be unfamiliar with the procedures, the manual will provide relatively specific information about their use at the Neuropsychiatric Institute, UCLA.

When using this manual, it will become apparent that effective parent training depends on two kinds of careful record keeping. First, at each point where there is an interaction between the therapist and the family, a record of the event should be made. This can be accomplished with minimum effort by constructing a chart with notations for date, place, type and duration of family contact, as well as an indication of which professional or paraprofessional made the contact. Second, progress records for the family are essential to provide weekly summaries of the family's current status in the program. Each week the therapist should summarize the data brought in by the family and add them to the ongoing family progress chart. *Only when records are available can the therapist properly assess the effectiveness and efficiency of treatment.**

To be maximally useful, this manual will include case examples to illustrate the effective application of systematic parent training. It is strongly recommended that those using the manual first *study* it carefully in its entirety, then attempt to *conceptualize* its application with families currently in treatment, and then perhaps begin to *gradually introduce* the various interventions until each one has been successfully applied. Finally, the systematic progression of interventions can be applied to an individual family or a small group of parents.

INDIVIDUALIZING PARENT TRAINING

In keeping with the cost-efficiency model presented in this manual it is important that families be treated with interventions appropriate to their particular needs. Some families respond to brief, simple interventions without involving the more complex treatments, while other families require more intensive and costly interventions.

In systematic parent training the emphasis is on the *criterion assessment* of family treatment response. In criterion assessment, a family's progress is determined by their weekly response to the interventions in effect at that particular time. Thus, in practice, treatment is truly "individualized" since the application of successively complex interventions is determined by the family's rate of progress.

The interventions in this manual should be utilized by having each family begin with "Social Learning Concepts" (Intervention I) and continue in a progressive fashion until they have approximated or achieved their intervention goal. Even in cases where it is estimated that the family has complex problems preventing rapid response to the simpler interventions, each of the procedures can be applied to (a) possibly alter severe current child problems, (b) provide additional information to the therapist concerning the adequacy of the child-rearing methods, and (c) provide a focus for later marital or individual parent treatments. The rationale for this step-wise approach to the interventions is also that when simpler, low-cost interventions are attempted first, little time is lost if they are insufficient, while much professional time and effort can be saved if the goals are met early in the treatment.

___

* The procedure for the therapist's "time and effort records" was suggested by G. R. Patterson at the Oregon Research Institute.

THE FLO-CHART MODEL

To facilitate the individualized application of the interventions, an idealized, hypothetical flo-chart is presented (p. 10) which summarizes the parent training procedures and the orderly progress of families through the assessment, intervention, and follow-up sequences. In practice, of course, treatment is not always orderly, and few families will require or should receive all the interventions and procedures described in this manual. The flo-chart is basically an oversimplified treatment guideline illustrating how the interventions in this manual are roughly organized according to the professional time and effort required to achieve the family goals.

The five major interventions which are discussed in systematic parent training are listed below:

I. Social Learning Concepts

II. Basic Discrimination Training

III. Home Contingency Program

IV. Punishment Procedures

V. Parent Counseling

These interventions will be identified in the flo-chart and throughout the manual by their numerals, e.g., Intervention I.

As shown in the flo-chart, there are several response levels indicating successful and unsuccessful treatment. First, the family can achieve their goals early, after Interventions I and II, and begin follow-up without further treatment. Second, problems remaining after Intervention II may require an *acceleration* procedure whereby low-rate behaviors which are incompatible with undesirable behaviors are increased in the Home Contingency Program (Intervention III). Third, if the acceleration procedures are ineffective or inappropriate, and a *deceleration* program is required to decrease intense disturbing behavior or interactions, then punishment procedures can be attempted (Intervention IV). In extreme cases a deceleration program may be necessary prior to any other interventions, such as when an intolerable behavior requires immediate reduction. Fourth, problems remaining after Intervention IV should be discussed directly with the parents in a series of parent counseling sessions focusing on the reasons for lack of success and, if necessary, a retrial of previous interventions should be recommended. These sessions, collectively referred to as Intervention V, can also be used to emphasize previous successes in parent training and to discuss methods to help the parents maintain treatment gains. Also, although it is not shown on the flo-chart, parent counseling can be utilized at any time during the treatment program when the parents' response to an intervention can be improved.

The flo-chart indicates how, after determining that family problems continue after the application of parent-child interventions, the focus of treatment may be changed to emphasize direct interventions for any or all family members. These more costly interventions may help prepare family members for a retrial or a continuation of systematic training procedures, if indicated. For example, occasionally a parent's progress in a given intervention may be enhanced by several sessions of individual treatment (such as desensitization or assertion training) or marital intervention. Thus, although the sequential order of Interventions I to V is important, any of these more intensive treatments for family members can be utilized whenever necessary to enhance a family's progress.

HYPOTHETICAL FLO-CHART FOR SYSTEMATIC PARENT TRAINING

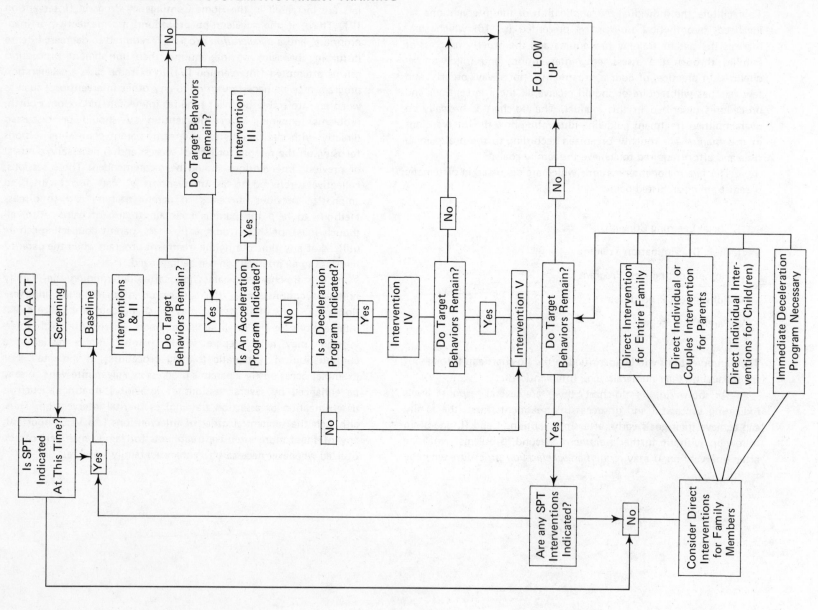

FOUR / PRETREATMENT PROCEDURES: Contact and Screening

The procedures in this chapter describe agency and family activities that are necessary to determine a family's suitability for systematic parent training.

CONTACT

The purpose of the initial contact is to arrange for screening procedures. The type of initial contact made between a family and the treatment agency depends on its location, size, and the type of services the agency provides. In larger cities and clinics families are often prescreened by other agencies, schools, or individuals and are finally referred to the clinic. In more rural settings a small community walk-in clinic often has families who are presenting their problems for the first time. While studies have not yet been made of possible urban-rural differences in families' responses to parent training procedures, the present system is designed to be applicable in many of the available child treatment facilities.

SCREENING

The purpose of screening is to assess the appropriateness of parent training as the treatment of choice when the family is referred to the clinic. In general, the procedures in this manual can be applied with any family whose reason for seeking help is to improve their child's adjustment or development, but the interventions here are especially effective when the child's problems are part of more general parent-child disturbances. In screening, a variety of procedures and materials are available to help determine the disturbing interaction patterns, actual and potential target problems, and personality and attitudinal variables in relevant family members (usually the referred child and his parents). Some of the suggested screening procedures are given below.

1. Physical examination for the referred child. Physical handicaps, sensory-motor problems, and transient medical problems can often contribute to a child's social difficulties and thus need to be carefully assessed.

2. Minnesota Multiphasic Personality Inventory (Hathaway and McKinley, 1943) for both parents. Important information about the parents' motivation to help their child and potential responsivity to treatment can often be assessed by the MMPI.

3. The Missouri Child Behavior Checklist (Sines et al., 1969) completed by parents for the referred child and one or more siblings. This checklist allows the parents to convey, in a relatively objective manner, important categories of recent and current disturbing behaviors in their children, and provides a rapid estimate of how parents see the referred child in relation to their other children. The behavioral categories on this checklist are aggression, hyperactivity, inhibition, somatic disturbance, sleep disturbance, and social maturity.

4. The Locke-Wallace Marital Adjustment Inventory (1959) completed by each parent. This procedure gives additional information about the likelihood that marital conflicts may interfere with the parent training.

5. Selected psychological tests to assess the referred child's mental, emotional and educational functioning.

6. Parental interviews, emphasizing the family behavioral and psychological history and current adjustment.

7. Direct observation of the family interaction, using a through-the-mirror observation room if available.

During the screening procedure it is very important that the therapist or intervention agent identify both *high-rate and low-rate* target behaviors. Examples of commonly observed problems which occur at a high rate (more than two or three times daily) are non-compliance, destruction of property, temper tantrums, negative verbal interaction, and excessively rough play and injurious behaviors.

Low-rate disturbances, which are serious because of the personal or social consequences, are lying, stealing, fire setting, running away, hair pulling, or sexual or drug problems. Using the present screening system with low-rate problems requires the therapist *to identify the high-frequency antecedents of the low-rate disturbance.* Thus it is assumed that infrequent behavior problems occur at the end of a chain of subtle but frequent activity (Patterson, 1974). Such behaviors as intense negative verbal interaction, criticism, or humiliation are examples of parent-child interaction sequences which often precede high intensity but low-rate behaviors. In these cases the probability of a serious behavior may be reduced by effectively intervening early in the emotional and behavioral chain (e.g., a family fight) which is terminated by the behavior (e.g., stealing). If these relatively high frequency antecedents of such intense or dramatic behaviors cannot be specified, then parent training may not be indicated since no meaningful baseline is possible. In fact, a good criterion for the appropriateness of systematic family intervention is that the intervention procedures here are intended for parent-child problems, including their relevant antecedents and consequences, that have a good chance of being documented using the available baseline procedures.

All the behavioral disturbances described above represent the most common presenting complaints in child treatment agencies, and all are examples of *behavioral excesses.* An additional area of concern to many parents and therapists is *behavioral deficits.* Many children are described as inadequate in the performance of various skills, having poorly sustained appropriate play or attention span, are socially withdrawn, or under-achieving in school. It is important that the therapist identify the referred child's deficit areas since both *acceleration* (behavior shaping and building) and *deceleration* techniques are emphasized in systematic parent training.

After the family has completed the screening procedures, the therapist should judge the suitability of systematic parent training and, if it is indicated, present this modality to the parents as the recommended treatment. When the parents express their willingness to participate, the therapist can plan the treatment with the family by specifying (1) the primary areas or daily periods which are currently disrupted due to inappropriate behaviors or interactions involving the referred child, and (2) an understanding of the unique clinical and historical factors which allow maximum individualization of the treatment plan.

SCREENING: CASE ILLUSTRATIONS

THE BA FAMILY: INTRODUCING SCREENING PROCEDURES

The BA family came to the clinic with the primary complaint that their six-year-old daughter, Beth, lied constantly at school and at home, was aggressive toward her five-year-old brother, and had frequent episodes of screaming and tantrums. Beth was an "affectionate, normal" child until age four when she became "sassy" with her mother and angry at her brother. Mr. A typically left all discipline to the mother and his work schedule prevented him from spending much time at home. Mrs. A resented having to do all the child rearing alone, but felt that Beth would be too much for any parent. The problem of lying had recently become much worse.

In a brief intake interview the parents had difficulty being specific about Beth's behavior. In the second interview, Mr. A was absent without explanation, and the therapist attempted to elicit more information from Mrs. A to determine the appropriateness of systematic parent training for this family. The therapist had considered, after the first visit, that parent training might be indicated for this family; the remaining questions were: Could the mother describe Beth's problems in more specific terms? Did she accept any of the responsibility for Beth's problems? Was it likely that the child's disruptive behavior could be effectively understood by studying the current family interaction? Were both parents willing to come to the clinic for ten or more visits and to follow the therapist's suggestions concerning how to better manage and help the child? "Yes" answers to each of these questions would not necessarily indicate success in parent training, but could provide a basis for accepting the family for this type of treatment.

Therapist	How are things this week?
Mother	About the same. Beth is driving me up a wall with her lying and bothering her brother. Why does she do that?
Therapist	We all want to find that out. Why don't we see if we can describe her lying point by point so that we can better understand what is going on. How often does she lie?
Mother	All the time. At school, with friends, wherever she is.
Therapist	When did she lie the last time?
Mother	Well, I caught her several times this morning.
Therapist	Please pick one instance and tell me about it.
Mother	It's hard to think of just one example. It's just her constant exaggeration and denial of what she's done, even when I catch her.
Therapist	I see—you confront her with something she's done, and she denies it.
Mother	Yes. She blames her brother or even says I did it. I don't know what's got into her lately.
Therapist	What did Beth say this morning that was untrue?
Mother	She lied about where she left her coat. She said she put it in the closet, and then made everyone late this morning. I found it outside and she said her brother took it out. I know she was lying because I've seen her do it many times. When I accused her, she started screaming and kicking and calling her brother names.
Therapist	Then what happened?
Mother	I spanked her and she started screaming at me. I was so mad I didn't know what to do. Every day it's the same.
Therapist	What happened next?
Mother	She made us all late. I picked her up, put her in the car, and took her to school. If she hadn't lied in the first place, none of this would have happened.
Therapist	What did your husband say about all this?
Mother	Same as usual. He said there was nothing wrong with Beth and that it was my fault for screaming at her. Then he left. I couldn't help it; the angrier I get, the more she aggravates me.
Therapist	You were screaming, too?
Mother	Of course. Wouldn't you be angry if your child lied to you? I can't cope with a child who lies.

Therapist	I see what you mean. Is the morning family period often as difficult as it was this morning?
Mother	Yes. It's been getting worse since she was about four.
Therapist	Any idea why it started getting worse?
Mother	No. Like I told you last week—she was not a naughty child. She used to be affectionate toward me and especially her brother. At first, when she was almost three, she wouldn't listen. Then she started being a troublemaker. She provokes everybody. She has absolutely no response to me but she wants affection—but I don't trust her. None of the kids want to be with her. After an hour they want to go home.
Therapist	What happens?
Mother	She controls them—can't stand to be second or share anything. But my husband says she doesn't have a problem.
Therapist	It sounds like you and your husband have a difference of opinion about Beth.
Mother	Not really. He just contradicts me on discipline. He undermines my punishments.
Therapist	Like how?
Mother	Well, I will admit I'm inconsistent too. Like the one-month punishment.
Therapist	What's that?
Mother	I caught Beth lying last week and restricted her for two weeks. Then when she screamed names at me, I made it a month. But then she was so sweet this weekend, I backed down. Isn't that awful?
Therapist	How do you usually punish her?
Mother	Spanking, restrictions, I've tried them all. Maybe I expect too much from a six-year-old. What do you think? Am I unreasonable to want her to be a good child?
Therapist	Of course not. Now let's go back for a minute. You must have thoughts about how Beth got to be this way—so oppositional. What do you and your husband think may have started all these problems?
Mother	I don't have any idea where her problems came from. I don't think she's a bad kid. She just started doing things to provoke me. Then after a while I started losing control and—I admit—sometimes I call her names, too.
Therapist	What do you think Beth will be like in a few years?
Mother	I hate to think. I know she needs help; that's why I'm here. I'll do anything to help her.
Therapist	What do you feel she needs?
Mother	Try a new set of parents (laughs). No—seriously, I think you should try to help her.

Therapist	Well, we talked a little already about our approach in treating these kinds of problems. Basically we think the therapy should take place in the home, where the problems are. I must tell you that it's possible that, without working on your relationship with Beth, any other treatment might not work.
Mother	What do you mean? My husband will never come.
Therapist	Here's my plan. First we have some questionnaires for you and your husband. I also want to meet your whole family. I'd like to set up a meeting for all of you to come in together at least once. Also, I'd like to get some tests done with Beth to see how she sees her problems and the rest of the family. But our treatment will be primarily through you and your husband. We'll need to meet for about ten times, on a weekly basis. If we can help you with this approach, we'll all know by then. What do you say?
Mother	I'll have to talk it over with my husband. What if he won't come?
Therapist	Then we'll do whatever we can for you when you come in. But we prefer to see you both.
Mother	I'll do anything you say. I just can't cope with her anymore by myself.

This interview was the final session required for the screening period since the therapist had accomplished his three goals: assessing the appropriateness of the case, eliciting an initial (although tentative) commitment from at least one parent, and planning the course of assessment and intervention. Mrs. A, with some help from the therapist, was able to begin specifying Beth's problem behaviors. However, her difficulty about being specific, together with her tendency to blame others for her difficulties with Beth, indicated that the treatment would have to focus on Mrs. A's problems as well as Beth's.

The screening tests supported the interview material: Beth was slightly above average in her development in all areas except social maturity. She felt a mixture of anger, affection, and confusion about her mother, little feelings for her father, and resentment toward her brother. The mother's testing revealed her to be a rather rigid, angry woman who had a very negative image of herself and who might resist therapy if it became too intrusive. She also reported a number of problems in her marriage in addition to the child-rearing issue. On a behavior checklist the mother reported a severe degree of behavioral disturbance in Beth, especially in aggressive behavior, and excessive shyness in her son. The father refused to take any tests.

Comment. The BA family illustrates many of the family attributes seen in children's clinics: an elementary school age child with average intelligence and a number of high-rate aversive behaviors, together with parental ambivalence and inconsistency about the target child and a willingness at least to try an intervention program. It is also not uncommon for the referred child's father to deny or fail to perceive any problems in his child. However, most fathers agree to participate in the screening and at least support their wives' efforts in the treatment.

THE MS FAMILY:
THE NEED FOR ABBREVIATED SCREENING

Mike, a two-and-one-half-year-old boy, was brought to the clinic by his mother who had been referred by her pediatrician (she was eight months pregnant). At the initial interview the mother appeared with Mike, saying that her husband wanted to come but couldn't get off work. A clinic volunteer was found to stay with Mike while the therapist interviewed Mrs. S.

Therapist	On the phone you sounded upset. Can you tell me about the problems you're having?
Mother	I can't handle it. Mike is scaring me to death. He says he's going to kill my baby. You've got to do something. (At that moment the volunteer knocks on the door and comes in saying she can't handle Mike's hitting her. Mike then runs into the room, snatches the therapist's note pad, and runs out again. Mrs. S runs after him, screaming for him to come back. They both return in about five minutes and the notebook is retrieved.)
Mother	(Holding Mike in his chair) Now you sit there and don't move—do you hear me?
Mike	(Laughing hysterically) No—no—no!
Mother	Doctor, do you see what I mean? (She then sits in the chair, holding Mike closely and rocking him.)
Therapist	Mike seems to be settling down now. Does holding him in your lap seem to help?
Mother	It's the only thing that works. If I put him down, he goes wild.
Therapist	Try making him sit by himself for a few minutes.
Mother	OK. You'll see. Mike, sit beside me in your own chair and be quiet while Mommy talks to the doctor. (She puts Mike in the chair and turns away. Mike jumps up, grabs the therapist's notebook again, and throws it into the wastebasket.)
Therapist	(Deciding to try *his* authority) Mike, come over here this second. Bring me that notebook. Right now! (Mike responds by laughing and bringing the wastebasket over and throwing it into the therapist's lap.)
Mother	You asked for it. Now you see why the pediatrician said he was going to be a madman. (She picks Mike up and holds him; he becomes relatively quiet, although he is squirming.) Mike, be careful not to hurt the baby.

Comment. The MS family illustrates what might be called a child-clinic emergency since the usual order of procedures has to be dispensed with and an intervention initiated immediately. For this reason the contact and screening procedures both occurred in a single abbreviated session, and the more complete screening activities were postponed until the immediate problem was treated. However, the therapist had the relevant material at hand to make a decision about proceeding with treatment: the child exhibited high-rate aggressive and destructive behavior that, at first look, appeared to be maintained (reinforced) by the mother's positive physical attention, and the mother was urgently asking for help. The therapist could plan to direct the intervention toward an initial deceleration program for Mike's behavior to reduce the mother's stress, and then later to develop the parents' management skills more systematically.

THE FJ FAMILY:
USING DIRECT OBSERVATION

Mr. and Mrs. J were referred to the clinic by their pediatrician who felt that their thirteen-year-old boy, Fred, was emotionally disturbed. At another clinic Fred was diagnosed as "presociopathic" and "impulse-ridden" with a "poor prognosis." He was said to be obsessed with sex and to lie constantly about his sex and drug exploits. During the intake session it was learned that family problems were much more general, involving constant negative interaction between Mr. and Mrs. J and Fred, as well as Fred's brother, age 11, and his sister, age 10. Both parents described the family life as having deteriorated in recent years, but "unbearable" at the time of referral. The therapist then met individually with Fred. While he verbalized his awareness that his family had many problems, Fred spent most of the time detailing his rather spectacular adventures, and seemed to be trying very hard to impress the therapist with the idea that he had no problems himself.

The family interaction was viewed in a clinic room through a two-way mirror in the second session. The problems described by the parents were all observed. There was a high rate of teasing and fighting among the children, and intermittent criticism and interrogation of Fred by the parents; at other times Fred and his siblings were completely ignored. In the third session the parents came in to discuss a preliminary disposition.

Therapist	How are things going this week?
Mrs. J	Much, much better. (Addressing Mr. J) Don't you agree? They're settling down quite a bit.
Mr. J	Oh, yes. The session last week seemed to help my wife a lot. She's really been on the kids this week.
Therapist	That's very interesting—we didn't talk much at all last week. We just observed you from behind the mirror.
Mrs. J	Yes, but I learned a lot from that. I think that recently I have dropped out from mothering and accepted the turmoil since my screaming at them hasn't worked. Last week I tried to put myself in your place while you were watching us, and all I could see was our saying "Don't do this" or "Don't do that" all the time and never following through. And I didn't like that at all. This week I tried following through each time they disobeyed—either by sending them to their room or with a strap. And they're much better. Much less teasing and griping about everything. But they still have a long way to go.
Therapist	Well, I'm certainly glad things are better.
Mrs. J	Oh, much better. We're really glad you're helping us.
Therapist	How else can we help you? We don't feel like we've done much yet—except try to list the problems you're having at home.
Mrs. J	Well, I know we have a lot more to do. My husband and I both need help with cutting down on all the fighting around the house. And Fred is about to get kicked out of school again, too.

The remainder of the interview was spent more clearly specifying the behaviors to be worked on and planning the initial steps in the baseline and intervention procedures.

Comment. With the FJ family the therapist was able to elicit the necessary information to accept the family for parent training in a relatively brief period. The behaviors pinpointed by the parents in the first session were observed in the clinic observation. The parents also indicated a need for assistance, and a tentative treatment plan was formulated. In this case, however, the therapist was curious about the mother's "insight" and initiative. Early indications of *parental initiative* often correlate with positive treatment outcome, but in the FJ case the child was relatively old, had a history of poor adjustment, and had been given a bleak prognosis in another clinic. It could not be known for certain if the mother was extremely responsive to even minimal "interventions" or if her "insight" was actually an indication of her desire to do all the work herself, thus perhaps indicating *nonresponsiveness* to the treatment ideas of others. Based on the screening observations, however, and the largely positive results of Mr. and Mrs. J's personality testing, the therapist accepted the family for a parent training program which involved all members of the family.

THE JB FAMILY:
SCREENING FOR A CHILD WITH MULTIPLE HANDICAPS

Mrs. B came into the clinic after several years of trying various treatments for her eight-year-old son, Jim, an only child who was mildly retarded, showed residual signs of cerebral palsy, and who had a history of chronic vomiting and behavior problems. The pediatric clinic could find no physical cause for the vomiting and referred Mrs. B to the children's psychiatric clinic. The therapist had discussed the problem briefly with Mrs. B over the phone, and had learned that she recently decided to try again, after numerous failures, to have Jim treated for the vomiting. During the initial interview the therapist attempted to determine the antecedents and consequences of the vomiting episodes.

Therapist	I've read Jim's pediatric chart and I see that his difficulties seem to be getting worse. Can you describe for me in your own words what the problem is?
Mother	Do I have to go through that again?
Therapist	I know you've done this many times—just try to tell me about Jim's problem.
Mother	Well, it's this vomiting thing.
Therapist	OK. Now I see you've been concerned with his vomiting for some time.
Mother	That's right, since birth. Jim has always had lots of problems. Even in pregnancy. Then not only was I having a hard time with Jim, when he was young, but there were marital problems, too. Finally I couldn't stand Jim's father running around and divorced him when Jim was seven.
Therapist	What have you tried before to help Jim with the vomiting?
Mother	A lot of different doctors with a lot of different advice. But he still vomits as much as ever. Lately it's more at school but they say they are taking care of him all right. But I keep hearing that there is no medical reason for it, so I'd like to do something to stop it.
Therapist	Fine. Now let's try to be as specific as we can about the vomiting problem. Please try to describe the last episode in detail.
Mother	OK, it was one week ago. It started, I think, when I told him on Monday that he was going to visit his father on Saturday.
Therapist	What tipped you off that the episode was beginning?
Mother	Jim said, "I don't want to go with daddy to the park." That made me begin to worry. Then the next morning, when I called, there was no answer and he wouldn't get up. Then I knew it was starting.
Therapist	What happened next?
Mother	I went into his room and found him drooling. He asked for some milk—he always does before vomiting—but I said I would bring him only some crushed ice. He said no, then

agreed, and I took him some ice to chew on. Then I started taking the TV out of his bedroom.

Therapist   Why?

Mother   He likes to have it there and I thought if he was thinking about losing the TV he wouldn't make a mess.

Therapist   Then what?

Mother   He said, "Are you taking away my TV?" I said I was. Then I told him I was going to work and for him to stay at home. Before I left, I got out his pads.

Therapist   His pads?

Mother   Yes, his pads so he wouldn't mess up the bed. I have to put them everywhere.

Therapist   Had he made a mess yet?

Mother   No, I put out the pads and left for work. Then I sneaked back in at lunch time, and he was still in bed. He had messed up the bed, floor, everything.

Therapist   Then what?

Mother   He asked for milk, but I gave him more ice. Then I cleaned him and the room, took his temperature, and went back to work an hour and a half late. When I got home later, he had made another mess. It's typical; once he starts it, it goes on for days like that.

Therapist   Is that the pattern?

Mother   Yes—first he gets upset, stays in bed, asks for milk, I put out pads, and then it's putting out pads and cleaning up over and over for several days.

Therapist   What's the first sign of an end to the episode?

Mother   He asks for food.

Therapist   Did he this time?

Mother   His grandmother cooked him some cabbage and it stayed down after he ate it. He also lets me know by greeting me when I come home. Then I know for sure it's over.

Therapist   What does he say?

Mother   General talk—he asks for his TV, and I give it to him.

Therapist   Then what?

Mother   Well, the next morning was Saturday, and I was afraid that he would mess up and not go with his father.

Therapist   What happened?

Mother	I woke him up on Saturday and he said, "Do I have to go?" I said he did. Then I told him to get ready and I left the room. Then when his father came he was dressed but still in bed. I got mad and told him to go, and he did.
Therapist	Then what happened?
Mother	I finished cleaning up his room.
Therapist	Is that the end of the episode?
Mother	Well, before he left he started to gag and I was afraid it was starting again. I told him to stop and he did. But when he came home the next day he was in a bad mood and got into bed. He started to gag again.
Therapist	Like before?
Mother	Yes, but I told him this time that he would have to be well or go to the hospital. Then he asked for milk but I told him first he would have to get out of bed and get dressed. He did, so I gave him some milk and bread.
Therapist	Does he mind you most of the time?
Mother	Yes, I would say he does.

During the remainder of the interview Mrs. B elaborated other problem areas in her interaction with Jim, mostly focusing on her indulgence of his lack of independent self-help skills. For example, Jim did not like to do anything for himself, and would have a tantrum which Mrs. B would terminate by giving in. Also, Jim was very demanding. One of his favorite ploys was to disassemble a toy and then manipulate his mother by demanding and whining for her to fix it. Mrs. B described herself as unable to deal with Jim when he started a tantrum.

Comment. The JB family illustrates one of the most difficult and challenging problems in parent training: the low-frequency, high-intensity aversive behavior. Following the conceptual framework presented earlier in the chapter for low-rate, high-intensity problems, the therapist attempted to determine *the chain of events* which led to vomiting. While the therapist could only speculate at that time, it was possible that Mrs. B was providing the important cues for many steps in the chain. The interview revealed the interactional context of the aversive episodes, as well as the negative, coercive atmosphere of the entire mother-child relationship. For example, it was likely that Jim's high-rate aversive behaviors, such as demands for attention, tantrums, and diversionary tactics, were maintained (positively

reinforced) by the mother's indulging consequences for these behaviors, and that her indulgence was maintained (negatively reinforced) by Jim's termination of the aversive behavior.

This analysis of Jim's problems, together with the mother's apparent high degree of motivation, provided a sufficient rationale for accepting Mrs. B for parent training.

SUMMARY

A simple Yes-No decision about applying the parent training method is not always as straightforward as presented here, but the therapist should seriously consider this approach in dealing with families who have problems similar to those described in this chapter. Many therapists would unhesitatingly consider psychodynamically oriented marital, child or family psychotherapy for these families, even though the evidence concerning the results of the traditional therapies in child guidance centers is not generally supportive.

This manual describes interventions which may not only be the treatment of choice for selected families, but can be applied and tested in a relatively brief period utilizing, to a degree, paraprofessional assistants. In such cases, the more complex, costly procedures can be delayed until specifically indicated, such as when systematic parent training procedures are shown to be ineffective.

FIVE / PRETREATMENT PROCEDURES: Baseline

PURPOSE

The purpose of the baseline in systematic parent training is to document, prior to treatment, the frequency and intensity of the disturbing behavior patterns pinpointed in the screening interviews. These procedures are important for several reasons:

1. They provide a basis for determining where to start in the intervention sequence that is based on the pretreatment level of parenting skills and child behaviors.

2. They provide support and clarification of the parents' stated problems.

3. They provide an estimate of daily variations in the problem areas.

4. They provide a record with which to compare the treatment effects and follow-up adjustment at a later period.

5. They begin the family intervention program with a structured record-keeping system which itself can significantly improve interaction patterns and help achieve intervention goals.

BASELINE TECHNIQUES

There are five specific techniques which can help determine the baseline behavior frequencies prior to intervention. These are (1) playroom observation, (2) home observation, (3) videotape analysis, (4) parents' home records, and (5) parents' responses on behavior checklists.

The first three procedures are primarily used to study the sequences of family interaction which will help determine the antecedents and consequences of the problem areas. Important chains of parent-child interaction to be studied include the *antecedents and consequences of the target child's compliance, aversive behavior, appropriate play and positive verbal interaction*. Playroom observation of the family is the least costly procedure to assess these behavior chains, but suffers from poor reliability and validity. Home observation can be the most "scientific" and reliable, but its merits are offset by the high costs of training home observers. Videotape analysis allows the most careful scrutiny (via playback) of the family interaction patterns, but requires expensive equipment.

The fourth method, parent home records, deserves careful consideration for two reasons. First, the majority of all published reports of parent training have relied on parent records for the "proof" of the intervention effectiveness (or lack of it). Its *advantages* include (1) helping the parents focus directly on daily problems in their own as well as in their child's behavior, (2) partial validity, since the parent records the same disturbances previously pinpointed during screening, and (3) very little professional time and effort. *Disadvantages* are (1) the records have poor reliability, caused by bias and fakeability, and (2) some parents are poor record keepers, for many different reasons.

Second, while at least one of the first three baseline methods discussed above is necessary to provide an objective, *independent* estimate of the family's interaction problems, daily parent records are in fact essential to Intervention III, the Home Contingency Program. As will be seen, the Home Contingency Program requires baseline parent records of a selected "disruptive time of day" which are then used to restructure the child's or entire family's behavior patterns. The parent records used in the Home Contingency Program are constructed to minimize the parent bias and record-keeping difficulties noted previously.

21

A different type of parent records is also available, and may be assigned to the parent during screening or baseline when continuous daily monitoring of a target child's behavior is desirable. In this procedure the parent can make hourly tallies of the child's behavior during specified daily periods. The results are subject to poor reliability, but when the therapist clearly defines the target behaviors, as with the Home Contingency Program, they can provide a useful estimate of the child's behavior. Also, the parent should be asked to make informal comments along with his or her tallies in order to provide important contextual information as well as particular perceptions of the daily events. These daily records are tedious to maintain, and they are best used by the parent(s) for only a few weeks during the baseline period.

The fifth method requires the parents to complete behavioral checklists for each of their children. The validity of behavior checklists is questionable, but the opinions that the parents have about the referred child relative to others in the family can be an important baseline measure. Often, changes in the parents' ratings of the referred child during treatment reflect the development of significant positive attitude change, which is seen in many successfully treated cases. Several behavior checklists completed by the parents in screening, such as the Missouri Child Behavior Checklist, can serve a dual function by determining the appropriateness of systematic parent training, and by providing pretreatment estimates of the parents' judgments of the child's problem areas.

BASELINE:
CASE ILLUSTRATIONS

Three cases are presented to describe the use of various baseline procedures preparatory to systematic parent training. While some of the cases involve the use of fairly sophisticated methods, such as home visits with raters or clinic videotape analysis, it should be noted that these procedures are not always necessary to provide the minimum baseline material required to begin treatment. In practice any objective assessment of the family interactions and attitudes prior to treatment can be used in most cases with good results. The only requirements are that the therapist (a) arrange the family interaction in such a way as to elicit behaviors which represent the family problems, and (b) categorize and objectify his observations in order to understand how the family members are influencing each other. Relatively more skill and experience are required when making a single observation in a playroom, but with practice in observing and recording important interaction sequences, the therapist can gather the needed information in any setting.

THE WS FAMILY:
VIDEOTAPING THE PARENT-CHILD INTERACTION

Mrs. S, a divorced young woman, was self-referred to the clinic. She was concerned about her six-year-old twins, Nancy and Wyman. Both children had always been "defiant" and recently had become unmanageable. Their school teacher also was concerned about their limit testing and lack of response to directives. During screening it was found that Mrs. S was unstructured in her management attempts, almost never had any positive interaction with her children, and had more difficulties with Nancy than with Wyman. The baseline procedure was introduced to Mrs. S at the end of the screening interview.

Therapist	Well, I have a pretty good idea what some of your difficulties are with the children at home. I agree that you need some help with them, and especially with Nancy. Now we've talked a little about our approach to these problems. In the time remaining today I think we should plan our work for the next few weeks.
Mother	The sooner the better. What should I do?
Therapist	Well, the next step is for us to have a good look at the problems you've been telling me about. First, we need everyone to come in next week so that we can make a videotape of you and your children. We have a room which is furnished somewhat like a playroom or living room. With the camera behind a window we can make a tape of you playing with Wyman and Nancy. It will take about 45 minutes. What do you think?
Mother	It sounds all right. But what if they don't behave?

Therapist	That's all right—we need to see how difficult it is for you. The tape will let us know where to start in our treatment program. After we have made the tape, we will need you to keep some records at home for a week or so on the kids' problems. Then we'll go over the tape and other materials together to see what we need to do to help you.
	(The following week Mrs. S came in with her two children, and they were directed into the clinic studio room. Toys were made available for the children and Mrs. S was taken outside for her instructions.)
Therapist	Mrs. S, what we want you to do now is to be in the room with your children for about 45 minutes while we make a videotape. We want everything to be as natural as possible, but there will be three parts to the session. Here is our plan for today. First we want you to play with the children any way you like for about 15 minutes. Then instruct the children to play together while you read your magazine. Then, about 15 minutes later, ask the children to pick up the toys. Don't help them, just try to have them clean up their toys by themselves. When everything is cleaned up, have them sit quietly until we come in. OK? Do you have any questions?
Mother	No, we'll do our best.
Therapist	Fine. Just try to spend the time here as you normally would at home.

Following the taping session, the therapist viewed the tape and recorded the frequency of parental commands, child obeys, and parental consequences for obeys for the three periods, which were roughly about fifteen minutes each. A time sampling scoring system was used whereby only the first observed behavior per category was recorded for the designated observation interval (in this case fifteen seconds). Also scored, using the time sampling system, were the children's rates of aversive behavior and appropriate play, together with Mrs. S's consequences for these behaviors. Graphs were then made to summarize the WS family's interaction prior to the interventions.

The points in Figure 1 (p. 24) were determined by averaging the observations for each behavior category for each fifteen-minute period. Each point reflects the percentage of fifteen-second intervals containing a behavior. Both children complied at a relatively low rate and their mother provided positive attention for the obeys at an even lower rate.

Figure 2 (p. 24) shows that the rates of aversive behavior for both children were quite high (relative to other referred children). Aversive behavior, which included verbal and physical aggression and destructive behavior, was observed to occur about once every three minutes for Wyman and once every minute and a half for Nancy. Most of the aversive behavior was shouting and criticism, although there were several occurrences of hitting and knocking down block constructions by both children. Mrs. S responded in some way to over 75% of the aggressive and destructive behavior, usually by mild threats, pleas for the children to stop, and criticism. Figure 2 also shows that the children's rates of appropriate play were fairly high, but Mrs. S ignored the appropriate play of both children.

As emphasized in Chapter 2, the use of social learning principles assumes that both desirable and undesirable child behaviors can be maintained by parental consequences. In the WS case it was clear that the mother attended to aversive behavior in an ineffective way, but did not praise appropriate play or compliance; yet noncompliance was her primary complaint. It was apparent from the baseline videotape that the mother's ability to understand and discriminate desirable from undesirable behavior would need improvement, and changes in the timing and frequency of her contingent, positive attention could then result in changes in the children's behavior.

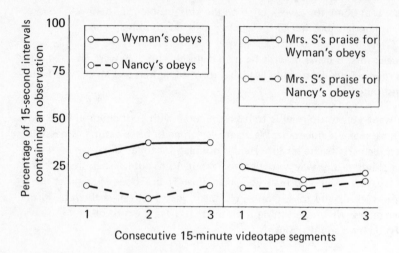

Figure 1   Baseline Compliance Variables for Wyman and Nancy S

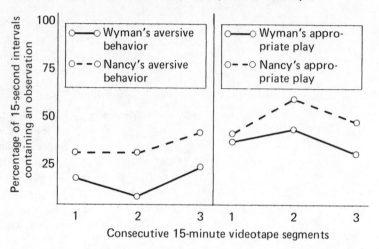

Figure 2   Baseline Rates of Aversive Behavior and Appropriate Play for Wyman and Nancy S

THE DA FAMILY: USING DIRECT HOME OBSERVATIONS

Mr. and Mrs. A were referred to the clinic by a friend. They were concerned that their youngest child, Danny, was becoming too aggressive and "wild." Danny, age 5, had a brother 7, and a sister 9. The screening interview indicated that the parents were particularly concerned about Danny getting into trouble at school for excessive swearing and hitting. He was described as always having been active, and much more so than his siblings. The mother, especially, was eager for treatment, and felt that she might be contributing to his problems since she tended to "favor" Danny. The interview material supported this hypothesis since both parents described themselves as very indulgent and reluctant to set limits, and quite adamant about wanting their children to develop "freely." Parental inconsistency was also a possible issue since the father reported no trouble with Danny at home while the mother, home all day, felt that life with Danny was a "constant struggle," and that recently she had resorted to spanking, but without results. Likewise, on the behavior checklist, Mr. A saw Danny as very active and extremely socially mature, while Mrs. A described Danny as extremely aggressive and destructive, but only moderately mature. It appeared that while they both saw many of the same behaviors they interpreted and responded to the behaviors differently.

In the DA case no problem was presented requiring urgent

attention, and the difficulties were longstanding, involving the parents' strong attitudes about child rearing. Therefore it was decided to use the baseline period to make an intensive study of the family interaction, focusing first on the mother-child relationship. The baseline was a two-week period in which the mother kept daily records in two-hour blocks of time while observers went to the home at a designated "difficult" time to record the interaction. Figure 3 shows the mother's home records on aggression, swearing, and screaming for fourteen consecutive days.

Each point represents daily totals for about seven or eight hours of observation. The rate of punishment (spanking) is not shown, but was administered one to two times daily. The most deviant overall period (not shown here) appeared to be immediately before school, although the afternoon period was the peak for swearing.

Three home visits were made during the two weeks that the mother kept home records, about four days apart. The home raters were trained to agree on at least 80 percent of their observations using a recording system similar to that described above for the videotape scores. Figures 4 and 5 show the results of the home observations.

Figure 4 shows that Danny had a relatively low rate of compliance, and that Mrs. A, like Mrs. S in the previous case, provided very little positive attention for compliance. Assuming that com-

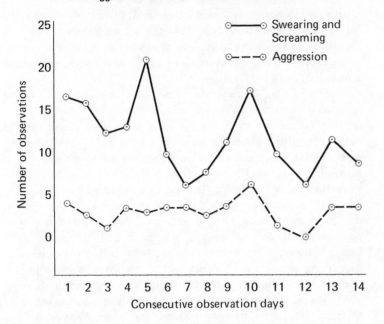

Figure 3 Daily Totals of Danny's Swearing, Screaming and Aggression (Mrs. A's Home Records)

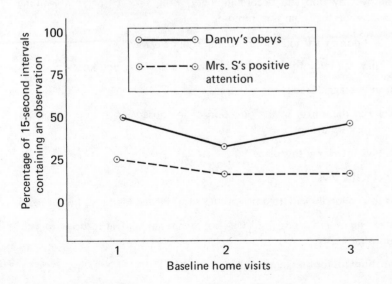

Figure 4 Danny's Obeys and Mrs. S's Contingent Positive Attention

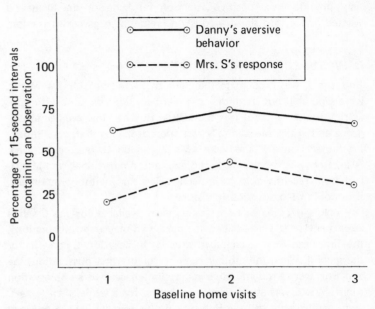

Figure 5 Danny's Aversive Behavior and Mrs. S's Contingent Nonpunitive Attention

pliance, like any other behavior, increases when it is followed by praise, it was no surprise that Mrs. A was experiencing a problem with *noncompliance*. Figure 5 shows the value of studying the sequence of parent-child behaviors. Relative to other cases with home data available, Danny's rate of observed, aversive behavior (sibling aggression, verbal and physical; tantrums; and destructive behavior) was quite high. Here the mother attended to Danny by turning toward him and attending in a nonpunitive manner following more than 70% of the aversive behaviors. Mrs. S was probably inadvertently maintaining the very behaviors she wished to decrease *by providing inappropriate consequences*. Other indications of the problematic mother-child relationship in the home data, not shown here, were (a) a moderate rate of appropriate play (45%) by Danny, but very little contingent praise from his mother, and (b) an extremely low rate of positive verbal interaction between Danny and his mother.

Both forms of baseline information data gathered in the DA case, the mother's records on the child and the observers' records on the mother-child interaction, supported the need for intervention. Also, the initial *direction* of the treatment was indicated by the baseline material. While the other family members, especially the

25

father, would play a later role in the treatment, *the initial goal was to help Mrs. A learn how to alter Danny's behavior.* The training would help provide more positive attention for behavior she liked and wanted to see, and simultaneously decrease the negative interaction.

THE BL FAMILY: USING DIRECT PLAYROOM OBSERVATIONS

Bob, age 7, was brought to the clinic by his mother. Mr. and Mrs. L were separated but the father still spent considerable time with Bob. During the screening it was found that Bob had low average intelligence and visual and auditory reception problems that were impairing his schoolwork and were serious enough to require tutoring. Also, Bob was reportedly withdrawn and oppositional, and Mrs. L had been recently told by a pediatrician that, without treatment, Bob would become seriously disturbed.

No videotape or home raters were available for the baseline assessment so it was decided to make two playroom observations, the first with Mrs. L and then attempt to have Mr. L come in for the second. When the mother came in for the first observation, she and Bob were brought into a playroom adjacent to an observation room. Mrs. L was asked to play with Bob for a while, then to read alone, and finally to have Bob pick up his toys. Using the one-way mirror and a speaker system, the observers could see and hear the interaction. The observers used a record sheet marked off in fifteen-second intervals to note (1) Mrs. L's directive, and whether they were initiating or terminating, specific or nonspecific commands; (2) the child's compliance to the directives; (3) the child's whining; (4) any appropriate play; and (5) Mrs. L's consequences to each of the scored child behaviors, in terms of positive or negative attention, or no attention. The observers also made informal notes during the interaction.

The session immediately began with problems. Bob didn't want to go into the playroom and, upon entering, began to whine and beg his mother to leave. She appeared desperate and tried to pacify him with promises to leave "in a little while." When he persisted, Mrs. L came to the door, and when the therapist went around to meet her, she said she didn't think she could keep Bob in the room since he was so upset. The therapist indicated that it was very important to complete the session, and for her to encourage Bob to stay by playing more actively with him. She returned and tried again, engaging Bob successfully in a game available in the room. Later, however, when she tried to read alone, Bob began whining and crying again, trying to get in her lap. After a while Mrs. L relented and let him sit in her lap while he sucked his thumb. After about ten minutes she told him to clean up his toys and to get ready to leave. Bob again started to whine, and when she repeated her directive, he went to the corner of the room and sat next to the wall whining. The following interaction then took place:

Mother   (Suddenly moving over by Bob and becoming angry) Bob, I'm sick of your whining. Now get busy and clean up the room this minute!

Child   You can't make me. I don't want to be in this dumb room anyway.

Mother   I can't help that. They want you to do it so do it now. I'm the boss, you know.

Child   No, I'm the boss, and you can't make me.

Mother   (Glancing frantically at the mirror in the direction of the observers) If your father was here he'd make you pick up the toys.

Child   But he ain't here. I want to leave this place.

Mother   Not until you pick up the toys.

Child   (Suddenly begins to cry loudly and hold his mother's leg) Please, Mommy, I want to go.

Mother   (Looks exasperated, sighs, and holds Bob) Oh, Bob, what am I going to do with you? Why won't you do what I ask?

Child   (Does not respond, hugs his mother, and continues to whine)

After a few minutes, Mrs. L picked up the toys herself and the session ended shortly thereafter. She was encouraged when told by the therapist that the observations would be very useful in helping her and that, if possible, she should bring her husband the following week so that the therapists could meet and observe him with Bob. She agreed this would be important, adding that she knew she did all the wrong things in the session, but didn't know what else to do.

After summarizing their observations, the therapists were able to confirm their informal hypotheses and to better understand the problems Mrs. L and Bob were experiencing. First, Bob complied with only 20% of his mother's directives, which were almost all nonspecific, and presented in a context of complaining. Second, Mrs. L's high proportion of ineffective initiating commands reflected her inability to get Bob to *initiate* activity, which contrasted with many clinic parents whose commands are largely worded to *terminate* some aversive activity. Third, Mrs. L attended to every instance of noncompliance by repeating the command, criticizing or threatening Bob, *while ignoring all of Bob's approximate obeys.* No positive interaction or praise was noted, except for the positive physical attention (hugging) which appeared to be contingent upon whining and crying.

In summary, Bob appeared to control his mother through *coercive interaction.* Mrs. L was negatively reinforced by Bob's reduction of oppositional behavior, and Bob was positively reinforced by his mother's delayed but predictable physical attention. It was clear that Mrs. L was caught up in a negative cycle, and saw Bob's behavior as almost totally aversive; and this attitude in turn interfered with her ability to identify the desirable behaviors which did occur. The therapists also noted Mrs. L's feelings of inadequacy, as well as her behavior deficits; she had appealed to both her husband and the therapists for support and a rationale for having her child pick up the toys. She was very much aware of the constant control struggle between herself and Bob, and seemed helpless to improve the situation.

The next session, with both parents present, also provided useful baseline material. Mrs. L was subdued and, each time she tried to interact with Bob, Mr. L criticized and contradicted her. Mr. L was also strict and domineering toward Bob and, after a few minutes of play, Bob began to whine. However, Bob complied with over 60%

of his father's directives in the session, although Mr. L used threats of punishment rather than praise to maintain compliance. In general, the interaction between Bob and his father was negative (very little positive verbal interaction was scored), and Bob spent most of his time sitting quietly by the wall.

It was important in the BL case to supplement the playroom observations with other available materials, such as the behavior checklist and parents' home records. The parents showed many areas of attitudinal inconsistency on the behavior checklist, with Mr. L reporting a high rate of aggression, and Mrs. L emphasizing somatic problems and inhibition. Also, Mr. L's overall responses indicated that Bob was doing well and did not have any serious problems. The two-week home records, kept by Mrs. L and her mother, showed that Bob had more than two tantrums per day, was compliant for his grandmother but not his mother, and had a consistently high rate of whining every day.

SUMMARY

The cases presented here illustrate the two types of baseline procedures which are recommended for each family treatment program. First, *independent assessment of parent-child interaction* and *target behavior problems* should be made utilizing home or playroom observations, or videotape analysis. Second, some kind of *parent reports* should be used, such as checklists and home records.

It should be noted that baseline techniques can be applied prior to any intervention in systematic parent training. The screening procedure provides baseline material in the behavior checklists and to a degree in the interviews; Intervention III has its own baseline in the initial private parent records of the Home Contingency Program; and the use of a punishment procedure (Intervention IV), which often is not indicated until later in the training, requires its own baseline. Thus, while the term "baseline" implies that a pretreatment period is set aside for certain procedures, *in practice any intervention, whenever used, requires some indication of what is going on before it is applied.* All forms of record keeping discussed here for the parents or the children, whether for specific interventions or the entire treatment, are important in assessing the effectiveness and efficiency of systematic parent training.

SIX / INTERVENTION I: Social Learning Concepts

PURPOSE

The purpose of Intervention I is to assess and improve the parents' understanding of basic social learning concepts.

DESCRIPTION

One of the defining characteristics of systematic parent training is the involvement of parents in all phases of the decision-making aspects of the child's or family's treatment. This process begins with the first family contact, but in Interventions I through V a major concern of the therapist must be sharing his treatment rationale with the parents. Parents may be better able to generate effective interventions on their own at a later time if they have some intellectual appreciation for *why* the therapist is directing the treatment in a certain way.

In practice, any available means may be used to convey and test the introductory concepts of social learning, which include the basic ideas about how family members influence each other through (a) prompts, cues, expectancies and rules; and (b) behavioral consequences (positive and negative attention and the absence of attention). A number of agencies have had success using Patterson and Gullion's *Living With Children* (1968), Patterson's *Families* (1971), and Becker's *Parents Are Teachers* (1971). Basic concepts of social and nonsocial reinforcements and extinction are presented in these books along with guidelines for best applying the procedures. In *Living With Children* each chapter has built-in tests of mastery in the form of statements requiring a response by the reader as each concept is presented.

The following social learning concepts summarize the major general ideas covered in these books and in other sources. Specific procedures for applying social learning concepts are discussed in the following section and in the next chapter.

1. *Interaction patterns are learned.* Interactions which constitute the relationships between people are based on learned behavioral, emotional, and attitudinal patterns.

2. *Interactions are maintained in present relationships.* These patterns have been learned in the past, but are often maintained by current, ongoing interactions with others who are significant. Thus, the relevant historical aspects of a given interaction pattern are continually being replayed in the present, and do not require extensive analysis in order for the interaction to be improved.

3. *Interaction patterns can be changed.* This *situational* description of learned desirable and undesirable behavior means that in any given interaction the contributions of relevant social agents (family members) can be studied and used to improve future interactions.

4. *The "Law of Reciprocity."* This social learning concept includes the following ideas:

   a.   If a person wants a positive input from another person, then he must give one first.

   b.   If a person gives a negative input to another person, then he must expect one in return. In short, "if you want a positive, give one; and if you give a negative, expect one."

The challenge for social learning therapies is the nonparity of positive and negative exchanges; a negative input is far more likely to be reciprocated than a positive input (Raush, 1965; Wills, Weiss, and Patterson, 1974).

5. *The Praise, Ignore, and Punish rules.* Successful social learning therapy is defined by an increase in observable positive family interaction and a concomitant decrease in negative interaction. At its simplest level these changes in systematic parent training depend upon the gradual development of the parent's application of the praise, ignore, and punish rules.

a. The praise rule. When a behavior or interaction occurs that a person likes and wants to see more of, he should respond with positive attention.

b. The ignore rule. When a behavior or interaction occurs that a person does not like, but does not warrant negative attention he should turn away and not respond to the other person.

c. The punish rule. If *any* attention is directed toward a person engaging in intolerable behavior, that attention must be negative and function to reduce the future occurrence of that behavior.

SUGGESTED APPLICATIONS

First, the therapist should explain to the parents in the first session, after baseline information is collected, that the next phase of their treatment will involve introduction and review of the procedures used in their family's treatment.

Second, the parents can be asked to purchase (or borrow) a copy of *Living With Children* and read it separately, *writing out* all answers on a separate sheet of paper.

Third, the therapist should emphasize that the parents' understanding of the ideas in *Living With Children* is essential to their further treatment and that they should call for their next appointment when they are ready to come in and discuss the book. If they do not call after one week, the therapist can contact them to arrange for a specific date when the book should be read.

Since parental response to the therapist's assignments is a major indicator of the treatment prognosis and also correlates highly with the treatment outcome, the response to the assignment of *Living With Children* is a good initial test of the parents' willingness to work for their family's improvement. In cases of parents with poor reading skills, *Living With Children* can be read to the parents and discussed in the same session.

Fourth, when the reading and test assignments are completed, and the parents come in to discuss *Living With Children,* the therapist can have them focus on portions of the book which remind them of their own family difficulties, and he can encourage them to verbalize the ways in which the techniques of praising and ignoring behaviors can be effectively utilized in their family.

Many families may be unaccustomed to taking an active role in their own treatment, and may resist the discussion of social learning concepts; but it is crucial that the importance of *active involvement, completion of "homework" assignments,* and *ongoing discussion of family progress* is conveyed to the parents early in the intervention sequence. Concepts presented above that are not included in the parents' readings should also be emphasized in the discussions.

ASSESSMENT OF INTERVENTION I

Following each intervention in systematic family training, it is important to assess the family's response to the treatment as well as the cost in professional time and effort to the therapist and agency. The therapist should carefully evaluate the records for each intervention in order to improve his methods and his effectiveness. In Intervention I, answers to the following questions can provide some indication of the family's progress.

How did the parents (and other family members) respond to the therapist's requirements (attendance, initiating discussion, and written answers to Living With Children*)?* Often, parents who are initially prompt and cooperative in systematic parent training continue to be "motivated" and treatment-oriented in later interventions. Also, parents who are frequently tardy and make many excuses for failure to complete their work may resist important suggestions later. If resistance to the therapist's assignments is encountered, it should be dealt with as it occurs, by an open discussion of possible alternative means of accomplishing the particular goal. It should be emphasized to the parents that *their cooperation in following the therapist's suggestions is essential in successful parent training.*

After the discussion of social learning principles, did the parents demonstrate an understanding or a mastery of the concepts? No particular psychological background or sophistication is required to master social learning concepts. If the material is presented clearly and succinctly, most parents will have no problem relating the ideas and examples in *Living With Children* to their own family. However, if parents do fail to comprehend the ideas which are basic to parent training procedures, the material should be rearranged and re-presented until all the relevant points are made. Some families have trouble relating written material to their life situation; others may find the ideas totally new or alien, and sometimes threatening. In these cases additional demonstration and supportive discussions for the parents may be necessary.

What were the effects of Intervention I on the family's interactions in the home? Did the parents' home records reflect any changes in the rate of target behaviors? All assessment in Intervention I should be brief since the social learning principles are usually presented as early as the third family session, often in conjunction with basic discrimination training (Intervention II). Each of the measures used to establish the baseline should be examined for possible changes. If the parents are keeping daily records on a few behaviors, the week following the discussion of social learning principles and *Living With Children* may reflect some change. If baseline home visits were made, there often will be observable changes in the parents' behavior although the intensity and duration are usually not sufficient to effect changes in the behavior of the children.

SUGGESTED PROFESSIONAL TIME AND EFFORT

In practice, Intervention I should not require more than two sessions and can be accomplished by any person experienced in the application of social learning principles to family problems.

SEVEN / INTERVENTION II: Basic Discrimination Training

PURPOSE

The purpose of Intervention II is to assess and improve, if necessary, the parents' ability to discriminate and respond appropriately to their children's behavior. An additional purpose is to prepare the parents for the Home Contingency Program (HCP) and other interventions where it is essential that family members know how to identify and respond to behaviors they like and do not like.

DESCRIPTION

As noted previously, Intervention I is concerned with the review of the basic principles underlying all the procedures in systematic family intervention. The common goal of these procedures is *to develop in the parents an awareness of their own importance in producing and maintaining desirable and undesirable behaviors in their children.* Intervention II involves the active application of these ideas, and is based on the assumption that effective child management and development depends, among other things, on the parents' ability to (a) perceive the subtle aspects of their children's desirable and undesirable behaviors, and (b) provide the appropriate consequences for the behaviors in a contingent (conditional) fashion.

All parents, prior to training, use the procedures emphasized in basic discrimination training to some degree, usually in patterns they themselves were exposed to as children or have learned by trial and error to be successful. Basic discrimination training attempts to improve existing parenting skills by helping parents understand the rationale for, and the correct use of, discriminating and responding to their children's behavior. Intervention II assumes the presence of the parents' motivation, cooperation, and potential to function consistently. If these important attributes are not present, the therapist should attempt to discover this early in the intervention sequence,

and the deficits should be worked on prior to, or concomitant with, basic discrimination training using parent counseling (see Chapter 12).

Intervention II developed from the observation that parents have only three major ways of responding to their children's behavior: (1) with positive attention, (2) negative attention, (3) or no attention. Thus, regardless of the child's behavior, a given parent's response can be conceptualized as occurring in one of these three categories. The specific goal of Intervention II is to insure that the parents are aware of *when* and *how* to respond positively, negatively, or not at all to their children's behavior.

This process of developing stimulus-specific responding is called *discrimination training.* For example, in the presence of a particular stimulus (the child's desirable behavior) a particular parent's response (e.g., praising desirable behavior) is reinforced (by the therapist's praise to the parent *and* by the child's increased desirable behavior) and learned, while a previous response (attending to undesirable behavior) is extinguished (by the parent becoming aware of its ineffectiveness and no longer responding). Simply put, in this example the parent learns to *ignore* what previously received attention, and to *praise* what was previously ignored. This parent is said to have *discriminated* the conditions under which a certain response will predictably yield desirable consequences, and the sequence will tend to be repeated when the parent is confronted with similar circumstances in the future. The process is of course not a novel one since all family interaction, both positive and negative, has developed and is maintained by discrimination learning. All people continuously teach those about them the conditions under which certain behaviors will be followed by positive, negative, or no attention. An effective school teacher clearly communicates to her pupils the kinds of responses that she will praise; the factory foreman teaches his subordinates how much they can "get away with"; and ineffective parents may communicate that the only way their child can receive their undivided attention is to have a tantrum, or to use forbidden language.

In systematic parent training effective treatment depends first on the parents becoming aware of their importance as dispensers of different kinds of attention, which produces and maintains significant behavior patterns in their children. The *modification* of undesirable child behavior then proceeds by the modification of the parents' discrimination skill; and the parent-child interaction can rapidly go from negative to positive as the parents discriminate and respond to desirable child behavior with positive attention rather than the previous negative attention or ignoring. Also, the dyadic, dynamic nature of parent-child interaction means that altering the parent's discrimination ability simultaneously alters the child's discrimination behavior. In successful training the parent learns that the child's behavior stimulates the parental response of "praise" rather than "ignore" or "punish." Likewise, the child learns that a certain parent behavior (and later the parent's presence) is a signal to behave appropriately rather than inappropriately; both parent and child are said to be under stimulus control of one another.

It is very important that this reasoning be explained simply and carefully to the parents prior to any attempt to alter their standards of responding to their children's behaviors. Assurance should be given that while the purpose of the procedure is to help them improve their parenting skill, their judgments will be respected.

SUGGESTED APPLICATIONS

The application of basic discrimination training consists of two main parts: baseline assessment and feedback training. Initially it is important for the therapist to determine the parents' present standards, consistency, and the timing of their positive and negative attention and ignoring for their children's behaviors. Then the therapist can utilize a "feedback" or practice-correction method to improve these primary parenting skills.

In practice there is rarely the opportunity to clearly separate the two activities of baseline and feedback in basic discrimination training. Both usually occur in the same treatment session since the therapist should provide immediate feedback (praise or correction) for strengths and weaknesses in the parents' behavior. Nonetheless, it is important that some type of baseline assessment be provided so that the effectiveness of the interventions can be measured.

ASSESSMENT OF DISCRIMINATION SKILLS

The following guidelines contain suggestions for assessing how the parents are functioning prior to intervention on the discrimination skills required in systematic parent training, together with methods for improving their abilities if necessary. It should be noted that the basic method for discrimination training applies equally to therapists, parents, and children; therapists may wish to use these guidelines to refine their own discriminative skills prior to introducing these procedures to the parents.

Any one of several treatment settings can be used for examining and developing basic parenting discrimination skills; the present procedures were developed in the home and in the clinic.

Videotape observation. If videotape facilities are available, the therapist can make a one-half-to-one-hour tape recording of the entire family using the procedure (abbreviated if necessary) presented on page 22. Basically, this procedure involves arranging the family interaction in the video or playroom so that the therapist can observe (a) the *nonstructured* interaction as it might occur at home with the parents interacting with the children, and with the parents engaged in another activity such as reading or talking to each other while the children play; and (b) interaction *structured* by the therapist (e.g., requesting the parents to have the children pick up the toys) to increase the likelihood that parent-child problems will occur. Later, with the parents and therapist viewing the tape together, the therapist should first pick out particular child behaviors and ask the parents to verbalize whether they should praise, ignore, or punish those behaviors.* The material on the tape can then be used to facilitate the behavioral practice exercises discussed in the guidelines below.

Playroom observation. If no videotape is available, a playroom observation can be made approximating as closely as possible the procedures for the taping activity described above. An observation room with a two-way mirror can be used to view family interaction unobtrusively. First, the therapist should have the family members interact while the therapist and one parent view the action together. Using the procedure described for videotape, the therapist should pinpoint behaviors and behavioral sequences and have the parents verbalize how they would respond. For example, the therapist can

---

* The initial systematic use of videotape feedback in parent training was developed by Martha E. Bernal at the Neuropsychiatric Institute, UCLA.

first pick out and label ongoing desirable behaviors (see list on page 36) and ask the parent how he or she would respond if they were in the room. Next the parent can pick out desirable behavior without cues from the therapist while the therapist records his agreement or disagreement with the parent's judgments. This procedure can then be used for "ignorable" and "punishable" behaviors and, finally, for whatever interaction occurs in the room. After one parent has practiced identifying particular behaviors vicariously with the therapist for a few minutes, the observing and the observed parent can exchange places and one can try the improved tracking and responding skills with the child(ren) while the other observes and rehearses the procedure with the therapist. A more direct but expensive method is to use a hard-wire "bug-in-the-ear" apparatus whereby the therapist communicates his suggestions and feedback to one or both parents from a microphone to a small earplug speaker. When playroom observation procedures are used, several training sessions are often necessary.

Home observation. If no two-way playroom for observation is available, representative family activity can be arranged in a large clinic room or in the home. Without interacting with the family, the therapist can observe carefully and record the parents' methods and timing when responding to their child's behaviors. The therapist may provide direct comments on the family interactions at a later time, or discuss his observations with the parents immediately following the observation period. By using this procedure for two to four sessions, it is possible to obtain baseline information in the initial session and then provide feedback training *during* the later sessions with the entire family observing. Additional sessions may be required for families whose members react excessively to the therapist's presence.

FEEDBACK TRAINING

Verbal rehearsal. Whichever setting is used for the assessment of the parents' skills the therapist should, early in the training, introduce the importance of parental consequences (reviewing social learning concepts) and the different categories of child behaviors that "earn" particular parent responses.

The therapist should define *praisable* behavior as that which the parents like and want to see more of, *ignorable* behavior as that which is inconsequential or which the parents do not like but is not serious enough to require the parents' attention, and *punishable* behavior as that which the parents would ordinarily punish. In each of the treatment settings discussed several examples should be available in the family interaction for praising compliance, approximate compliance, appropriate play or positive interaction; for ignoring roughhousing, mildly disturbing attention-seeking behaviors, or whining and crying; and occasional examples for responding negatively to destructive or aggressive behaviors or continued noncompliance or limit testing. The therapist can acknowledge and support the parents' appropriate decisions and have them verbalize, according to the definitions above, why a particular choice was made. If the parents disagree with the therapist's judgment, the therapist should verbalize the reasoning for his opinion, and try to reach some mutual decision about the appropriate response.

Several sessions may be required for the parents to attain the ability to rapidly recognize and verbalize the appropriate consequences for any given behavior they observe in their family. Reference to examples given in *Living With Children* and the therapist's other family treatment experiences may facilitate the parents' acceptance of this approach to improving family interaction.

Behavioral rehearsal. As soon as the parents have demonstrated the ability to correctly *verbalize* appropriate responses to their child's behavior, the therapist should introduce procedures for *behavioral practice*, which is a major modality for all the interventions in systematic parent training. There are three features of behavioral practice which are of special significance in training parents to effectively provide consequences for their children's behavior.

First, *all interventions, including basic discrimination training, attempt to increase positive family interaction and should emphasize positive reinforcement skills early in the practice sessions.* Just as the therapist praises the parents for achievements and effective parenting behavior prior to correcting faulty habits, the parents should demonstrate the ability to provide effective positive attention *before* working on the supplemental skills of ignoring and punishing.

Second, *the therapist must be active and convincing in his demonstration of appropriate parental consequences.* Most parents learn best when the therapist *shows* them, rather than tells them, what to do.

Third, *the therapist must carefully structure his training procedures.* The degree of structure required is determined by the degree of difficulty the parents experience in learning the skills. For example, some parents may need only a brief demonstration and some discussion about the timing of their consequences for behavior. Others, however, may require several sessions of highly structured role playing and clinic practice, beginning with the simplest aspects of praise.

INCREASING DESIRABLE BEHAVIOR: POSITIVE ATTENTION

The following guidelines summarize the important features discussed here concerning the use of positive attention and praise in training parents, including techniques for teaching parents *how* to praise, *what* to praise, and *when* to praise.

1. *How to praise.* The therapist can initiate behavioral practice for improving positive reinforcement by helping the parents (a) identify praisable behavior, and (b) provide positive attention by turning toward the child, establishing eye contact, and pleasantly delivering verbal and physical praise. The timing, wording, and manner of effectively delivering praise often require careful attention and practice. For example, parents who are just learning to use praise effectively often have a tendency to "spoil" the positive effect of their responses by adding a habitual criticism, like "that's good—now why couldn't you do that before?" The therapist can help parents learn to listen to their own responses to their children, and learn to communicate clear and simple positive messages. Much variation in the timing of praise is observed even in parents of nonreferred children, but immediate reinforcement after identification of praisable behavior should be emphasized. Also, the wording of a praising response can vary a lot and still prove effective; the only guideline for the wording is that a positive unambiguous message be conveyed to the child as he responds in a way the parents like and want to see increase in frequency.

2. *What to praise.* Parents should praise any behaviors they like and want to see more of, such as:

   a. Compliance to the parents' directives.

   b. Approximate compliance.

   c. Age-appropriate play and task performance.

   d. Pro-social peer and sibling interaction.

   e. Positive verbal interaction.

   f. Self-initiated positive responses to others.

   g. The conspicuous absence of unwanted behaviors.

3. *When to praise.* Parents should praise behavior in the above categories immediately contingent upon their occurrence, if at all possible. If immediate delivery is not possible, delayed praise is also effective since the predictability of praise is probably as important as its immediacy. The schedule or rate of praising is important. In training, praise should be delivered virtually every time a behavior being accelerated occurs, even if initially the process is somewhat artificial. Later the schedule can become intermittent as less praise is required to maintain the desirable behavior.

Many parents rapidly learn the concepts and techniques of praise, and in these cases it is not surprising to observe significant behavior change in the referred child as the parents apply their skills in the home. However, other parents require considerable structure in the training methods before they are proficient in discriminating praisable behavior and dispensing contingent positive attention in an effective way. With these parents the therapist should be prepared to use a gradual, step-wise procedure, such as the following:

1. Training the parents to verbalize how, what and when to praise.

2. Role playing the verbal skills until they can satisfactorily apply positive attention in a contingent fashion.

3. Arranging a playroom situation in which a light or sound signal (using the bug-in-the-ear device) is presented by the therapist to cue the parents to praise their child.

4. Repeating the playroom interaction without the cue until the parents have mastered the *in vivo* application of positive attention.

The family observations in the clinic and home will provide many examples of child responses where the parents have the opportunity to identify and attend to desirable, and approximations of desirable, behavior. Common problems seen in family interaction, and alternative patterns which the parents can learn and apply, are described in the following three case examples.

EXAMPLE A

The child is hyperactive and has no sustained play. During the session she often scribbles briefly with a crayon, then jumps up and runs about the room. The parent has rehearsed the use of praise to increase appropriate play, and now tries to implement it with her child.

Interaction		Comment
Parent	(Sitting near child) Susan, sit here by me and draw a picture of our house. I'll help.	Parent prompts child to produce praisable behavior.
Child	(Picks up crayon and makes a few marks)	
Parent	(Begins to draw) Very good. Tell me if you need help.	Initial praise is for any approximation of sustained play. Parent also models desired behavior.
Child	I can't draw a roof (begins to get up).	
Parent	Susan, sit down. That's it. Now watch me draw a roof on my house. Now you try it. Go ahead, you can do it.	Parent provides many ongoing cues when structure is needed.
Child	(Tries briefly, then stands again) Yours is better. I can't do it.	
Parent	Look at your roof! I like that. Is anything missing?	Parent praises, prompts small extension in productivity.
Child	The chimney (begins to squirm).	
Parent	Give it a try. Go ahead.	
Child	(Tries) That's the best I can do.	
Parent	Very good! You've worked hard and made a good picture. What would you like to do now?	Parent accepts small efforts as a beginning, offers open-ended reinforcement.

EXAMPLE B

The child does not comply with parent requests. The parent has practiced shaping approximations of compliance, and in this example demonstrates what she has learned.

Interaction		Comment
		Parent uses specific initiating command to provide unambiguous prompt.
Parent	Danny, please pick up your toys.	

Child	(As he puts his hand on one toy) I don't want to.		
Parent	That's good; you've got one in your hand! Go ahead and put that one in the box.	Parent ignores refusal, selects desirable portion of response to reinforce.
Child	(As he throws the toy in the box) No! You do it first.		
Parent	That's a good start. Now go ahead and put the rest of the toys away.	Parent again acknowledges only the behavior which is desirable, and keeps behavior continuous by new prompts.
Child	If I put some in, will you help?		
Parent	Sure. Tell me when you've put away half the toys and I'll help with the rest. You're doing a good job.	Parent accepts compromise in early stage of building independent child skills.
Child	(Begins to rapidly put away toys)		
Parent	Danny, I really like the way you're working hard to clean up the room.	Parent praises independent compliance.
Child	(Finishes about half the work, then starts for the door)		
Parent	Danny, you're doing a good job. Now come on over and I'll help with the rest.	Parent follows through with promise.
Child	(Starts to open door and looks back at his parent)		
Parent	That's it. Come on over. Let's finish up together.	Parent ignores all but relevant desirable behavior (i.e., looking back), which is praised.
Child	(Returns to toys, picks one up) OK. But you have to help.	
Parent	You bet. You get those over there, and I'll get these.		
Child	(Complies, and then wants to leave)		
Parent	Danny, I'm really proud of you. You did a beautiful job. We'll go in a few minutes.	Parent indicates pleasure at watching the child's appropriate behavior.

Comment. In these brief examples, the total emphasis is on the quick identification of approximations of desirable behavior and the immediate positive feedback so that *the child rapidly learns the connection between improved behavior and positive attention from his parents.* Both examples have a number of subtle but important parent behaviors, such as prompting, tracking, and well-timed praise. For example, these parents were in the process of developing the skill of identifying instances of the desirable response, *however brief,* and quickly providing, simultaneously, a reinforcement and a prompt for continued behavior. In this way the parent facilitates a chain of desirable behaviors rather than having to confront the child's noncompliance.

Both examples emphasize interactions which can get desirable behaviors started so that praise can become more frequent. Later, increased appropriate behaviors can occur with fewer reinforcements required. Some parents, who are motivated, cooperative, and already have a good repertoire of parenting skills, will be able to rapidly initiate or imitate praising behaviors in training, and subsequently to practice them. Other parents, however, as in the example presented below, must receive additional training in social learning concepts

(Intervention I) *and* basic discrimination in order to develop the timing, wording, and manner for effectively dispensing praise.

EXAMPLE C: THE TL FAMILY

Tracy L, a four-year-old girl, was brought to the clinic by her mother for help with her extreme noncompliance and self-destructive behavior. From the start of the interventions Mrs. L had great difficulty following through with the intervention procedures because of her verbalized, very negative attitude about Tracy. She understood and could discuss the elementary social learning concepts after reading *Living With Children,* but she refused to praise Tracy for any behavior. In her words Tracy's behavior was "entirely negative." Also, she admonished the therapist for asking her to praise by saying, "If you lived with Tracy, you'd see that the reason I can't praise her is that she never does anything praisable."

In basic discrimination training, in which the concept of praising very small "approximate obeys" was discussed, Mrs. L still maintained that interventions based on praise were futile for Tracy and that she needed to learn how to "control" her daughter. Mrs. L even stated that Tracy's self-destructive, accident-prone play was designed to punish her mother.

Mrs. L's nonresponsiveness to the low-cost, routine interventions indicated the need for more intensive treatment. The therapist thus arranged a series of meetings for brief parent counseling (see Chapter 12, Intervention V) in which the emphasis was on (a) the understanding of how parents often project and displace the expression of anger onto their noncompliant children; and (b) the importance of working hard to start a new relationship with Tracy based on positive interaction. After several sessions, Mrs. L understood and accepted the concepts presented by the therapist, but still doubted that she could change her negative interaction with Tracy.

The next week the therapist went to the home three times and used modeling, direct instruction, and feedback to demonstrate to Mrs. L that she could identify and increase Tracy's praisable behavior. During the initial visit the therapist first got Tracy's permission to play with her while building blocks on the floor. Then every few seconds the therapist gave Tracy a directive, like "please hand me that yellow block." With the first indication of compliance, the therapist praised Tracy. After a few minutes of pleasant play, also acknowledged by the therapist, Tracy was asked to build a small bridge as part of a larger construction. She resisted at first but, with the therapist praising approximations of her building attempts, she was able to complete the bridge.

Next, the therapist named all the things Tracy had done that were "nice and showed how well she could play." Mrs. L was then asked to play briefly with Tracy in the same way she had just observed, and to try to respond to Tracy only when she saw a behavior she liked and wanted to see more of. Mrs. L willingly tried to imitate the therapist and, although the therapist had to interrupt the play session a few times to remind Mrs. L to respond *only* to behavior she liked and wanted to see, she did get Tracy to comply with her simple requests. More importantly, Mrs. L began to praise Tracy, although in an unnatural, stilted fashion. Also, the therapist encouraged Mrs. L to name the behaviors she liked in the interaction.

After the play session, Mrs. L acknowledged the improvement, but informed the therapist that she didn't like using praise when she didn't "feel" it. The therapist encouraged her to keep trying and indicated that she might feel better about the interaction later when she saw that Tracy could respond positively to her.

The therapist repeated the procedure in Mrs. L's home on two other occasions; Tracy and her mother demonstrated increased positive interaction in each visit. After the third visit, the therapist asked Mrs. L to have a regular time each day when she could practice improving Tracy's compliance with the shaping procedure.

After two weeks, Mrs. L reported that she was beginning to see things in Tracy's behavior that she genuinely liked for the first time since Tracy was an infant. A clinic observation supported Mrs. L's report, and she not only showed considerably more praise for Tracy's increased compliance, but appeared to be much more natural in her wording and in her manner of praising Tracy.

Comment. The TL case illustrates the importance of *behavioral rehearsal and feedback* in improving parent-child interaction and the parent's attitude about her child. Additional interventions were required, including a deceleration procedure and parent counseling, to resolve the family's other problems. However, until the home-based, basic discrimination training provided visible proof of Mrs. L's ability to influence her daughter in a positive way, it was not likely that she would be responsive to further suggestions by the therapist.

An additional area of importance in training parents to provide positive attention involves the determination of *what is reinforcing* for a given child at a given time. When assessing what is reinforcing the child's desirable and undesirable behavior, the therapist often must examine a number of personal and developmental factors, such as the child's age, social maturity, and feelings about himself and his family. It may also be helpful for the therapist to focus on the issue, "What does the child need that he can only get by engaging in disrupting behavior?" In this way both the child's critical reinforcers *and* the parents' potential role of providing positive attention for desirable behavior can be elucidated. It should be emphasized, however, that the final test of what is reinforcing depends upon the *child's response to the social contingencies present in the family environment.* The reference to the child's personality and individual needs is made here to indicate that the therapist can sometimes utilize his experience and skill to determine the child's important reinforcers without having to test out all the possibilities.

DECREASING UNDESIRABLE BEHAVIOR: THE ABSENCE OF ATTENTION

After practicing the delivery of praise with the therapist and their children to everyone's satisfaction, the parents can begin to improve their ability to ignore undesirable behavior. In the training examples above (on praise) several occasions were described where the parent, confronted with several behaviors, *discriminated* the child's responses which earned "praise" from those which earned "ignore." When training parents to effectively ignore certain behaviors, this discrimination is essential. The therapist can begin by helping the parent label categories of "ignorable" behaviors. Two commonly observed categories are given below:

1. Child responses which function to change the subject, avoid or delay the issue, or distract the parent. These responses are collectively called *diversionary tactics,* and are maintained because the child has learned to avoid or postpone certain activities by getting parental attention for the diversion. Some examples of interaction which include diversionary tactics are:

   Parent   Pick up the toys.

   Child   Mother, can I have this toy?
   I hurt my finger.
   You can't make me.
   You can pick one up first.

   Parent   Stop pushing your brother.

Child   He pushed me first.
I didn't push him.
Mommy, are you mad at me?
What's that you're cooking?

2. Recurring child responses which are aversive and bothersome, but which do not merit negative attention. Examples include rough physical play, hyperactivity, whining and crying, emotional outbursts, and a variety of excessive, attention-seeking, and coercive behaviors.

Behavioral practice for improving the parents' ability to ignore aversive behavior begins by the therapist first having the parents demonstrate their ability *to recognize* ignorable behavior, as described above, and then having them respond to those events by one of the following methods:

1. *Turning away from the child* and, if necessary, walking away. This response is used when the child is engaged in repeated aversive behavior such as whining, complaining, demanding, or noisemaking that the parent does not wish to directly terminate by punishment.

2. *Making no response at all,* including no eye contact. This response, or lack of it, is especially effective for young children who have been accustomed to commanding their parents' attention by aversive behavior. It is usually most effective when, after the attention-seeking behavior momentarily decreases, the parent responds to an approximation of desirable behavior. This procedure teaches the child that he can get positive attention only by engaging in nonaversive behavior.

3. *Continuing to respond to desirable behavior,* or the desirable portion of a behavior, while ignoring the accompanying unwanted behavior. Demonstrations of this method were presented in Examples A and B in the previous section on Positive Attention.

It should be emphasized that *it is difficult and probably erroneous to train parents to ignore behaviors in isolation.* As noted in the previous examples of the application of positive parental attention, ignorable behaviors usually occur in a broad context of both positive and neutral interaction.

An additional important consideration in training parents to ignore certain of their children's behavior concerns the difficulty many parents have in altering habitual emotional and behavioral responses to children, and perhaps to others as well. Very often, when a child engages in an unwanted behavior that has been problematic for a parent, the parent responds both *emotionally* and *behaviorally* to the child. The emotional component may continue even if the parent is capable of the behavioral aspects of "ignore" listed above. Also, many parents complain that the emotional "gut level" response is so intense that they are unable to prevent the behavioral component that is observed by the child. For these latter parents, who usually do not learn to ignore by the therapist's use of *verbal rehearsal* alone, four step-wise techniques can be applied, with each succeeding procedure contingent on remaining problems after the preceding one:

1. *Support.* First, the therapist should discuss the problem of "emotional responding" with the parent, and inform the parent that such responses are natural. Further, it should be emphasized that as soon as the child begins to respond to the parent's behavior of ignoring and praising incompatible behavior, the aversive behavior will decrease and, with it, the parent's negative reactions. Encouraging the parent's patience and perseverance is an important aspect of all new skill-building.

2. *Covert Labeling.* Next, the therapist should teach the parent to develop *cognitive control* over his responses by a mental reminder not to respond when the child makes an "ignorable" response. Thus the parent can practice thinking a particular phrase or word *that provides an inhibitory cue in the presence of emotional arousal.* Many parents, confronted with a difficult-to-ignore behavior, simply think or say "ignore" or some other practiced word. This technique can momentarily *terminate* the emotional response and allow the parent to exercise more rational self-control of his behavior. The therapist should use verbal and behavioral rehearsal to help the parent practice covert labeling prior to its application with the child.

3. *Systematic Desensitization.* This is a procedure to gradually extinguish irrational, counterproductive feelings, and was originally described by Wolpe (1958). The procedures involved are too complex to describe here, but basically involve the development of muscle relaxation as well as the therapist's presentation of emotionally provoking stimuli followed by relaxation, which has the effect of reducing the anxiety or emotional arousal. This procedure should be reserved for parents whose overreaction to their children is extreme, and who do not respond to the previous, less complex techniques.

4. *Parent Counseling.* Continued difficulty helping parents decrease behavioral and emotional nonresponding, which is not uncommonly observed in the very punitive or indulgent parent, is an indication for the use of parent counseling (see Chapter 12).

DECREASING UNDESIRABLE BEHAVIOR: NEGATIVE ATTENTION

Procedures for improving parents' delivery of negative attention can be introduced concurrently with their development of the ability to ignore aversive behavior. Negative responses are often more complex and difficult to teach than "ignoring" or "praising," but parental competence in using responses that can limit or terminate undesirable behavior is essential in systematic parent training for several reasons. Early in the child's development his natural, impulsive style of meeting his needs confronts reality, which in all cultures is characterized by standards of acceptable and unacceptable conduct. Parents naturally impose their own standards on their children, and their ineffectiveness at limit setting is often a major cause for referring the child for treatment.

In this manual the emphasis is on improving children's behavior and the parent-child interaction by developing the parents' ability to provide *positive attention* for *desirable behavior.* This procedure allows the child to meet his needs by behaving in acceptable ways. However, both in the natural development of the child, and in the modification of undesirable behavior, negative attention is often required. Thus the therapist must be prepared to help the parents identify and appropriately respond to disruptive behavior as it occurs.

In Intervention II, the training in punishment procedures is limited to helping the parents clarify their standards and improve their timing and effectiveness when dispensing negative feedback. The application and behavioral practice of more complicated punishment procedures is presented in considerable detail in Chapters 10 and 11 where the focus is on Time Out and other effective methods for severe or persistent aversive behaviors.

As noted earlier, in basic discrimination training punishment is defined for the parents as behavior "which the parents would ordinarily punish." Using this open definition, the therapist can determine the behavior by the parents' responses to the videotape (if present), by family interaction, and by discussion of what their current standards are. The therapist can then further specify the meaning and appropriate use of punishment by emphasizing the need for a procedure *to limit or reduce the rate of disrupting behavior.* It may also be useful to distinguish between the child's *aversive behavior* (lesser but potentially serious disruptions) and *intolerable behavior* (physically dangerous disruptions). These distinctions concerning the child's behavior can make possible the parents' awareness of the need for different levels of negative attention; milder limiting consequences should be used for aversive behavior and more intense punishment for intolerable behavior.

Together, the parents and the therapist can determine if negative attention, including the use of punishment, is an area which warrants improvement in their family. General features of the parents' responses which need to be examined are the possible excesses, deficits, and ineffective manner of providing negative consequences using the observational guidelines described above for positive and neutral attention. Then, if indicated, the basic method in basic discrimination training can be applied by using available data and observational materials to provide the parents with direct feedback (praise or correction) regarding their selection of punishable child responses. For example, this method is effective for many parents who, for various reasons, do not like to punish, or to be seen as "punitive," and thus withhold punishment until the children respond with a total outburst. By providing these parents with feedback to better *identify* and *label* the increasingly aversive behaviors, and encouraging them to use milder, firm responses, the therapist can help them learn to prevent outbursts. Other parents punish frequently but erratically, leaving their children anxious and retaliative. In this case the parents can utilize discrimination training to learn that *many instances of child misbehavior are best ignored, and that effective punishment is a highly selective procedure.* "Screamers" are a third common problem; they are parents who nag, criticize, and scream at their children, having learned that occasionally their vituperations are followed by a reduction in aversive behavior. The feedback procedure can be especially useful for parents like this who can see that their own behavior is aversive and occurring at a high rate. These parents readily learn that much of what they consider "punishing" to the child *actually functions to maintain the child's behavior,* and that selective, specific firmness is more effective than a tirade for reducing serious, unwanted behavior.

The parent's systematic, objective application of firm limit setting for common parent-child conflicts is called *negative feedback.** As distinguished from the corrective feedback provided by the therapist to parents in discrimination training, negative feedback is provided to the child by parents who wish to reduce aversive interaction without having to utilize an intense or lengthy punishment plan. This procedure is so named because it helps children to develop an awareness of the negative effects of their behavior, and to participate in a plan to reduce future negative interactions with their parents. In many families negative feedback is often the treatment of choice when serious conflicts arise between parents and older children.

For the parents, negative feedback has five basic components:

1. *Obtaining the child's attention.* This may require the parents' directive for the child to attend, or a simple request for a discussion about the current conflict or problem or, when necessary, a postponement of the discussion until the child complies with the directives or requests. This *setting* aspect of negative feedback is crucial, and parents should not attempt these procedures prior to securing the child's attention. In fact, unsystematic and haphazardly given negative feedback is often the substance of criticism and humiliation, which can insure further conflicts with the child.

2. *Stating the problem.* After establishing an environment in which a rational discussion can occur, the parents should *briefly, simply,* and *unambiguously* state what has just occurred or what the problem area is. Great care must be taken lest the parents become critical of the child with excessive personal statements like "you've really disappointed me with your behavior," or "sometimes you really are a brat," or "you are headed for serious trouble." Instead, the statement must be

* The concept and many of the procedures of negative feedback were suggested to the author by Susan Price.

42

factual and unarguable, if possible without labeling the child in any way.

Many children who have often been criticized respond initially to the statement of the problem with defensiveness and diversions. Parents can prevent most of these problems by stating the problem in a neutral, matter-of-fact manner. However, when the child does become defensive, the parents must try to ignore all discussion except the issue at hand, which is the clarification of the negative interaction. If necessary, the parents can simply repeat their objective statement of the problem until there is minimal acceptance by the child.

3. *Stating the feelings and interpersonal consequences of negative behavior.* As soon as the child acknowledges the existence of the problem, the parents should state briefly and honestly their feelings about the problem in a language that the child can fully comprehend. The feeling statement should be a non-apologetic, matter-of-fact statement. Excessive wording and punitive intonation becomes a kind of "guilt induction" whereby the parent hopes to influence the child's behavior by stimulating anxiety and guilt. Simply and correctly presented, however, the feeling statement is not an attempt to stimulate punishing feelings in the child, but rather to demonstrate the parents' appropriate displeasure when their standards have been seriously transgressed. For example, if a ten-year-old boy has cursed at his mother, a "guilt-induction" statement might be: "After all my work to make a happy home, look how you mistreat me." But a *feeling statement,* which could constructively express the same intensity of emotion, would be, "I don't like it at all when you use that language," or even "It really makes me angry when you call me those names, and I won't tolerate it."

In another example a mother, who has previously found that screaming is the only sure way to stop her seven- and eight-year-old girls from running and yelling in the house, can learn to calmly but firmly say, "Girls, it really upsets me when you are so loud and overactive in the house." Likewise, a parent disturbed by a twelve-year-old's constant complaining that her friends all have better clothes can say, "I know you want nicer things, but it bothers me when you complain so much. Perhaps we should talk about it." Finally, a father who

is extremely irritated to the point of yelling by his son's fast eating pace at dinner can say, "Son, I think you eat too fast—and it makes me nervous at dinner." It can be seen from these examples that the parent's statement of feelings often directly follows or accompanies the statement of the problem.

4. *Elicitation or suggestion of alternatives.* The constructive phase of negative feedback is based on a discussion of ways to avoid the conflict-producing interaction. Depending on the age of the child or the nature of the conflict, the parent may choose to share this responsibility for a new plan by a statement like "Do you have any suggestions about how we can improve this situation," or "What do you think we should do about this?" or more specifically, "What would be a way for you boys to avoid fighting over clothes every morning."

If these elicitations are not productive (or not used), then the parents must directly suggest appropriate alternatives, but still consider several options and attempt to secure the child's acceptance of the plan.

5. *Ending with positive interaction.* After a plan is proposed and agreed upon, the parents should *always* end the discussion pleasantly, and perhaps acknowledge the child's participation in the discussion. Many parents remain quite angry with the child, or perceive that the child is angry, and assume that the child's role in the discussion is mandatory and not praiseworthy. But a simple positive acknowledgment such as, "I'm glad we were able to talk about this," or "I like the way we were able to work out a plan to solve this problem," or simply "Thanks for helping us work this out" is an important response for parents to make. Often this step can influence in a positive way the aftermath of the "confrontation" as well as future discussions in which negative feedback is a part.

The following examples further illustrate the parents' application of negative feedback. In the first example John, age twelve, continues to come home late for supper after promising to be on time. The family's dinner routine has been disturbed since when John previously arrived late, there usually were arguments and swearing between John and his father. After receiving training in negative feedback, the following exchange takes place on the next evening when John is late.

Father   Son, I think now would be a good time for us to sit down and discuss a problem we're having. For three afternoons this week you have come in late for supper, and now we're going to try to find a way to help you be home by suppertime.

Father obtains child's attention and states the problem.

John   But I couldn't help it. The kids made me late.

Father   Whatever the reason, you're late again. Do you agree we have a problem?

Father acknowledges excuse, then refocuses on the issue.

John   But you don't care about why I'm late. It's not my fault.

Father   Do you agree that we have a problem?

Father ignores diversion, and restates the issue.

John   I guess so.

Father   Good. We are all effected when you are late, and we need to work this out. Also, I get concerned about you when you're late.

Father states interpersonal consequences of tardiness and expresses his own feeling.

John   OK. I'll try harder tomorrow.

Father   Well, that's a problem because you promised your Mom last week you wouldn't be late anymore. I think we need some kind of plan to help you remember. Do you have any ideas?

Father wants more than additional promises, suggests a general strategy and solicits John's participation.

John   Please, Dad. I can do it. It's no big deal.

Father   What would you like to do?

John   I guess what I'll have to do is watch the time closer.

Father   That's a good plan, if you can stick to it. Now see if you can be on time the rest of the week. If you still have a problem, we'll have to try another plan. I'm glad we could talk about this and work it out together.

Father decides to give John another chance to demonstrate responsibility and solve the problem himself. Discussion ends with positive acknowledgment.

In the next example Mike, age nine, has begun to swear at his little sister when they are playing in the afternoon. His mother doesn't want to punish him for this unless she has to, and agrees to try the negative feedback procedures. When Mike swears even after several of his mother's terminating commands, she tries the new procedure.

Mother   Mike, come sit beside me on the couch. I want to talk to you about something that is very important to me. (Mike sits on couch) Good. Now let's talk about what just happened between you and your little sister. I overheard some very bad language a moment ago while you were playing checkers.

Mother gets Mike's full attention and states the problem.

Mike	She cheated!	
Mother	There's no excuse for swearing at your sister, and I don't like it. Also, I don't like swearing and don't want to hear those words again in the house. Do you understand?	Mother expresses strong feelings about the behavior and firmly sets a limit.
Mike	OK. But what about her cheating?	
Mother	Why don't we all play a game of checkers together so we can teach your sister the rules? This will help all of us.	Mother ends the discussion with a pleasant response to the child.

In another example, the mother is very upset with Kay, age six, for repeatedly yelling at her three-year-old sister.

Mother	Kay, look at me. Good. Now let's talk about what just happened. You really screamed loud at your sister when she took your doll.	Mother gets child's full attention and states the problem.
Kay	She always does that! Make her stop.	
Mother	I don't like it when you scream at her and, anyway, screaming only makes things worse. Your sister is only three, and needs to learn not to grab. Why don't you just tell me when she does it and we'll try to help her learn how to ask for things, OK?	Mother expresses feelings and states interpersonal consequences of child's negative behavior. Mother suggests a simple plan and solicits child's acceptance.
Kay	Well, all right.	
Mother	Very good. I like the way we worked out this problem. I don't want her to grab things either, but we have to help her.	Mother ends discussion with positive acknowledgment and supportive statement.

A final example concerns Gary, a nine-year-old boy who is very careless around the house. He repeatedly borrows and uses other people's things and then forgets to return or replace them. When confronted in the past, he has denied taking the things, but they always turn up in his room. His single parent mother, brother and sister are all very concerned about his carelessness and apparent lack of concern for other's property, and are now attempting to apply negative feedback procedures.

Mother	Gary, would you sit down with me for a few minutes? I have something very important to talk about.	Mother gets child's attention.
Gary	Why? What do you want to talk about?	
Mother	Please sit down and I'll tell you.	
Gary	All right. But I want to go out. What is it? (Sits down)	

Mother	I am very concerned about your habit of borrowing other people's things. I've decided that now is a good time to work out a plan to help you be more thoughtful.	Mother expresses concern about the undesirable behavior.
Gary	You're always picking on me. I didn't take anything.	
Mother	You don't think we have a problem?	Mother solicits child's acknowledgment of the problem.
Gary	What's the big deal? They borrow my stuff.	
Mother	I think we have a problem. Maybe we can work it out so that everyone is more responsible. But we have to face the facts. Just last week your brother and sister found several things in your room that they thought were lost. And yesterday you borrowed my brush without asking.	Mother now restates her concern and cites unarguable facts.
Gary	I can't help it. I lost my brush.	
Mother	Now I'm very concerned about this, and I am serious about our need to change this habit of yours. Each member of this family is going to respect the property and rights of others.	Mother ignores the child's diversion, emphasizes need for change and firmly states the general family policy at issue.
Gary	What are you going to make me do?	
Mother	What do you think about what I said about respecting other people's property?	Mother again solicits child's response to her statements.
Gary	I don't know.	
Mother	Now let's make a plan to remind you to ask permission before borrowing things. What do you suggest?	Mother accepts child's denial, and attends to more important issue of need for change. Again she tries to involve the child in the discussion.
Gary	I'll do better.	
Mother	How?	
Gary	I don't know, but I will.	
Mother	I'm very glad you want to work on this problem. Can I suggest something?	Mother praises first positive response from child, but wants more than a general promise.
Gary	Sure.	
Mother	OK. For this week I want you to try very hard to ask permission before you take anything, no matter how little, that belongs to someone else. When you do that, I'm sure everyone will gladly let you use most of the things you need. Why don't we list the things you like to use that belong to others in the family. This may help you	Mother suggests specific plan for child and indicates willingness to be involved in the plan.

46

remember and maybe I can get you some of the things. (Gary and his mother then construct the list and mother agrees to get him some of the items.)

Now there is still the problem of your taking things that belong to others, like sugar and cereal, to your room and not replacing them. But this week we want to work on improving your asking permission before borrowing things. When we talk next week, we'll see how much you've improved and whether or not we need a different plan. What do you think about what I'm suggesting?

Gary   I guess it's all right.

Mother   I'm very glad you feel that way. And I appreciate your sitting with me and helping me work out a plan.

The procedures discussed so far show how parents, having been trained, can effectively utilize negative feedback in a variety of situations involving mildly disruptive behavior patterns.

For the therapist, there are three aspects of training parents that should be emphasized. First, the *training* must occur under close supervision, with both parents present when possible, and utilizing the verbal and behavioral rehearsal methods discussed earlier in this chapter. The therapist should first elicit precise details of current problem and conflict areas, and then ask parents to briefly act out (role play) how the conflict actually occurred. Then the step-wise procedures should be verbally and behaviorally rehearsed, with the therapist and parents taking different roles and practicing them until they are competent and confident in applying the procedures at home.

Second, in each session the parents should be assigned the task of making a record or note of similar problem areas that arise during the week so that each session focuses on current issues in the family life. As more negative interactions are improved, the parents should be encouraged to apply the procedures more on their own, utilizing the therapist as a consultant.

Finally, parents should be advised of the importance of their own emotional stability *during* the negative feedback discussion. Many parents should actually *not* attempt to apply the procedures during a conflict until they are completely rational and have planned how to conduct the discussion. In the "heat of the moment," when parents perceive that their standards have been repeatedly violated, there is often a natural tendency to express strong feelings and there

Mother recognizes the need to begin with a simple plan that might work. Additional negative feedback sessions, or more complex methods such as a Home Contingency Plan or a punishment procedure may be necessary later if the problems continue.

Mother praises child's participation, even though child was largely negative.

is little opportunity for positive or rational interaction. But the parent can still have the negative feedback discussion later when constructive interaction is possible.

PATTERNS OF PARENTAL CONSEQUENCES

The previous sections have described the basic method and principles of discrimination training. The following section continues with the analysis and modification of parent-child interaction, with special attention given to the qualitative aspects of parental consequences.

COMMON ERROR PATTERNS

An analysis of the parents' pattern of providing consequences is extremely useful in understanding their level of parenting skill and in facilitating their improvement. The therapist should examine the relative number of appropriate praise, punish and ignore responses used by the parents, keeping in mind that the child's problems may arise both from parental *failure* to respond appropriately as well as by *excessive* parental responses. The extreme use of praise and ignore in some clinic families may indicate that the parents are reluctant to set limits, and are perhaps giving too much attention to undesirable behavior. If the pattern is in the opposite direction, the parents may be excessively punitive, and are depriving their children of the positive attention needed to maintain appropriate interaction. Either pattern can usually be modified with effective shaping (reinforcing small approximations of the desired response) and guidance by the therapist. Finally, many parents "take for granted" their child's compliance and appropriate behavior, or they complain that their child exhibits no praisable behavior and attend only when there is a problem. This common pattern, when observed, also points to the need for replacing some portion of the parents' "ignore" responses with positive attention for approximations of any desirable behaviors.

PARENTAL CONSISTENCY

Together with the parents' error pattern, their responses throughout basic discrimination training should be examined to detect poorly timed, inconsistent, and unpredictable styles of responding to their children. Many parents possess minimal praising, ignoring, and punishing habits, but their inconsistent responses leave their children confused, producing a high rate of attention-getting behaviors as the children seek to establish a pattern of interaction with their parents. This "pattern" often includes deviant behaviors *since the children usually will learn any behavior pattern which produces predictable parental attention* even if the attention is at times "punishing."

Intraparental Inconsistency. Parental inconsistency is a behavior pattern which can be defined and improved just as any other aspect of parent-child interaction. *Intraparent* consistency is a measure of how an individual parent behaves over time and in different settings. Thus, the highly consistent mother will frequently praise her children whenever she sees them behave in ways she likes and wants to see more often, *regardless of external circumstances.* Most parents vary their responses somewhat which, up to a point, provides a healthy variety for their children. It is when the child finds that he cannot predict the consequences of his behavior, or cannot discern a meaningful pattern in his parent's response to him, that he may initiate maladaptive, trial-and-error behavior to establish a pattern.

Parental inconsistency occurs for many different reasons, and is often caused by realistic, external circumstances. A mother who is usually quite firm may report that she is "unable" to terminate poor behavior in church or in a moving car. Other parents may be distracted and fail to praise good child behavior when away from home. In most cases these omissions are inconsequential since the total parent-child relationship may include enough intermittent reinforcement to maintain an acceptable level of appropriate child behavior. However, when the parent complains that the child's aversive behavior is excessive, or that a child is withdrawn or has behavior deficits, then the therapist should closely examine the consistency of the parent's praise, punish, and ignore response pattern, and try to determine if the child's problems reflect the parent's inconsistency.

If intraparent inconsistency is observed in any of the settings described above, or is reported by the parent or other family members, the basic method in basic discrimination training should be applied (ideally with both parents present) so that the parent can (a) better discriminate (become more aware of) the praise, ignore and punish categories of parental attention, and the kinds of child behaviors he or she wishes to alter; (b) practice (rehearse) specific application exercises in the clinic (e.g., immediate and delayed negative attention for in-church or in-car disruptions); and (c) work out a simple schedule or recording system to keep track of their response patterns in daily interactions with their children. Often it is best to begin the schedule by focusing on *one* category of parental attention (i.e., praise) and the appropriate corresponding child behaviors. Thus, for one or two weeks a mother's records should reflect how she consistently praises every instance of compliance or approximate compliance during a brief but difficult daily time period. Later, she can indicate how she provides effective, brief, negative attention for each occurrence of child disruptions during the selected time period each day. This procedure will increase her *awareness* of her consistency as well as her *effectiveness*.

Interparental Inconsistency. A second type of erratic parent behavior is *interparent* inconsistency. Here the parents may or may not show intraparent inconsistency, but they disagree overtly or covertly (or both) with each other. Almost any of the problems noted in children who are brought to child guidance centers may be caused by this problem. A moderate degree of interparent differences, reflecting their personalities, can stimulate and promote adaptive child behavior as the varied problem-solving styles are modeled and learned. However, intense, constant and open disagreement between parents can produce confusion in the child concerning standards of behavior, and even severe emotional reactions in cases where an *expectancy* of one parent is the *prohibition* of the other.

In basic discrimination training the therapist can increase interparent consistency by the following methods:

1. Meeting with the parents to pinpoint and discriminate areas of disagreement in their parenting behavior, emphasizing similarities in the parents' standards, attitudes, expectancies, and positive and negative feelings for their children (comparing parent scores on child behavior checklists can facilitate the discussion).

2. Pinpointing the family or parent conflicts which are usually observed by the children.

3. Defining interparent consistency as agreement and similar timing in the use of praise, ignore, and punish; setting up mutually agreed upon categories of child behaviors which earn parental attention; rehearsing common parental application of contingent consequences; and planning a schedule for daily application (practice) of consistent responding.

4. Setting up family *rules* for practicing consistency such as "no policy debates with children present," or beginning statements with "*we* want" or "*we* like" whenever possible.

The therapist can further help by monitoring a session or two in which the parents rehearse and plan their policy-making behavior for the home, keeping the issues clear and initial goals simple.

In cases where the parents' inconsistent child management practices persist after the application of the techniques presented here, the therapist should recommend concomitant parent counseling as described in Chapters 12 and 13.

THE COMPLIANCE STRUCTURE

Another important area of basic parenting skill which may need attention is the means the parents use to teach their children to comply with requests. Compliance is generally agreed to be a significant aspect of the socialization process in all cultures and, as a primary area of concern for many parents and child guidance clinics, it can be a sensitive indicator of the parent-child relationship. When assessing the family by any of the procedures discussed above, it is important to examine three parts of the behavioral chain which produce compliance. These components are shown schematically in the diagram below.

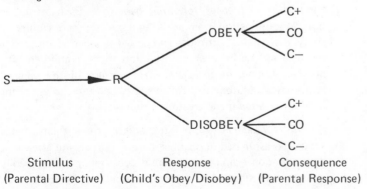

| Stimulus (Parental Directive) | Response (Child's Obey/Disobey) | Consequence (Parental Response) |

First, there is a parental directive or "command," which may be specific or nonspecific, or initiating (with the intent of having the child *begin* some action) or terminating (with the intent of *stopping* some action). Research at the Neuropsychiatric Institute has shown that the important areas to assess are (a) the relative frequency of parental *specific commands,* since the child's noncompliance is frequently related to the parents' high rate of ambiguous directives; (b) the relative frequency of *terminating commands,* since this information can help focus the intervention on decreasing parental negativity as well as high-rate aversive behavior by the child; and (c) the *total number* of commands since a low rate (relative to other clinic parents) may reflect insufficient communication by the parents, while a high rate can produce confusion or overstimulation in the child.

Second in the compliance chain is the child's response, which must be either compliance or noncompliance. Consistent with social learning principles, the relative frequency of obey or disobey in most cases depends on the parental antecedents (directives) and consequences.

The third and most important of the elements in the compliance chain is *the parental consequence of the behavior.* The principles and procedures for responding to compliance and noncompliance are the same as discussed above for any other desirable or undesirable behavior. Thus, if the parents value compliance, *they should attend positively to the child's obeys or approximate obeys, ignore incidental disobeys, attend negatively to extreme noncompliance, and try to be consistent at all times.*

MAINTENANCE TRAINING

The purpose of maintenance training is to increase the likelihood that the treatments will have a lasting effect, and that the parents will be able to continue the improved family interaction relatively independent of the therapist. Thus maintenance training is an integral part of each intervention in systematic parent training. The general guidelines presented here are applicable for Interventions III and IV as well as for basic discrimination training.

1. If the family is in or is about to be in follow-up, maintenance training should be recommended. The concern with *maintenance of progress* is a standard and routine aspect of every family's successful course of treatment. As will be discussed in Issue No. 3, Chapter 15, a major criterion for judging

"success" in systematic parent training is the parents' ability to produce and maintain effective family interaction independent of the therapist. Maintenance training increases the probability of independent parent behaviors, such as generalization over time of previously practiced skills and interaction patterns, and generalization of these skills to new situations not yet encountered.

2. In the initial maintenance training session the therapist should emphasize the family's successful response to the interventions and then discuss the importance of family members working to maintain the progress after they no longer come to see the therapist. In Intervention II, the procedures used are less structured and complex than those suggested in later chapters, and often one or two sessions will be sufficient to help the parents prepare for the follow-up period.

3. The therapist can utilize *behavioral rehearsal* and *overlearning* techniques to test and develop the parents' maintenance skills. In applying the behavioral rehearsal technique to maintenance training the parents are asked to verbalize and practice solutions to current child and parent-child difficulties as was done earlier in the treatment. Then, in overlearning, the therapist goes beyond the parents' initial demonstration of competence in Intervention II skills and suggests additional problems for which the parents can practice applying what they have learned. Initially these techniques can be applied for behaviors similar to those which have been recently treated, and then extended to problems that may arise in the near future.

Each week the parents should be advised to make informal notes of conflict situations and negative interactions as they occur each day and to bring these examples to the session. The therapist can then encourage the parents to state how they might resolve these problems by the consistent and contingent application of parental consequences. Also, by helping the parents improve their ability to observe, reinforce, and model each other's appropriate problem-solving behavior, the therapist can increase their independent functioning and begin to change his own role from therapist to *consultant*. In this way the parents can learn to deal with day-to-day problems on their own, and to consult the therapist only when there are serious problems.

In summary, new and old problems, which arise after successful parent training, usually reflect subtle errors in the timing and consistency of parental consequences for their children's behavior. In the maintenance training sessions the therapist can help to minimize the occurrence of these difficulties by having the parents overlearn the careful, consistent application of positive attention for desirable behavior, and negative attention and the absence of attention for undesirable behavior. Specifically, it should be emphasized that (a) successfully applied interventions, when the child is relatively young, may *prevent* serious problems later, and (b) the parents' skills of maintaining consistent, contingent, and positive family interaction by the judicious use of parental consequences can help *reduce* the child's problems at any age. The more parents practice these skills, both in the interventions and in maintenance training, the better prepared they will be to facilitate their child's development in the future.

ASSESSMENT OF INTERVENTION II

As with other systematic parent training procedures, it is important that the therapist keep careful records and summaries of the family's responses to the intervention. In basic discrimination training this is especially true since no standard data-taking form is available, as in Intervention III. Thus the therapist's records and treatment log show less formal estimates of individual family responses on dimensions such as the following:

1. *Parental cooperation.* Intervention II is the first intervention where the therapist is influencing what the parents actually *do* with their children, and the parents' response to the feedback training is extremely relevant in deciding if it is appropriate to proceed with more demanding home interventions.

2. *Parental consequences for child behaviors.* Each session in basic discrimination training is an excellent opportunity to study the parents' attitudes and actual practice of dispensing positive and negative or no attention to their children. The number, timing, manner, and error pattern of the parents' responses should be recorded regularly and used to assess the need for treatment and treatment change.

3. *Parental consistency.* Both intra- and interparent consistency should be estimated, if possible, before, during, and after basic discrimination training. Interparent consistency can be readily assessed any time both parents respond on the same issue,

whether it is in the initial interview, questionnaire and checklist responses, or clinic and home application of the principles. When consistency is presented as a significant area of parenting, and is constantly a focus of the parents' behavior in treatment, they should observably improve their ability to work together. Poor or little improvement in interparent consistency may reflect rigid attitudes in one or both parents about the child or the marital relationship and, as noted previously, these problems should be evaluated for possible intervention using parent counseling. *Intra*parent consistency is assessed by estimating the variability of an individual parent's behavior during treatment. In successful training a parent should show decreased variation in the delivery of praise, ignore, and punish responses for his or her child's behavior, both in the clinic and in the home.

4. *Compliance.* When parents effectively provide the prompts and consequences for their child's behavior, the behavior usually improves and is judged to be appropriate and desirable. This finding applies especially to the child's compliance to the parents' directives. Also, since compliance is so frequently a presenting complaint in child treatment settings, changes in this area should be carefully documented so that the conditions for improvement can be specified for the parents. For example, clinic observation records of the family pre- and postdiscrimination training can reflect changes in the parents' type of directives, the frequency of child obeys, and the parental consequences. Successfully treated families almost always show greater specificity of commands, reduced terminating commands, increased compliance, and increased parental praise for compliance. Parent records, however informal, can further document improvements in their child's compliance.

5. *Response to other interventions.* As will be seen, Intervention III (the Home Contingency Program) and Intervention IV (Punishment Procedures) are reserved for treatment plans in which basic discrimination training is not sufficient, that is, when more structured or intensive procedures are needed to accelerate desirable behavior or decelerate serious aversive behavior. Thus, an indirect test of the effects of basic discrimination training is the parental success observed later in Inter-

vention III. The Home Contingency Program may prove difficult for many reasons, but it is assumed that when it *is* effective the parents possess the tracking and contingent responding skills emphasized in Intervention II. In fact, as noted earlier, one would not ordinarily expect the parents to be able to effectively utilize a family restructuring plan, such as the Home Contingency Program, until they are able to praise appropriate behavior in a contingent, consistent fashion. Similarly, it will be emphasized that in most cases punishment procedures probably should not be used unless the parents are already utilizing a rich schedule of contingent positive attention.

In summary, the therapist must examine all the available data after applying the procedures in Intervention II and, together with the parents, reach a decision about what additional interventions, if any, are indicated. After each of the interventions in systematic parent training, there are several major alternatives for the therapist to consider based on the family's response to treatment.

First, after basic discrimination training, many parents are able to demonstrate improved confidence and competence in their parenting skills, and some may even demonstrate significant improvement in their child's behavior. When the parents' goals for the family are attained following the intervention, the therapist should suggest a few sessions of maintenance training (see above, p. 49).

Second, most parents who receive basic discrimination training show improvement in their own ability to interact more positively, consistently, and contingently with their children, but continue to report problem behaviors in the home. Intervention II focuses primarily on parent-child relationships, and very often more complex and structured treatments are needed for the child's specific problems. Thus in most cases the therapist should be prepared to recommend either a home contingency plan or a punishment procedure following discrimination training.

Third, some parents may have so much difficulty accepting or responding to parent training procedures that continued interventions focusing on the child are not indicated. In these cases the therapist should recommend parent counseling (Intervention V). If the series of parent counseling sessions is sufficient to resolve the factors which are interfering with the parents' response to training, the therapist can then suggest a retrial of basic discrimination training. If the problems continue, the therapist should make available more intensive therapy for the appropriate family members (family, couples, or individual parent or child treatment).

FOLLOW-UP PROCEDURES

In systematic parent training "follow-up" refers to the period that begins as soon as the family has attained its intervention goals and completed maintenance training. Follow-up assessment is essential for an analysis of the effectiveness and efficiency of the treatment; and "successful" treatment requires that the family maintain their gains beyond the termination of active treatment.

Follow-up can be initiated at any point during the parent training. For example, although the treatment flo-chart on page 10 indicates that Interventions I and II should *always be applied,* an occasional industrious, highly motivated family may resolve their problems after mastering the social learning concepts (Intervention I). More commonly, however, families will begin follow-up after Intervention II, III, or IV.

The procedure for beginning follow-up is similar for each intervention, and the follow-up guidelines suggested here for Intervention II are applicable at any time during the training. At each regular meeting with the therapist the parents should routinely discuss their progress in the training program. Then, if the parent and therapist records after maintenance training clearly indicate a diminution of behavioral and interactional problems and the development of effective family interaction, the therapist should recommend that follow-up be initiated. Generally it can be suggested that all record keeping be stopped for a while, although some families may wish to continue their records for a period of time.

Finally, the family should be advised to recontact the therapist whenever they need help with additional problems. The therapist may then consider a retrial of the initial intervention procedures or, after assessing the problem, decide to continue the intervention sequence at a later point. However, the parents should be advised that whether or not they report new difficulties they will be contacted at posttreatment intervals (usually every three to six months for at least a year), during which time they may be asked to reinstitute their record keeping for a week or two and possibly to have a few home visits made.

The follow-up procedures should approximate as closely as possible those used in the baseline period to originally document the child's behavior and the parent-child interaction. If possible, home, clinic or videotape observation should be made, and behavior checklists and parent records should be repeated during the follow-up period. An additional form that the parents should complete is the Parent's Assessment of Therapy; examples are presented in Chapter 14.

SUGGESTED PROFESSIONAL TIME AND EFFORT

Generally, basic discrimination training requires two to four hours of professional time depending on the parents' responses and the procedures used. Some professional experience is probably necessary for assessing parental discrimination skills and providing clinic or home training by feedback, modeling, and rehearsal techniques. However, while certain of the specific techniques used may require some preparation by the therapist, the majority of the procedures and principles suggested here can easily be integrated into the therapist's existing skills.

EIGHT / INTERVENTION III: The Home Contingency Program

PURPOSE

The purpose of Intervention III is to restructure and improve family interaction during disruptive daily periods, using social and nonsocial reinforcements contingent upon the occurrence of certain specified, desirable behaviors or behavioral sequences.

DESCRIPTION

The Home Contingency Program (HCP) is fundamental to the application of systematic family intervention. With the exception of some families whose "target" children are severely retarded, autistic, or less than three or four years of age, this procedure can provide the tool whereby actual behavior change in the family will occur. The HCP is *valid* since the parents and children themselves provide "target" disruptive periods to be restructured, is *reliable* since it rapidly becomes "public" and available for all family members to monitor, and is almost always *beneficial,* even when there is a minimum of parental cooperation and consistency.

Many variations of home contingency programs for arranging contingent family interaction have been used, usually with success. The present HCP is based in part on these previously reported reinforcement plans, but is unique in two respects. First, *no behavioral problem is treated in isolation.* Instead, the focus on a particular behavior is changed to the focus on high-frequency behavioral components, usually three to six, of a *daily time period* with significant family disruption. For example, instead of specifying a particular behavior, such as "temper tantrums" or "noncompliance," the HCP specifies a recurrent, daily time during the week when the behavior of family members prevents effective family functioning. If there are morning disruptions which "make everyone late and unhappy," this intervention period may be labeled "Getting Ready for School." If

the problem is "after-school resistance to riding quietly home in the car," the period might be referred to as "Coming Home from School." Other examples are "Playing After School" for "fighting and noncompliance in the house after school"; "Homework Time" for "problems with homework"; or "Getting Ready for Bed" for "bedtime problems."

Second, *the HCP uses a counterconditioning, or incompatible response procedure, for treating components of the disrupted period,* thus insuring that the program is *accelerative* and is always *increasing desirable behavior.* For example, a common complaint in a disruptive morning period is that the child is never ready to leave the home when everyone else is, thus making everyone late. But instead of specifying and recording the child's disruption, the HCP item could be "ready to go by 8:10 a.m." Other examples of specifying the components of the troublesome periods in a positive way are "eating breakfast without teasing brother," or "begin homework by second request," or "in bed by 9:00 p.m. without being reminded." The advantage of this acceleration program is its total emphasis on increasing *positive interaction,* thus making previous negative interaction improbable.

The HCP is developed gradually when possible, starting with the parents' private records, then applying social, nonsocial and negotiable reinforcements, and finally testing the effectiveness of the intervention in short- and long-term follow-up periods.

It is important that the HCP be applied after basic discrimination training for several reasons. First, it was emphasized in the previous chapter that the skills in Intervention II are basic to the successful use of the HCP. Second, it is important to consider that the HCP is time consuming and deals with the standing or routine problem areas which disturb the family. Thus Intervention II is best suited for parent-child interaction difficulties which are not observed at a recurrent time, or which occur at a low rate, or at a time when a point system is inappropriate. If after a reasonable trial the problems worked on in Intervention II are not improved, or are improved but problems in daily interactions still occur and an *acceleration* program is possible, then a contingency program should be developed. The primary effect of the HCP is *to restructure* or *improve* existing family interaction. The HCP should be used when the child-family problems are related to poorly organized daily patterns, or inter-action characterized by poorly defined behavioral expectancies.

SUGGESTED APPLICATIONS

The suggested application of the HCP occurs in a step-wise sequence in which the parents first keep private records, then apply social and negotiated contingencies, and finally test the maintenance of their program. Each of the steps used in the HCP are summarized in Table 1 and fully described in the following sections.

Table 1   Summary of HCP Procedures

Procedure	Description	Expected Minimum Duration	Expected Professional Time
Program Planning	Selection of problem period and chart components	1-2 sessions	1-2 hours
Private Records	Pretreatment parent records of problem period (private records)	1-3 weeks Daily	1-2 hours
Social Contingency	Social feedback and praise for daily earnings (public records)	2-4 weeks Daily	2-4 hours
Negotiated Contingency	Social contingency and negotiated rewards for earnings	2 weeks Daily	2 hours
Short-term Follow-up	Reinstatement of private records immediately after termination of public programs (social or negotiated contingency)	2 weeks Daily	1-2 hours
Long-term Follow-up	Reinstatement of private records at posttreatment intervals	1-2 weeks Daily Every 3-6 months for at least 1 year	1-2 hours
		Total:	8-14 hours

PROGRAM PLANNING AND PRIVATE RECORDS

If the therapist and parents agree that a behavior acceleration plan is indicated, the therapist should explain to the parents that the next part of the family treatment will focus on their keeping records on the daily recurring problem areas.

Record keeping should be presented to the parents as essential to their progress in parent training. The therapist can show the family how to construct a chart to register weekly averages in points earned and thus obtain visible evidence of their efforts during baseline, treatment, and follow-up stages of the HCP. The charts should also provide the focus of the weekly meetings with the family.

It should be noted that the private records for the HCP can be planned during the regular baseline period before any interventions begin. Thus the family often can begin keeping private records on the HCP components as early as the third family session (or even by the second session, when intake and screening are done during the first meeting). The treatment session order for such cases would be:

Session 1:   Intake.

Session 2:   Screening.

Session 3:   Baseline (home records, including HCP private chart, can begin here).

Session 4:   Reading materials for Intervention I assigned.

Session 5:   Interventions I and II; baseline records continue.

Session 6:   Family and therapist review three-week, private HCP records and decide if the HCP should continue.

Occasionally a referred family consists of parents whose discrimination abilities are so poor they cannot provide accurate HCP private records without discrimination training. In these cases it is necessary to develop the prerequisite pinpointing and documenting skills *before* proceeding with the HCP baseline records.

When developing the private records, the therapist can help the parents divide the "average family day" into three to six time periods when there are several parent-child or child disruptions. It should be emphasized to the parents that previous family treatment has shown the importance of beginning the day with positive, pleasant interaction, and that the first time period worked on should be the earliest daily period that presents problems. This first period is referred to in many family programs as the "AM Program" and is usually emphasized first in applying the HCP unless the family indicates the total absence of early AM conflicts or problems. In such cases the parents can focus on an afternoon or early evening period, such as homework or bedtime.

It can also be emphasized that families who start their day with pleasant interaction may have fewer problems later on since the skills applied by the parents early in the day are often used by parents on their own in subsequent times of daily conflict. Finally, it is relatively easy to demonstrate success with the AM Program since it is usually characterized by a more or less structured routine. Thus it can provide a foundation for the parents' acceptance and successful application of the HCP for more difficult, less routine daily disruptions.

After the observation period is selected, the parents should name five or six specific behaviors in the period which, if observed, would result in a more amicable or pleasant period. As many as two of the five or six behaviors should already be occurring regularly and not represent any problem or conflict in order to insure that the child shows some earnings *at the beginning of the intervention.*

The best way to elicit the components of the selected period which will comprise the data sheet is to have the parents pinpoint, step-by-step, each succeeding event until the items on the record sheet are decided upon. The following is an example interview with parents when the baseline HCP chart is being constructed.

Therapist	What happens first in the morning?
Parent	Well, Larry always gets up without being called.
Therapist	And then?
Parent	He never makes up his bed. That's a problem.
Therapist	OK, I'll make a note of that. What happens next?

Parent	Larry goes into the bathroom and does his chores—except that somebody always has to remind him to brush his teeth. Then he usually starts teasing his little sister and they get into a fight that goes on the rest of the morning. When we punish him, he goes to school in a bad mood. We need to do something about that.
Therapist	Right. Let's include an item about teasing. What else happens that we should have on our chart?
Parent	We have a problem getting them to come to breakfast. They won't leave the TV and come to the breakfast table. Especially Larry; we have to threaten him to get him to the table.
Therapist	Any problems with breakfast after he comes?
Parent	No.
Therapist	Any other problems?
Parent	No—somehow the kids are all ready to go when we are.
Therapist	At what time do you like to leave?
Parent	By ten after eight.
Therapist	Fine. For your record keeping, let's have six items for Larry. How about

1. Gets up without being called.

2. Makes up his bed without being told.

3. Brushes teeth without being told.

4. No teasing sister.

5. At the breakfast table after second call.

6. Ready to go by 8:10 a.m.

Notice that two of the items on the chart, the first and the last, are already occurring without any problem. We do this so that when we begin our program Larry can be certain to start out with some earnings. Now it is very important that you know when a given item is earned or not earned. Do you think this will be a problem?

Parent	No, the items are clear enough. But do we both always have to agree that Larry has done the things on the list? That will be difficult.
Therapist	I'm sure it would. Which behaviors can you both observe without much trouble?
Parent	Let's see—items 4 and 6, and maybe 1.

Therapist I'll make a note of that. OK, do the best you can. Remember, the important thing is that at least one of you is always certain whether or not each behavior on the chart occurred. How many points do you think Larry will earn each day during your private record keeping?

Parent I guess maybe two or three at best.

Other problem periods can be discussed and defined in the same way. Common examples of other charts are given below:

A. *Problem:* Refuses to do homework.

   Period: "Homework Time."

   Components:

   1. Is in house by 5:30 p.m.

   2. Has homework materials out without being told.

   3. Requests Mom or Dad to review assignment prior to starting.

   4. Works on homework for 30 minutes without more than two brief breaks.

   5. Requests Mom or Dad to check homework.

B. *Problem:* Refuses to go to bed when told, then stays up talking with brother.

   Period: "Bedtime Period."

   Components:

   1. TV off by 9:00 p.m.

   2. Dressed for bed without being told.

   3. Teeth brushed without reminder.

   4. In bed by second request.

   5. Lights out by 9:15 p.m.

   6. No talking after 9:20 p.m.

C. *Problem:* Runs away from mother after school and causes a disruption in the car, then refuses to come into the house when home.

   Period: "After School Period."

   Components:

   1. Comes to the car by first request.

   2. Is in car within 15 seconds after request.

   3. Plays quietly with brother during ride home.

   4. Comes into house by second request.

   5. Puts away coat or sweater without being told.

D. *Problem:* Generally disruptive and noncompliant after school.

   Components:

   Pick one hour of the disrupted period, divide the hour into six ten-minute periods. Each ten-minute period becomes an item on the HCP record sheet. Score one point for each period free of limit testing (noncompliance to *terminating* commands). Later extend the period to include more of the total problem time.

In order to facilitate the construction of the HCP record sheet, forms can be made available to the parents so they can fill in the behavioral components as they are being discussed. A blank HCP chart is presented on p. 58. Features of the chart that require comment are listed below:

1. *Program Name:* A brief title of the daily period being treated, such as "AM Program" or "Homework Time."

2. *Token Value:* In the negotiable contingency the value of each point earned, such as "one token earns two cents," or "four of six points daily earns a surprise treat."

3. *Pay Day:* The day selected for exchanging points for earnings, such as "daily" or "Saturday, 10:00 a.m."

BLANK HCP CHART

Target Behaviors	Sat.	Sun.	Mon.	Tues.	Wed.	Thurs.	Fri.	
								Weekly Dates
								Family Name
								Program Name
								Token Value
								Payday
								Total Earnings
Daily Earnings	=	=	=	=	=	=	=	

Week No. and Program: | 1 | 2 | 3 | 4 | 5 | 6 | 7 | 8 | 9 | 10 | 11 | 12 |

(circle one each)   PR   SC   NC   T

PR—Private Records; SC—Social Contingency; NC—Negotiated Contingency; T—Program Test

4. *Week Number and Program:* A weekly indication of the program status so that "6" and "NC" circled would indicate that the HCP was in the sixth week and a negotiated contingency was in operation. Other symbols are "PR" for private records, "SC" for social contingency, and "T" for program test.

Following the completion of the items on the chart, the private record phase of the HCP can begin and the parents can be instructed to mark "+" in the appropriate space if a behavior was observed, "O" if the behavior was not observed (in the time allowed), or "—" if there was no opportunity to observe the behavior. The parents should be encouraged to use the back of the sheet to note any informal observations made during the day.

Important: The therapist should stress to the parents that during the private record keeping weeks the records should be *unknown to the children.* Also, the parents should observe the behaviors for occurrence or nonoccurrence only, and not structure or respond to the target behaviors in any new or different way. During this observation period, the records should accurately reflect the present state of affairs in the home and thus, if possible, *the parents should not be concerned with trying to change or improve the child's behavior at this time.* Additional examples illustrating the development of the HCP are presented in the following chapter (see especially the GW and JB cases).

THE PUBLIC PROGRAM: SOCIAL CONTINGENCIES

The steps which follow can be used as guidelines for proceeding in the HCP after baseline is completed. It should be emphasized that each of the steps assumes that the parent records are complete and weekly attendance with the therapist is regular.

If the daily earnings are stable at two or three items earned out of a possible five or six items, then after one week of private records (two weeks are even better), the therapist should instruct the parents to announce and describe the plan to the family and post the record sheet in a conspicuous place, such as on the refrigerator door. This procedure is referred to on the record sheet as "SC" and means that the family should give social, positive attention for each point earned, as well as for daily totals. The family should emphasize only the positive aspects of the child's responses; no criticism or negative verbal interaction should occur when there is a lack of accomplishment. A statement such as "You'll have another chance tomorrow," or "Don't worry, tomorrow is another day" should suffice.

When using social contingencies, it is very important to indicate the child's accomplishment in a very direct manner, and many successful families even develop a small ritual around publicly posting the child's earnings. For example, instead of using "+" for earnings once the program becomes public, it is usually more effective to allow the children to register their own points using some kind of special stamps, stickers, or marks while being praised for their efforts (see the SP case in Chapter 9).

The therapist should not assume that the parents can always effectively provide the necessary social praise for points earned, even after completing basic discrimination training. In order to increase the likelihood that the desired parent-child exchanges take place in the home, *the acknowledgment for points earned should be rehearsed* in the clinic or home (or both). First, in the clinic office the therapist should ask the parents to role play the delivery of praise as they would at home after a point has been earned. Then if the parents' style is consistent, effectively encouraging, and their praising message is clear, the social contingency phase should begin.

If the parents have any problems applying social contingencies, the therapist should *model* the effective parent behaviors and the parents should imitate the therapist until they have mastered the sequence and expressed confidence that they can be as effective at home. In some cases it may be necessary for the therapist to go to the home and have the entire family practice this procedure.

A particularly common and serious error that parents make in the public contingency phases of the HCP is to threaten the child, using the chart items. For example, unless specifically cautioned, many parents who want their child to perform better might say "OK, now get to work—remember your chart," or "This is your last chance to earn the point." In these interactions the parents' emphasis is on the *penalty for absent behavior* rather than *praise for observed behavior.* The therapist must teach the parent to relate to the child in terms of the chart *only* concerning the *prompt* (if included in the item) and the *consequence, if positive.* In the HCP there are *no threats* and *no penalties.* The chart should never be used as a verbal inducement to perform or as the subject of negative interaction or criticism. The child's development of self-management is facilitated only when the HCP chart is a stimulus for self-initiated behavior and the subject of positive family interaction.

The social contingency portion of the HCP in systematic parent training is often the first concrete indication to the children that a new "plan" is being used in the family. Not only the "target" child but the other children can be expected to have questions about the program. In general, it has been found that the entire family responds best to a public HCP when it is *explained to all the children* and applied to the target child and at least one sibling. In fact, many siblings see the chart as a kind of "status" and are eager to have their own charts. There are several benefits of having charts for two or more children at the same time: more of the family interactions are structured during a difficult period; it prevents the isolation of the target child as "special"; and it often induces in the children a healthy, competitive spirit to accomplish expected chores and positive interaction. The items on the siblings' charts can be similar to or completely different from the target child's, and the children themselves can often help "pinpoint" chores or daily tasks they are willing to work on, even if there is no major problem involved (see Chapter 14, Case No. 2).

In general, the family should maintain the social contingency plan for a minimum of two weeks. There are many individual response patterns to the social attention for points earned, and while some children improve immediately (with most points being earned) and the parents keep the chart up as a way of continuing to structure the children's behavior for a while, others like to take the chart down after a few weeks and begin follow-up. Still other families indicate the need for more intensive procedures such as the use of negotiable rewards (referred to as "NC" on the HCP Chart).

THE PUBLIC PROGRAM: NEGOTIATED CONTINGENCIES

When two weeks or more of the social contingency show little or no improvement, or when the social contingency is not used, then the procedure utilizing the negotiated exchange of tangible reinforcement for earnings should be considered. Here the chart is publicly posted as before, and the child is provided with direct knowledge of earnings so that the systematic use of negotiated rewards is possible. While it is not essential, it may be important in the beginning for the therapist to help the parents communicate the details of the reward procedure to the child. Only a few minutes of the therapist's time (in the clinic or home) are required to describe the entire plan, and this information may prevent confusion at a later time. *In all programs involving older children (over seven or eight years) the child should be included in the negotiation of the rewards used.*

The reward procedure can be applied in several different ways, such as short-delay primary rewards (e.g., treats for young children immediately contingent upon each point earned), or longer delay rewards utilizing secondary reinforcers (coins or exchanging points for special privileges on "payday"). The sample chart (p. 61) illustrates an HCP in which the family has just begun negotiated rewards with an AM Program and are in their fifth week of the program. At the end of each AM period the parents give the child a token for each item earned; on "payday" the tokens are exchanged for his allowance. In this example, the child has earned 83%, or 25 of the available tokens, but he is still having difficulty making his bed.

Basically, the reward procedure works by utilizing the child's performance in the social contingency period to determine the initial "criterion" level for the administration of the contingent rewards. The rationale for determining the criterion or starting level is always based upon the unique aspects of each family's treatment plan, but general guidelines include the following:

1. The initial criterion should be equal to or only slightly higher than the level of items earned during the social contingency, insuring a successful beginning for the procedure.

2. If the social contingency level is very erratic, such as an HCP sheet showing maximum earnings some days and zero earnings on other days, it is usually best to attempt to stabilize the baseline record before beginning the negotiated rewards. This can usually be done by first examining the daily antecedent and environmental factors which might be contributing to extremes in daily earnings. Then the therapist can have the parents attend especially to the target behaviors on days with very poor earnings and attempt to improve the child's performance using positive attention for *approximations* of the desirable behavior.

3. The criterion level should always be based on the *developmental age* of the child and the *reward* which the parents anticipate using. For younger children who require more immediate reinforcers or feedback for their performance the rewards can be administered directly after the daily period is over, or perhaps at the end of each day when both parents are present. For older children weekend "payday" is often more effective, and in some cases a long-term program can be used, e.g., when the child has weekly earnings that count toward a major reward such as a bike or a trip.

SAMPLE HCP CHART

Target Behaviors	Sat.	Sun.	Mon.	Tues.	Wed.	Thurs.	Fri.	
Gets up without being called	____	____	☺	☺	☺	☺	☺	**Weekly Dates** 2/4-2/8
Makes bed without being told	____	____	☺		☺			**Family Name** Smith
Brushes teeth without being asked	____	____	☺	☺	☺	☺	☺	**Program Name** A. M.
No fight with brother over clothes	____	____	☺		☺	☺	☺	**Token Value** 1 = $.05
At breakfast table by second call	____	____	☺	☺	☺	☺	☺	**Payday** Sat. 9:00 A.M.
Ready to go by 8:10	____	____	☺	☺		☺	☺	**Total Earnings** 25 Tokens = $1.25
Daily Earnings	=	=	6 = 30¢	4 = 20¢	5 = 25¢	5 = 25¢	5 = 25¢	

Week No. and Program:

1	2	3	4	(5)	6	7	8	9	10	11	12

(circle one each)

PR	SC	(NC)	T

PR—Private Records; SC—Social Contingency; NC—Negotiated Contingency; T—Program Test

Several considerations must be made when using negotiable rewards. First, the act of making rewards conditional upon the explicit completion of some child's behavior is probably not a "natural" interaction between parents and children. Experiments have shown that, given a choice of working for rewards or having their needs met without an explicit reinforcement program, most organisms, including humans, choose the latter (Fisher, 1973). Thus, since the goal of systematic parent training is to arrange conditions which are conducive to a "natural" positive social interchange, the reward condition should be utilized primarily *to get a positive behavioral sequence initiated or maintained at a higher rate.*

Second, it is important, whenever possible, to tap into ongoing family activities and exchange systems rather than introducing a new reward into the system. For example, it is most parsimonious to make an existing family exchange system more explicit, such as utilizing an ongoing "allowance," daily "treat," or desired activity as the reward for HCP earnings. In many cases, of course, it will be necessary to introduce fairly novel rewards, at least initially, but even in these cases the choice of the reward should be carefully worked out with the parents to approximate as closely as possible the existing family exchange and interaction system.

Third, whenever negotiable rewards are introduced, the use of *bonuses* should be considered. Bonuses add incentive and interest to the HCP, and can be arranged for daily or weekly earnings. In a typical HCP program with six components, a daily average of five items earned out of the six is usually sufficient for a weekly bonus, while daily bonuses are best for perfect days (all items earned). The value of the bonus can be quite small, since the purpose is to provide simple *recognition* for the child's extra work.

SHORT-TERM FOLLOW-UP: THE INITIAL PROGRAM TEST

As soon as the appropriate behaviors are present and stable (i.e., when the daily level of HCP items being regularly achieved is at 80% or better), the procedure should begin to return to nonnegotiable reinforcement, or the "natural" exchange of positive social interaction, again using private records. The use of private records after the application of social or negotiated contingencies is important because the records provide the first test of treatment generalization and maintenance without the public charting system or earned rewards. The specific procedure involves the parents keeping private records once again, precisely as described earlier.

When changing the HCP from a reward to a postreward condition, the parent first informs the children that they have been doing very well, and that the chart will be taken down for a while. Second, the children are told that the rewards that they have been earning, based on their appropriate behavior, will continue, but *will be given to them without having to earn any specific points.* Thus, the children continue to receive all the benefits of the chart earnings, usually at the same "payday" time as before, but with no contingency applied (although the parents continue to record daily "earnings" using private records). Third, the parents should emphasize how pleased they are with their children's recent behavior, and how they hope that the improved, pleasant interactions will continue without having to use a chart or point system. Finally, the parents should be reminded that their continuing praise for desirable behavior is essential if the improvements are to be maintained.

An example of a parent-child discussion prior to beginning private records after a negotiated reward condition might be as follows:

Parent	John, we are really pleased with your behavior during our family chart plan. You have tried hard and earned your rewards very well. Now this week we want to see how well we can do without using the chart or the daily points. You will keep getting your daily allowance.
John	OK, but do I still have to do my homework after school?
Parent	Yes, we want you to continue to do as well as you have been. We'll help you any time you want us to.

The private records in the HCP can be reinstated after the social contingency as well as after a negotiated reward condition. In either case, after beginning the initial program test, the therapist should watch the weekly records closely to assess possible losses in daily earnings. If the losses are greater than two or three items in the daily average after returning to private records, then either a social or reward contingency should be reinstated. Some parents have trouble returning to a contingency procedure after point losses, especially when rewards were used, but it should be emphasized to the parents that behavior change often takes time, and that a retrial of a previous condition should be accomplished as matter-of-factly as possible. When the criterion is reached and maintained again, parents can then go on to a new test period with private records.

CONCOMITANT AND COMBINED PROGRAMS

Most parents pinpoint more than one daily "disruptive" period when beginning the HCP. In these cases the family should begin baseline private records on the second target period as soon as a successful level of behavior is achieved in the contingency phase of the first program attempted, or even at the beginning of the initial program. Thus the family may have, for a while, overlapping home contingency programs for different periods of disrupting behavior. Whenever possible the parents should be encouraged to develop the details of a second HCP, using the therapist as a consultant. This procedure can promote generalization of parent skills.

Concomitant programs are especially appropriate when the therapist determines that a severely disrupted daily period is best dealt with by first developing a successful HCP on a less troublesome period that is likely to be more responsive. The SP case, presented in Chapter 9, illustrates how concomitant programs can be developed by the therapist and parents, and also shows how the therapist can effectively utilize the available HCP procedures when the child makes a poor response in the short-term follow-up of the intervention program.

Following the initial test phase, many families are successful at combining certain features of two programs into a single HCP for maintaining specific behaviors. A simplified, combined HCP is especially useful for newly acquired, desirable behaviors which do not remain stable during the short-term follow-up. For example, during the initial HCP a child may achieve and maintain each target behavior except "ready to go" in an "AM Program." Thus, during the next program this item can be included in the new chart. Also,

since some behaviors are difficult to maintain without daily structure, some families have combined "maintenance" public programs that last for three months or more (see Case No. 2, Chapter 14).

Interpretations of the Initial Follow-up Response. There are probably two primary factors that produce the desired results in the public social contingency procedure: the *structural cues* (from the chart and the parents' directives), and the *contingent, positive, social attention* (from the parents). Thus, when there are losses in the daily behaviors previously achieved in the public program after the parents reinstate private records, it may be assumed that one or both of these factors are related to the losses. In general, reinstating social contingencies after poor results in the test phase has excellent results, but it cannot be known if the attention or the structure is the primary factor responsible for the improvement since both are usually present. Nonetheless, when returning to the private records, it is important at least to demonstrate that the parents can effectively maintain the desired behaviors using social reinforcement without the chart since without this skill future maintenance of the child's desirable behavior may be difficult.

A clearer understanding of the factors producing desirable behavior is possible when, after the negotiated reward procedure, a test trial of private records results in a loss of previous earnings. Here, it is likely that the negotiated tangible earnings function as more powerful incentives than the parental social praise for good behavior. In this case the therapist should consider repeating the essential ideas and practices in basic discrimination training by using the behavioral rehearsal method, described on page 35, in which the parents and therapist role play (rehearse) the exchange of social or negotiated reinforcement in the clinic or home until the parents have a "natural" style of delivering positive attention. Then, when the parents reinstate the reward condition, they should be able to provide the positive social consequences for the target behaviors which will continue and maintain them when private records are again used to test the program.

A final note about the test phase concerns the parent-therapist relationship. The HCP is often difficult work for parents, and for most it is a new experience. Also, some parents may have tried a "point system" previously which was unsuccessful. In any case, the therapist should be encouraging and positive in his recognition of both success, and approximations of success, in the HCP by the parents. In the initial test of the HCP the therapist has tangible results of the parents' efforts and an excellent opportunity to give the parents and children direct, weekly feedback about their efforts.

MAINTENANCE TRAINING

After the postcontingency private records indicate continued acceptable performance of the charted behaviors for two or three weeks, the parents should come in for a few sessions of *maintenance training* in preparation for follow-up. The guidelines for maintenance training on page 49 can be used, with some modification. The first step in maintenance training, after an HCP, is for the therapist to specify the changes made by the parents which contributed to the effectiveness of the treatment. While there are several additional factors which are important in a successful HCP, the therapist should especially emphasize the *reorganization* and *restructuring of family interaction* and the parents' increased positive social attention for desirable behavior. Next, the therapist can discuss the preventive aspects of a successful HCP since the parents have developed skills which can prevent persistent disrupting interaction by continuing to provide positive consequences for the child's appropriate behavior. Also, as noted earlier, this preventive maintenance can be further facilitated in some families by encouraging them to maintain a public chart and social reinforcement for a few months in the follow-up period.

Finally, the therapist should point out that both old and new problems may arise for which the parents can use the procedures in this chapter. By helping the parents *verbalize* and *rehearse* how they might apply or reapply an HCP for daily problems occurring later on, the therapist can reinforce the parents' confidence in their ability to deal with problems more independently. Of course, the therapist should also reassure the parents of the availability of professional help if serious problems arise for which the HCP is not indicated or effective.

OTHER APPLICATIONS OF INTERVENTION III

MODIFICATION OF THE HOME CONTINGENCY PROGRAM

The application of Intervention III has emphasized the highly structured HCP to help build desirable behaviors, but there are other, less formal procedures which should be mentioned here since they make possible wider use of the basic method. First, there are specific treatments which can be improved by using them in conjunction with modifications of Intervention III. An example of this would be the treatment of nocturnal enuresis. This disorder is often thought of as an aversive behavior requiring a deceleration program. However, in Intervention III enuresis would be conceptualized in terms of "number of dry nights." In this way the private and public charts could be used prior to, in conjunction with, or to the exclusion of the highly successful bell-and-pad conditioning apparatus. The parents could prepare, and privately keep, a chart on "dry nights" and perhaps one or two other nighttime chores or desired activities, and then have the child keep his own records by marking his chart in the morning. Since there is some evidence that the child's chart-keeping coupled with mild parental acknowledgment and praise can increase dry nights by over one-third (Dische, 1971), the parents can assess the effects of the child's record keeping, or a bell-and-pad conditioning device (if used), for a few weeks later on.

Second, the HCP can be used in modified form to improve a number of problem behaviors that are isolated, very low in frequency, or do not occur at a regular, daily time period. Examples are whining, pouting, criticizing, nailbiting, messy eating, or continuous failure to perform a singular behavior, such as helping with household chores or cleaning one's room. As noted in Intervention II, the consistent, effectively timed application of contingent praising, ignoring and negative feedback is often sufficient to improve these "bad habits"; but, if they continue, then a modified HCP, or what is really a more structured application of Intervention II, is needed. In practice a simple contingency, with or without the chart, is stated and the child earns a social or negotiable reward for performing a desired response that is incompatible with the bad habit, or for simply *not* performing the unwanted behavior. Examples of task and reward combinations which can be used in less formal home contingency programs, all sharing the focus on *increased structure* in parent-child interaction, are listed below. Any combination of items may be indicated for a given family problem.

Child's Tasks	*Child's Rewards*
Good daily school report.	Daily use of TV.
Homework completed.	After-school treats.
No fighting with siblings.	Extra play time with parents.
No swear words (specify).	Having friends visit.
Household chores completed (specify).	Playing outside after school.

SCHOOL APPLICATIONS

The principles and procedures in Intervention III can be readily extended to improve academic and behavior problems that children manifest in the school setting. Most commonly, the HCP can help reduce school problems by first developing a successful HCP using an AM or other nonschool period, and then developing a second HCP *with component items relating to school,* such as homework. In cases where there are no home disturbances, and thus no basis for the application of an HCP in the usual manner, the therapist should still begin with Interventions I and II, however abbreviated, prior to the school intervention. Then the parents can facilitate the school-based plan by providing home contingencies for improvements in school work or behavior. The therapist can use the following guidelines to set up a school program:

1. The school problem should be carefully evaluated (pinpointed and documented), by a school visit and by discussing the situation with the child's teacher.

2. The therapist should develop a simple rating system with one or two items that the teacher can easily observe and record, and he should attempt to get at least one week of baseline records. Common examples of problems, which teachers will usually agree to keep records on, are "work completed on time," "followed teacher's directions well," "no tantrums or hitting all day," "no problems on the playground," or "no visits to the principal."

3. The therapist should arrange a meeting with the parents and teacher to carefully plan and coordinate all aspects of the intervention program. Considerable attention should be given to the daily communication between the parents and the teacher. The simplest arrangement is usually for the teacher to present the child with a card containing his daily score of points earned for each item, and for the child to give the card to his parent when he arrives home. The points can be registered publicly on a chart similar to the HCP record sheet.

4. The therapist should carefully evaluate the weekly progress of the child by meetings with the parents (and child), and by phoning the teacher if indicated. Usually school interventions are a week-to-week arrangement and the therapist should be prepared to modify his plan to better meet the needs of the school or the family at any point.

The therapist's and the parents' involvement in the child's school problems is often complex and deserves careful study in its own right. However, the therapist can help to improve the child's school functioning by planning and carefully monitoring the parents' involvement with the school, based on Intervention III procedures. When more complex or serious school disturbances or problems in functioning are reported, it may be best for the therapist not to include the parents but to develop classroom interventions by consulting directly with the teacher. *How to Use Contingency Contracting* (Homme, 1970) and *Modifying Classroom Behavior* (Buckley and Walker, 1970) are both excellent classroom intervention manuals written for teachers that can facilitate the therapist's school consultation.

ASSESSMENT OF INTERVENTION III

In Intervention III assessment occurs at each stage of the procedure, as provided by the parent records. The initial records provide continuous information on the children's early response to the restructuring process as well as the parents' ability to utilize materials learned in Intervention II. Later, the records provide data needed to judge the attainment of the parents' own short-term goals; finally, the follow-up private records can reveal important information about the parents' ability to function effectively without direct professional or paraprofessional support.

SUGGESTED PROFESSIONAL TIME AND EFFORT

The time required to produce effective follow-up response in the HCP varies considerably, ranging usually from three to twelve hours of professional contact. Thus, while the *effectiveness* of the HCP is generally good based on the attainment of family goals, the *efficiency* varies with the number of sessions and programs required, the intensity of the problem behaviors, and the degree of parental motivation (assessed by response to the therapist's assignments). Any clinic personnel experienced in child and family intervention can direct the HCP development, maintenance and follow-up.

SUMMARY

It has been emphasized that the general purpose of systematic parent training is to restructure negative interaction so that it is replaced by positive interaction. Intervention III can play an important role in this restructuring process. As such, the goal of an HCP is to teach family members to meet their needs without engaging in disruptive interaction, using naturally occurring social reinforcement. The various stages of the HCP offer different degrees of support in accomplishing this goal. In the social contingency phase the parents increase the predictability of parental attention while providing special cues and praise for desirable behaviors that are arranged to be incompatible with undesirable behaviors. When utilizing negotiated rewards, more potent contingencies are applied in addition to positive social reinforcement. Also, there are tests for maintenance of the improved child behaviors and parent-child interaction, and opportunities to reinstate the HCP for recurring or new problem areas.

It is assumed that the primary effective ingredients in the HCP are the parents' increased structured expectancies and positive consequences associated with their children's behavior. Often these factors begin operating during the baseline, such as when the parents' records reveal significant improvements in the private record keeping compared with previous reports. When the formal intervention begins with the application of public social contingencies, the therapist should utilize these factors to the family's best advantage, and also later improve the generalization of the treatment by communicating to the parents the possible mechanisms underlying the family's improvement.

Many variations on the basic HCP method are possible, and several examples have been presented. Concomitant, overlapping programs for the same child can often optimize and accelerate the benefits of the treatment. For maintenance purposes the difficult features can be combined later in a single public chart. Also, concomitant programs for two or more children can provide a rapid treatment response and improve generalization by adding positive peer interaction and reinforcement to the basic method. Other applications of Intervention III are possible, such as for relatively isolated problem behaviors that continue after Intervention II.

NINE

THE HOME CONTINGENCY PROGRAM: Case Illustrations

INTRODUCTION

In this chapter three cases are presented to illustrate the application of HCP procedures. While the procedural descriptions and discussions in the previous chapter are fairly detailed, many readers find that case examples provide a more intimate understanding of the techniques used than do the "suggested applications" alone.

The first two cases in the present chapter examine the process of setting up the all-important record-keeping procedure in the HCP. The third case shows how the therapist's evaluation of the family's response to the short-term follow-up of the HCP facilitates the flexible application of available procedures to produce a positive intervention outcome.

THE GW FAMILY:
DOCUMENTING GOOD BEHAVIOR

The complete intervention program for the GW family is presented in detail in Chapter 14 (Case No. 2). Mrs. W came to the clinic shortly after she had divorced her husband; she was concerned about her two boys—George, 9 and Lee, 10. George was having many problems which Mrs. W thought might relate to the parents' separation. During the screening it was learned that George was lying to her about his schoolwork, was stealing money from her purse, and was constantly provoking his brother and fighting with him. The negative sibling interaction was most intense around bedtime, but there were minor disturbances and hassles every morning which caused Mrs. W much duress. Other screening data showed George to be a very impulsive, angry boy with learning and behavior problems in school in addition to his problems at home. Lee was having a reading problem and was very shy but otherwise showed no major problems in his behavior. Mrs. W was quite anxious in the initial interviews, but expressed relief when told that her family would

be accepted at the clinic. It was decided to begin HCP charts for both boys as part of the regular baseline procedures, together with the other home records and clinic observations.

In the baseline interview Mrs. W and the therapist constructed an AM Program for the boys, involving five items each. Since George and his brother usually began fighting as soon as they woke up, and were extremely competitive, the chart contained some items that, if observed, would preclude negative interaction, and some that reflected the individual difficulties of the children.

The items on George's chart were:

1. Out of bed after first call.

2. No fighting over which clothes to wear.

3. 10 minutes maximum in bathroom.

4. No teasing Lee.

5. Ready to go by 8:00 a.m.

Lee's items were:

1. Out of bed after first call.

2. No stepping on George's bunk bed.

3. No fighting over clothes.

4. 10 minutes maximum in bathroom.

5. Ready to leave by 8:00 a.m.

Mrs. W was asked to keep these HCP charts privately for a few weeks, at which point they would be made "public." The therapist pointed out that the private records might not reflect the full degree of the problems usually observed since Mrs. W wanted to use a kitchen timer to determine the amount of time each boy spent in the bathroom. In the past, the "time-in-bathroom" issue was the event which set off much fighting and complaining that often lasted the rest of the morning. Nevertheless, it was decided to proceed with the baseline charts and Mrs. W agreed to try her best not to change any other variables and to keep the records unknown to the children.

In the next session Mrs. W brought in her HCP records. Surprisingly for both the therapist and herself, Mrs. W's records showed that George had earned over 55% of the available items per day, or nearly three of the five items possible. Lee did even better, earning over 60% of his possible points. Also, she reported that the morning period was more pleasant and without major disruption or argument for the first time in many months. Obviously something had changed. Mrs. W thought the previous week that the boys might earn the item "Ready to go," but never guessed they would change so drastically on the other items. Looking over the weekly HCP chart, the therapist found that on the first day of the program George had earned *no* points prior to the item "10 minutes maximum in bathroom" (his number 3 item), and afterwards he earned the other two. Lee likewise earned no points on the first day before the timed bathroom activity (his number 4 item). Mrs. W reported that when she introduced the timer for the bathroom chore, both boys thought it was a very good idea and made certain to be finished before the timer went off. In fact, on each day of the week both boys earned the bathroom point.

The question still remained about why the other problems decreased so much. Mrs. W was certain that the timer was the only feature of the morning routine that had been added. During the session the therapist speculated about the changes which had occurred. Some of the possibilities were:

1. As a result of structuring the bathroom routine, the boys had less opportunity and stimuli for provocative and negative interaction later.

2. On subsequent days the boys, *expecting* the morning to be more structured, ceased their excessive provocations.

3. Mrs. W had, without being aware of it, communicated to the children her expectancy that they would reduce disruptions and perhaps even her pleasure at seeing them improve.

It was agreed that the HCP records should continue, and that in the following week something more definite could be said about the changes. It was suggested that perhaps Mrs. W could ask the boys if they saw the mornings as being different.

The following week the records were much the same; a slight decrease for Lee and an increase for George were observed, but overall a high rate of target behaviors was performed. The boys had attributed some of the change to the timer, but couldn't verbalize any other difference, although they both liked the improvements in each other.

The therapist was hesitant about suggesting an intervention for the AM Program in view of the uncertainties about why the changes were occurring. Also, Mrs. W complained again that the bedtime problems seemed more difficult than ever. Therefore, the therapist asked Mrs. W if she would like to begin private record keeping on the PM problems in the same way she had kept the AM records. She was eager to do so and, after some discussion, the following items were decided upon for both George and Lee:

1. TV turned off after first request.

2. 15 minutes maximum for bath.

3. Clean tub after bath.

4. Go to bed without being told.

5. No fighting about who turns off the light.

Private records were maintained for the PM Program for two weeks. George earned about 40% of his points for both weeks, while Lee earned about 55%. Mrs. W's records also showed that the improvements during the AM period were continuing. These records, together with the other baseline materials, provided the basis for developing an intervention program for the GW family.

Comment. The GW case illustrates a common finding when developing private HCP records or any baseline: an increase in desirable behavior prior to treatment. In similar cases, therapists have suggested that the events associated with baseline procedures can communicate information to the child in terms of either behavioral antecedents or consequences, which then can function like an intervention to alter the behavior (the so-called "baseline cure"). Also, there was the possibility that Mrs. W had exaggerated her estimates of disturbing behavior in the AM period. In any case these findings point out that baseline data can often (a) minimize speculation about what the pretreatment level of behavior is, and (b) indicate quickly what areas of the child's behavior require formal intervention.

THE JB FAMILY: DOCUMENTING
THE ANTECEDENTS OF UNDESIRABLE BEHAVIOR

The JB case was presented in an earlier chapter as an illustration of the application of screening procedures. The case was accepted for treatment based on the screening information in which it was learned that (a) Jim's primary presenting problem of vomiting had many antecedents which might provide a basis for treatment, and (b) the more general mother-child interaction involved a number of areas which needed improvement. In the next session the therapist decided that while it would be difficult to treat the high-intensity, low-frequency problem of vomiting directly, a baseline could be constructed on high- and low-frequency behaviors which might compete with the antecedents of vomiting. During the interview the therapist attempted to pinpoint the baseline items so that an HCP chart could be started for Jim.

Therapist   At the end of the session last week we learned that Jim has some problems other than vomiting. The first thing we should do today is to spell out some of Jim's daily problems that we can work on. I think that by improving his general interaction with you he will learn to control himself better. Are there any problems early in the morning with Jim?

Mother   Yes, he usually makes me late because I have to do everything for him.

Therapist   Would you like him to do more things for himself to get ready in the morning?

Mother   Yes, but that will be difficult. He's used to me taking care of him.

Therapist   Let's try to work on the early AM Program to see if we can help. OK?

Mother   Sure. What do we do?

Therapist   First, we have to pick several components of the AM period and make a chart to keep private records for a week or two so that I'll know exactly what's going on. We need about six items in all (therapist hands Mrs. B a copy of the HCP chart so that she can begin to fill in the items). Four of the items we choose should be things that you want to see happen that would make the morning easier for you and also help Jim learn some self-help skills. Two items can be things he is already doing regularly so that when we make the chart public he will "earn" some points from the start. What's the first thing in the morning that we want to work on?

Mother   That's easy. I have to call him three or four times before he gets up.

Therapist   OK. Now we have to define the item so that there will be no doubt in your mind about whether or not Jim has earned it. How about "Jim is out of bed after the first call"?

Mother   Do I wait and see if he gets up? That may take a while. The way it is now, I just shout at him from the kitchen until I hear him getting up.

Therapist   Well, you may have to restructure things a bit to use this item but I think that's all right. Try this: go to his room and wake him. Instruct him to get up. If he is up already, or gets up after one request, give him one point, marked as a "+" on the chart later, without Jim knowing. If two or more requests are needed, then give him a zero. How does that sound?

Mother   Fine.

Therapist   OK. Now we'll practice how you can best use these items when we have completed our list. What happens after he's up?

Mother   He goes to the bathroom and washes his face and brushes his teeth by himself.

Therapist   By himself?

Mother   Yes, there's no problem with that.

Therapist   How about having "washes face by himself" and "brushes teeth by himself" as our two free items?

Mother   He'll always get two points then.

Therapist   Good, that's what we want. Now what can be our fourth item?

Mother   Well, I don't know whether to add "getting dressed" as an item. He usually needs my help, and I don't mind because he can't button or tie anything.

Therapist   What can he do that you would like for him to do more of?

Mother   He could do everything but button his clothes and tie his shoes.

Therapist   OK, how about "clothes and shoes on after first request"? You can use this item without having to change the routine about dressing at all, right?

Mother   Yes, I think so.

Therapist   Fine, let's try that. What should be our next item?

Mother   Well, breakfast might be a problem. I have to take breakfast into his room for him. This has always been the morning routine.

Therapist   Would you like for him to eat in the kitchen with you?

Mother   Of course, but he never has and I know he'll refuse.

Therapist   Why?

Mother   Because he wants to watch his TV while he eats.

Therapist   Can you bring his TV into the kitchen?

Mother   Yes, but is that the right thing to do?

Therapist   Let's try it and see. At first these changes may be difficult for Jim. But we can make it easier by changing just a few things at a time. Perhaps later we can have him watch TV after breakfast. Now this item will also involve some change from the routine, but it is necessary. Let's name the item "Jim eats breakfast in the kitchen." Tomorrow morning, when you fix his breakfast, go to him and announce that breakfast is ready and is on the kitchen table and that you would like him to come in. If he wishes, you can bring in the TV. Then continue with whatever you were doing. If he comes in without a reminder, he earns the point. Would you like to try that?

Mother I'll try it, but remember, he's never done this before.

Therapist That's all right. If it doesn't work out to be a good item on the chart, we'll try something else. Now we need one more item. You said Jim is never ready to go in the morning when you are.

Mother Right. I would love it if you could have him be ready and not make me late.

Therapist What time do you like to leave?

Mother At about 7:30.

Therapist What makes him late?

Mother Oh, he's just in his room playing around. I have to call him again and again.

Therapist Then I think the last item should be "ready to go by 7:30." We now have six items for you to keep track of in the morning:

1. Out of bed by second call.

2. Washes face by himself.

3. Brushes teeth by himself.

4. Clothes and shoes on after first request.

5. Eats breakfast in the kitchen.

6. Ready to go by 7:30 a.m.

Some of them will require changes in your routine so I think we should practice exactly how you will present the instructions to Jim.

The remainder of the interview involved Mrs. B rehearsing methods for keeping the baseline HCP records with a minimum of change in her daily routine.

Comment. In general there should be no changes in the daily family activities during the private records, but in the JB case it was necessary to provide additional structure for some of Mrs. B's interactions with Jim in order to assess his performance on desirable but low-rate behavior. To the extent that *structured expectancy* is an important aspect of behavior change in the home, Jim's behavior could improve during baseline as did George's and Lee's in the previous case. However, the baseline does not always require an *au naturel* assessment of characteristic events; in some cases an adequate, objective, pretreatment measure of the child's behavior is possible even with minor alterations in what might be the "true" state of affairs.

THE SP FAMILY: DEVELOPING AN EFFECTIVE PROGRAM

The SP family was referred to the clinic by a friend who had previously been involved in systematic parent training. Mrs. P, a single parent, was concerned about the problems of her seven-and-a-half-year-old daughter, Susan. The primary complaint involved Susan's extreme noncompliance, temper tantrums, and what was described as her "negative attitude." Mrs. P stated that she was aware that she was doing many things wrong with Susan, but that she was having problems herself trying to work, go to school at night, and somehow deal with Susan's problems at the same time.

The therapist suggested a plan to help both Susan and Mrs. P by arranging intervention programs for significant disruptive periods during the day. Mrs. P was anxious to start since most of her daily interaction with Susan was negative, and the problems usually started each morning when Susan woke up "in a bad mood." It was decided to start with an HCP for the morning problems and, when a stable level of desirable interaction was achieved, to then begin to work on after-school and PM problems. Together with other baseline procedures, an HCP chart was constructed for the AM period with the following items:

1. Out of bed after the first call.

2. No arguments about getting dressed.

3. Twenty minutes maximum for eating breakfast.

4. Brushes teeth after breakfast.

5. Gets books and lunch ready in five minutes.

6. Ready to go at 7:30 a.m.

Items which Susan was expected to earn were No. 4 and No. 5, although occasionally Susan was reported to be slow in getting her things together.

During the three-week, private records phase of the HCP Susan responded considerably better than her mother had expected, achieving 60% or more of the available earnings. However, other baseline results in the initial week of private records indicated that the general interaction between Susan and her mother was indeed very negative; Mrs. P lost her temper frequently and screamed at Susan, and Susan continued to noncomply with most of her mother's directives. Also, Mrs. P's judgments about how she would respond to Susan's behavior while viewing a videotape of parent-child interactions revealed that she often failed to praise appropriate behavior and "punished" excessively. For example, her pattern of

positive and negative attention and ignoring indicated that she ignored behaviors she should have praised and punished what she should have ignored (according to the therapist's and others' judgments).

Prior to the second week of the baseline Mrs. P and the therapist discussed social learning principles and she was given a copy of *Living With Children* to read. In the third session Mrs. P reported that the book and social learning ideas were helpful. In the same meeting she was given feedback about her deficits in praising and excesses in punishing, and she responded by increasing her use of positive responses in a second videotape viewing session. However, she reported that she was still a "screamer" at home with Susan.

Figure 6 shows graphically Susan's progress in the HCP.

Figure 6   Susan P's HCP Progress

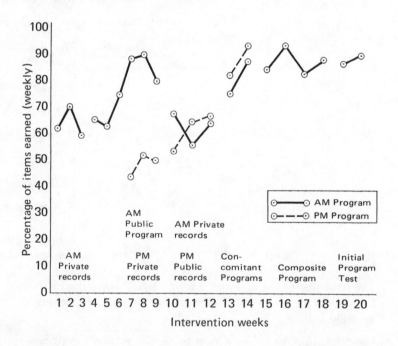

The private records of the morning program show the 60% earnings in the first week (baseline), improvement in the second week (after assignment of *Living With Children*), and a decrease in the third week (after Interventions I and II). Thus, although Susan's earnings were higher than expected during the baseline week, Mrs. P's experiences in Interventions I and II were not sufficient to further improve Susan's behavior.

At the fourth session the therapist presented Mrs. P with the procedure for the social contingency. Most of the session was used to behaviorally rehearse the delivery of positive attention after Susan earned each point. Again, Mrs. P's response to the role playing was very favorable in the clinic with the therapist present. However, as Figure 6 indicates, there was no improvement in the morning program for the initial two weeks of the social contingency procedure.

One consideration discussed at that point was that Susan might respond better if she were more involved in the program, and allowed to register her own points. Previously, Mrs. P had registered Susan's earnings by simply putting checks on the chart. Thus the therapist provided Mrs. P with a roll of silver stickers and suggested that she have Susan record her own points by placing a sticker on the chart for each item accomplished. During the following four weeks the mother's records showed a considerable increase in points earned. Throughout these sessions Mrs. P indicated that the mornings were much more pleasant and that she was providing profuse daily social praise for items accomplished.

The therapist had originally planned to begin a PM Program earlier in the treatment sequence since Mrs. P felt that the major problems occurred in the evening. The therapist reasoned, however, that until the AM Program had stabilized at above the 80% level a new program should probably not be attempted. Thus, when Susan's earnings reached 88% following the addition of the AM stickers, Mrs. P was asked to keep records on the evening problems. The items for the PM Program were:

1. Hangs up clothes after getting home from school.

2. Gets homework started by 5:30 p.m.

3. Works independently on homework for 15 minutes.

4. Comes to dinner without argument.

5. Starts bath by 7:30 p.m.

6. In bed by 9:00 p.m.

Items No. 4 and No. 5 were selected as the two relatively high-frequency behaviors.

After three weeks of private records on the PM period, during which the AM Program was maintained at an acceptable level, it was decided to test the AM Program by returning to private records and to begin a public intervention during the PM period. Mrs. P was asked to tell Susan that she was doing very well in the morning and that she wanted to help her now with some of the evening difficulties by using the same system. The therapist stressed the importance of Mrs. P's continued praise for morning "earnings," even though Susan would not be aware of the private AM records.

During the first week after the change, and the tenth week of the program, Mrs. P's charts showed a decrease in the AM Program and no change in the public PM Program. Neither finding was anticipated. Mrs. P reported that she had been on vacation that week and perhaps was not as observant of points earned for the AM Program. Also, Mrs. P had failed to utilize the stickers for the first week of the public PM Program, so it was suggested that she reinstate them for the remainder of all public, chart-keeping procedures.

The following week's records indicated further problems with the HCP. The morning problems had returned to their baseline level, although in the evenings Susan was earning, on the average, about one additional daily point after the stickers were added.

During the twelfth session there was much discussion of Mrs. P's problems with the procedural aspects of the entire HCP. She reported, for example, that she indeed had been praising Susan less in the morning since the changeover of programs, and that her scheduling problems in school and work had made it very difficult to always follow through as requested by the therapist. Both Mrs. P and the therapist agreed that the delayed response and improvement with stickers in the social contingency period, as well as the loss of earnings in the test phase, all pointed to the need for a more highly structured plan at that time. The therapist also planned to spend more time discussing Mrs. P's own difficulties, and to help her develop a less stressful routine. It was emphasized that improvements in Susan's daily behavior could provide an important source of reinforcement and relief for Mrs. P, and that it would be well to continue working to improve the HCP.

The therapist suggested that the first important step in restructuring the program would be to try public interventions for both programs since Susan had responded so well to the stickers-for-points-earned procedure. Figure 6 shows the results of weeks thirteen and fourteen with concomitant morning and evening social contingency programs. The losses of the previous weeks in the morning program were regained, and continued progress was made on the more difficult evening problems.

The next step in simplifying Mrs. P's HCP was to suggest that she *combine the two programs* so that Susan could continue to earn points and praise for her daily accomplishments, and in the process make the procedure even easier to maintain. The therapist and Mrs. P agreed on the following items for the combined chart, based on Susan's relative difficulties with these items in previous programs:

1. Out of bed by first call.

2. Ready to go at 7:30 a.m.

3. Hangs up clothes after getting home from school.

4. Gets homework started by 5:30 p.m.

5. Works independently on homework for 15 minutes.

6. In bed by 9:00 p.m.

For the next four weeks the therapist had brief contacts with Mrs. P by clinic visits and phone contacts while the combined HCP was in operation. Weeks fifteen through eighteen on Figure 6 show the excellent maintenance of Susan's morning and evening desirable behavior. Then Mrs. P, on her own initiative, suggested that she and Susan try another test phase with private records. She reported that the entire interaction between her and Susan was now quite positive, and wanted to try maintaining Susan's improved behavior and accomplishments without a public chart. The therapist agreed, although pointing out that the private records should be carefully

kept and monitored for two weeks before beginning a long-term follow-up period with no records. Figure 6 shows that Susan's earnings in the following two weeks of private records were maintained at greater than 85%. On the basis of these results it appeared that Mrs. P, after a slow start, was indeed able to effectively utilize the HCP to achieve her goals.

Comment. When working with the SP family, it was the therapist's judgment that many of the problems Mrs. P experienced were realistic and caused by a difficult, stressful life style, as well as a difficult child. The therapist determined that although increased professional time and effort would be required, the training program would have to become even more structured and simplified in order to develop Mrs. P's independent ability to maintain successful application of the programs in the future.

In this case the test phase of the morning HCP provided significant information about how to better direct and apply the available home contingency procedures, including brief parent counseling. With the mother's weekly records and informal reports, the therapist was able to utilize the results of the test phase to redirect the treatment response with improved results.

Finally, the SP case shows how the HCP is developed gradually based on a week-to-week assessment of the parents' records. Although the intervention program covered twenty weeks through the short-term follow-up, many of the contacts with Mrs. P were made by phone and in brief office meetings, and less than twelve hours of professional time were required.

TEN / INTERVENTION IV: Punishment Procedures

PURPOSE

The purpose of Intervention IV is to train parents to use procedures which can reduce persistent or intense aversive behavior. Successful training is judged by the parents' ability to reduce these unwanted behaviors in a relatively short period without extended negative interaction, so that the procedures themselves rapidly become unnecessary and, more importantly, by reducing aversive and intolerable child behavior, more time is available in the daily interaction for praisable behavior. Most parents will probably not require a punishment program when Interventions I through III are used as described in this manual. However, when a direct deceleration program is necessary, it must be applied correctly and with caution.

DESCRIPTION

Although punishment techniques of some kind are probably used in all cultures, the term "punishment" often produces negative feelings in both professionals and parents, so that the factors which define the use of punishment in systematic parent training must be carefully considered.

First, *the application of a punishment procedure for severe family and parent-child interaction disturbances does not add to the punitive exchanges already existing in the family.* Usually the disruptive behaviors to be decelerated are already very punishing to the family members, and the parents are already engaging in various types of "punishment," such as screaming, spanking, threats, and various penalties. The use of punishment in systematic parent training reorganizes the context, timing, quality, and consequences of punishment so that the negative family interaction is actually minimized and decreases over time.

Second, in this manual *the term "punishment" implies "deceleration" since it always describes a procedure which slows down, or decelerates behavior.* Three procedures which have been successfully used for slowing down behavior are: (1) the termination of reinforcing activity by a brief isolation period ("Time Out" or TO); (2) the application of penalties; and (3) the application of an aversive stimulus. In this chapter the focus is on the successful application and management of Time Out. The use of penalties or removal of a reinforcer is emphasized as a backup for the TO procedure and in some cases as an additional deceleration method. Aversive stimulation, such as spanking and criticism, has a very restricted role in systematic parent training and will not be discussed here.

It is important to note that any of these methods, however used, can only be considered an effective punishment procedure if the result is *a reduction in the behavior it follows.* Therefore, these procedures may provide different levels of success in limiting different kinds of problems, but they ultimately must have the same function. Also, *punishment is only used to decelerate serious, intolerable behavior.* Procedures other than punishment can be used to decelerate less aversive, milder disruptions, such as negative feedback and extinction by well-timed ignoring discussed in Chapter 7, and the reinforcement of behavior incompatible with disruptions using an HCP, as discussed in Chapter 8.

Third, *some kind of punishment procedure should be considered whenever intense aversive or intolerable behavior (1) has not diminished following Intervention III,* or *(2) is so frequent or intense that the time available for praisable behavior is seriously diminished,* or *(3) must be dealt with immediately anytime during the parent training program.* The MS case on page 15 is an example of a family problem which was so intolerable for the mother that the usual sequence of procedures in systematic parent training had to be postponed until the aggression was reduced by a deceleration procedure. In other families (like Case No. 3, Chapter 14) the problem behavior pattern required deceleration, but not urgently; and when an HCP was only partially successful, the mother requested a more intensive procedure.

In practice, the decision to use the procedures in this chapter to punish certain behaviors must be made individually for each family and child using the above criteria as guidelines. The procedures in this chapter have been found to be effective for children between the ages of two and twelve years who exhibit verbal and physical aggression, destructiveness, and continued nonresponse to any of the parents' terminating commands (limit testing). Other interventions should be considered when the problems involve repetitive delinquency, truancy and law breaking, self-destructiveness, bizarre behavior, or behavior accompanied by extreme anxiety or withdrawal (see Chapter 12).

Fourth, *punishment should be defined in the training as a transient, expedient method to help parents reduce serious problems.* In successful programs the punishment is not applied more than a few times since the child rapidly learns to respond to the warning signal which precedes the punishment, and thereby learns to avoid committing the behavior which earns the punishment. Thus, the common goal of each method described is to teach the parents to effectively use the cues (terminating commands) and stated contingencies (warning signals) which, having been previously followed by TO or a penalty, can replace the punishment.

Fifth, *the application of a punishment procedure is complex and necessitates a careful integration into the total treatment plan.* Even when a deceleration plan is applied prior to other interventions, the therapist should continue to work with the family to help them develop future alternatives to punishment even though their presenting problems are reduced. More commonly, Intervention IV will follow other interventions in the more systematic order presented in the treatment flo-chart, where the family can more easily understand the total context in which punishment should be used.

THE PROS AND CONS OF PUNISHMENT

There are a number of possible benefits and potential hazards in utilizing punishment procedures which the therapist should be aware of prior to suggesting that the family apply the methods of Intervention IV.

PROS

1. Punishment is the most rapidly effective available technique for reducing unwanted behavior.

2. Punishment can help initiate and maintain appropriate, productive, and nonaversive behavior patterns by reducing negative interaction.

3. Effectively applied punishment reduces its own necessity and can thus be relatively brief.

4. Punishment can teach children self-control when they learn to manage themselves in order to avoid the contingent loss or termination of reinforcing activity.

5. When TO is used, it removes the child from an environment which provides (a) cues for aversive behavior *and* (b) sources of desired incentives; thus TO terminates aversive behavior and at the same time can make possible the development of incompatible behavior (e.g., appropriate play) which prevents isolation from incentives.

6. Punishment, as used in systematic parent training, eliminates the need for negative physical interaction (spanking or fighting) between parents and their children. Effectively used, punishment allows parents to terminate intolerable behavior in a minimally intense, matter-of-fact manner (the emphasis is on the child *earning* TO, just as he earns other parent responses).

CONS

1. Even when punishment is successfully applied, the procedure can model negative social interaction for children as a means for solving interpersonal problems.

2. Punishment may have other side effects:

   a. The child's negative reactions toward the punishing agent, possibly including counteraggression.

   b. Strong emotional arousal and avoidance of the environment in which punishment occurs.

   c. Resistance in parents and professionals who for any reason wish to avoid negative confrontation or aggressive-like interaction.

d. The reduction of opportunities for appropriate, praisable behavior; usually TO only involves a loss of five or ten minutes, but when a response-cost procedure is used, the child may be required to lose an entire social activity period as a penalty for seriously disturbing behavior.

3. Punishment can be easily misused or overused by parents and therapists, and must be very carefully monitored by the therapist; thus the procedure can be costly in professional time and effort. Both parents and therapists often observe an immediate decrease in unwanted behavior when punishment is correctly applied. This effect can reinforce the use of punishment rather than procedures for improving desirable behavior.

SUGGESTED APPLICATIONS

The previous discussion focused on the therapist's preparation for the application of punishment procedures. In this section guidelines are presented for introducing the procedures to the parents.

Previous authors have described guidelines for using punishment, especially TO, which should be studied by the therapist prior to introducing Intervention IV to the parents. The best of these guidelines, written for parents as well as professionals, are Patterson's *Families*, Chapter 9 "Time Out" (1971); Becker's *Parents Are Teachers*, Chapter 5 "Punishment" (1971); and for professionals, Rose's *Treating Children in Groups*, Chapter 7 "Decreasing Maladaptive Behavior" (1973). Both the concepts and application of behavior deceleration programs are presented in these sources.

After meeting with the parents to discuss their progress, and having determined that Intervention IV is indicated, the therapist should attempt to get some *objective estimate of the rate and intensity of aversive behavior,* however informal, so that at least a one-week baseline for Intervention IV is available. This may be in the form of currently or previously acquired home records, family observation, and behavior checklist responses. Often the seriousness of the behavior can be estimated by the parent counting its occurrence during selected hourly blocks of time each day.

When the preintervention estimate of the problem has been made, the therapist can present the rationale and pros and cons of punishment, as described above, to the parents. The therapist should emphasize that the parents study and read about TO (e.g., in Patterson's *Families*) prior to planning its use in the home. Then the details of the methods chosen can be tailored to fit the particular problem observed.

The BR and RS cases in Chapter 11 illustrate the introduction of the TO procedures to the parent, as well as the principles and sequential steps relevant to TO and other punishment procedures. As described in the BR and RS cases, these procedures are summarized in the following points.

First, *meet with the parents to plan, rehearse, and review each of the steps in the TO sequence in advance, with the child present whenever possible.* Usually the best procedure is to (1) work out the details with the parents in the first part of the session, and then (2) bring the child in to present the plan to him and request his assistance and participation. Only a few minutes are required for the therapist and family to role play the entire sequence of TO. The effects of behavioral rehearsal can of course be maximized if it takes place in the home. The therapist should emphasize the positive aspects of the child's performance in other intervention programs used in the family, and the concept of the child's *earning* either pleasant or unpleasant consequences for his behavior.

Second, *select a suitable place in the home for the TO room.* Finding a place for TO can be difficult since most families do not have an available unused room free of stimulation. However, in almost all cases an approximation of the optimal conditions is quite adequate. There are probably increasing degrees of behavior control associated with increased stringency and isolation up to a point, although this is unproven. In practice any setting is effective when it accomplishes the goal of "time out from positive reinforcement." Therefore, some degree of restriction and isolation *is* necessary. Some families have had success with the "chair in the hall" or "chair in the corner" procedure, but this requires that the family members close by be very good at ignoring the punished child since the procedure is easily rendered ineffective by subtle attention perceived by him.

For the majority of families involved in systematic parent training careful planning and preparation of an available closed-off space is effective. The TO space should be well lighted, not too confining, void of stimulating or fun potential, void of dangerous materials such as glass objects or medicines, and readily accessible and easily monitored. Problems which arise in the child's adaption to the TO space usually occur in the first few instances of its use. When the difficulties are dealt with by the parent providing a brief explanation and by ignoring diversionary tactics, they usually are not recurrent.

Third, *determine an optimal time for TO duration.* The little evidence which is available indicates that five minutes is an optimum TO duration for most schoolage children (White, Nielsen and Johnson, 1972). Other anecdotal data and clinical observations support the notion that for very young children (aged two to four years), TO can be very effective only so long as it represents an interruption of reinforcing attention or activity. Thus two or three minutes may be sufficient for toddlers who often cease complaining or crying within this time period, and who then become engaged in distracting activity or self-stimulation, which can be reinforcing and countereffect the deceleration program.

Another consistent clinical observation is that periods of TO greater than five minutes are effective only if the extra minutes are contingently added to the basic TO period, as described in the cases in Chapter 11. Also, the study by White et al., reveals that there were no increases in the decelerating effect of TO periods which lasted longer than five minutes. Thus extended periods of TO add little, if any, to the desired effect, and may actually have a negative effect because less time is available for the child to engage in positive interaction.

Many parents and therapists may have previously applied a behavior contingency rather than the time duration contingency for TO suggested here. For example, most parents who come to the clinic will have tried the "go to your room" penalty for disruptive behavior. Usually a behavior contingency is then added, such as "when you calm down," or "when you think you can behave yourself, you may come out." However, this procedure usually results in the child's learning to avoid *being in* TO by temporarily terminating his disruptive behavior rather than learning to avoid *going in,* which occurs when the punishment has a nonnegotiable, absolute time duration. This is important because the success of the TO intervention is assessed by the child's ability to *stay out* of TO rather than to simply *get out*. Also, learning to stay out means more time available for reinforcing interaction.

Fourth, *integrate the TO procedure into existing interventions.* In most cases the parents will have applied Interventions II and III before beginning a punishment procedure. At every phase of applying TO the parents will need to utilize their skills of positive attending and ignoring. Often the child's diversionary tactics (whining, complaining, name calling, excuse making) are at a maximum during the initial stages of the TO procedure, and all behavior that detracts from the issue of completing the TO sequence should be ignored if possible. The parents' ability to ignore diversions is crucial since, in order for the punishment to be effective, the TO sequence must be completed once initiated.

As emphasized previously, the therapist should probably not suggest TO or any punishment procedure to the parents before determining that they are capable of effectively dispensing positive and negative attention consequent to their child's behavior. If a punishment procedure is ever indicated at a time when the parents are having difficulty mastering the skills emphasized in basic discrimination training, the individualized assertion and effectiveness training procedures discussed in Chapter 12 may be warranted.

The TO procedure can also be integrated into, or used concomitant with, an HCP. Aversive and intolerable behaviors can be treated at the same time an HCP is in effect. In this way the child can receive systematic positive attention or a reward *for not* performing the proscribed behavior, or *for* performing its incompatible counterpart; he can then receive the decelerating consequence if he breaks the rule. If the punishable response is not incompatible with an HCP item, or occurs at a different time of the day, the HCP should continue while the punishment procedure is applied concomitantly. When the punishment procedure is necessary *prior* to other programs, the therapist should introduce procedures as soon as possible to systematically increase positive interaction at times other than the occurrence of punishable behavior.

Just as the referred child's siblings are involved in other aspects of the family treatment plan, they should be included in the TO or other punishment program. Thus the contingencies stated for earning TO are not just proscriptions for a particular child, but *house rules* which apply equally to everyone. The siblings can be involved at any phase of the TO planning or application and can, in many cases, facilitate the acceptance of the plan by the referred child.

The previous guidelines have emphasized the general considerations which are necessary when preparing the parents to institute TO procedures. The remaining guidelines summarize the specific behavioral sequence for applying TO.

SPECIFIC GUIDELINES FOR PARENTS

The Specific Terminating Command. Once the aversive or intolerable behavior is observed, the parent should learn to use a verbal directive that states unambiguously that the child should immediately cease the activity. Parents are usually already using a large number of terminating commands; but without the all-important consistency of consequences, the commands have no discriminative stimulus value for the child. The first step in initiating the TO chain is usually the directive to terminate unwanted behavior or interaction. The exception is the use of a directive for the child to proceed directly to the TO room, which is necessary in cases of repeated disturbances that have previously earned TO. Examples of specific terminating commands, which communicate a clear, unambiguous message to the child, are:

"Richard, don't use the words ____ and ____ in this house."

"Brooke, stop hitting your sister right now."

"John, I want you to stop playing so rough with your brother."

The Warning Signal. The child may comply with the terminating command, in which case the episode ends with the child being praised. In most instances parents can terminate unwanted behavior by teaching their children to expect positive attention as a consequence of complying with the terminating command. However, the child's *noncompliance* and persistence in seriously aversive behavior is the occasion for the parents to present a warning signal. The warning signal is always followed by specific aversive consequences when ignored, and is thus distinguished from the parents' previous vague, excessive, or "doomsday" threats, such as "cut it out or else"; or, "just keep it up and see what happens"; or, "you do that once more and you can't watch TV for a month"; or, "either control yourself or go live somewhere else."

The effective warning signal always has two parts: *a clear statement of the transgression* and *the consequence of noncompliance with the terminating command,* in this case TO. Like the terminating command, the warning signal is only effective when it becomes a discriminative stimulus for a highly predictable consequence; also like the terminating command, the signal is omitted for repeated disruptions and TO is applied immediately. Commonly used warning signals are:

"This is a warning. If you use the words ____ or ____ again, you will earn five minutes in the TO room."

"I've asked you to stop hitting your sister. If you do it one more time, you'll have to go to Time Out."

"I'm not going to tell you any more not to play rough in the house. If you continue, you must go to Time Out."

The Beginning of the Time Out Period. Time Out is earned as a consequence of noncompliance with the terminating command, the warning signal, or with a "standing command" or ongoing house rule. When the child earns TO, he must receive it every time, just as if he had earned a point in the HCP. Most children, having actually rehearsed the procedure with the therapist and parents, begrudgingly will go to the TO room when instructed to do so. When the child moves toward the TO room, the parent should acknowledge the compliance with a simple "thank you" or, if necessary in the beginning, a more explicit shaping procedure to facilitate the child's compliance. A timer should *always* be used and shown to the child to indicate the exact beginning and end of the punishment period (small kitchen timers are readily available for a few dollars).

Parents and therapists often differ on whether or not to lock the TO room. Although it may be necessary in some cases the first few times the procedure is used, the child probably learns more from the experience if the controls are *social* rather than physical. Thus, while the locked door is not recommended, there must be contingencies for the child's noncooperation when punishment is being administered, such as the social backups discussed below.

The *manner* of sending a child to TO is of great importance, and often requires considerable supervised practice by the parent. In all phases of applying punishment the parent must show displeasure and firmness *without excessive emotional responses*; a nonapologetic matter-of-factness about the child's having earned a nonnegotiable consequence for his behavior; and *physical distance,* which means the parent should avoid using physical force to have the child enter the TO room.

The Use of Backups. As noted above, most of the problems which might arise in applying the TO procedure, especially resistance by the child, can be dealt with in advance by adequate preparation and behavioral rehearsal. However, in many families children do resist going into the TO room at one time or another, if for no other reason than to test the new system. Social backups for the TO procedure are therefore an essential part of the plan, and the deceleration program should not begin until the details of the backup are well understood and rehearsed. Thus, *parents should probably not seriously use a warning signal or even a terminating command until they are willing to back it up when necessary.* One or two instances of the parents not following through with the stated consequences in a deceleration program are probably reparable, but if the child perceives that a severe test of the program can render it inoperative, then the procedure obviously will not be effective. Even worse, the child's aversive behavior may escalate as a result of the parent's inconsistency.

The backup for TO must be a consequence the threat of which will motivate the child to follow the parent's instruction, "Go to the Time Out room." Perhaps the optimal backup is the loss of a reinforcing stimulus or the privilege to engage in a highly reinforcing activity. This technique has been called *response cost* since the child's response, or failure to make a response, produces a consequence which is "costly." Common examples are fines, or loss of the privilege to watch TV, play outside, stay up late, or ride one's bike. When planning the TO procedure at the beginning of Intervention IV, the therapist, parent and child should choose what the contingent backup will be. The therapist should advise the parents to try to arrange the backup so that the response cost occurs on the same day as the TO resistance so that the child can start each day without carrying over previously earned penalties.

As in other aspects of TO application, the parent's manner in using the backup is very important. Children who resist TO often also resist the backup, and may try to negate the cost of the penalty by such remarks as "I don't care if I have to stay in," or "I don't want to watch TV anyway." These statements should be ignored and the procedure followed through as planned; the effect of the backup can only be determined by the child's future cooperation, or lack of it, with the TO plan. Continued difficulty is an indication to find a more potent backup, or perhaps reassess the appropriateness of Intervention IV.

Interaction with the Child During and After Time Out. It is very important that the child receive no interaction or attention while in TO unless he creates a disturbance, in which case *additional time is earned.* Parents who provide attention or sympathy to the child during or after TO may find that the procedure is ineffective or, worse, that the TO makes possible a highly valued kind of interaction. A child being punished should receive the parent's displeasure, *if anything.* The brevity of the TO procedure makes this possible without extended negative interaction or separation.

Often the parents have their greatest difficulty in the post TO period, in the first few minutes after the child leaves the TO room. In general, the best procedure is for the parents not to respond to the child until he engages in some appropriate activity, or until a few

minutes have passed. In the RS case, in Chapter 11, Mrs. S, after the few minutes when Richard was very quiet after leaving the TO room, initiated the interaction. Often this response by the parent can serve as a prompt for the child to begin to engage in reinforceable activity.

Once the TO period is completed, it should be treated only as a past event. Any discussion in the family concerning TO after it is established policy should be in terms of encouragement for the children to avoid TO in the future by maintaining their desirable behavior.

The Use of Time Out for Problems Away From Home. A problem commonly observed in children when they are first exposed to TO is their continued or increased disturbances away from home when it is not possible to implement TO. Many children with this problem simply have not yet gained sufficient self-control for their behavior in settings different from home. Others may be testing the program by design to see if their parents will follow through in a difficult situation. However, regardless of the individual considerations, the TO procedure is jeopardized and may become ineffective, or at best situationally effective, unless away-from-home disruptions are reduced. Common examples of this problem include fighting, swearing, teasing or the commission of other punishable behavior in a moving car, or in the market, in church, or in a neighbor's house.

In general, the TO procedure should be extended to cover all previously specified, punishable behavior wherever it occurs, provided that the actual punishment follows within a few hours of the rule infraction. Parents often will have to exercise some ingenuity in applying the TO for away-from-home misbehavior, but with the therapist's help in rehearsing the plan, the parents usually are successful.

The primary ingredient which makes TO succeed so well is probably not so much its immediacy as its absolute predictability. The child learns that certain disruptions, wherever committed, will be followed by TO. All the steps in the TO sequence leading up to TO should be carefully followed. If the child is fighting or causing a disruption in the moving car, the parents should, if necessary to get the child's attention, stop the car and issue a terminating command, and perhaps at the same time a warning signal. If the behavior continues, the child is taken home as soon as possible and placed into the TO room. In cases of extreme disturbance both the terminating command and the warning signal can be omitted, and the child's punishment simply announced with a clear statement of what the offending disruption was. Many of the child's away-from-home disruptions can be handled using this procedure: the parent should first make eye contact with the child and get his undivided attention, then issue the command and warning and, if necessary, announce the punishment.

Usually this special use of TO only has to be applied a few times. The *consistent use* of TO can rapidly decelerate disruptive behavior as the child experiences the ubiquity of aversive consequences for intolerable behavior.

OTHER DECELERATION PROCEDURES

The primary deceleration technique used in systematic parent training other than TO is the response-cost method described above. Response cost was originally used to penalize someone by assessing a fine for misbehavior after he had already earned a number of reinforcers or tokens. In systematic parent training the procedure is modified somewhat since *the child never loses or is never fined for an item he has previously worked to possess.* Rather, in systematic parent training the procedure is a deprivation or penalty measure since the child must "pay" for his disrupting behavior by temporarily losing a reinforcing item or activity. Unlike TO, which terminates an ongoing episode of undesirable behavior, even in the context of a preferred activity, response cost denies the child an anticipated reinforcer. As used in the RS case, on page 88, for example, the penalty measure illustrates a number of features which make it ideal for the child's resistance to TO since it provides the parent with a strong decelerating consequence for the undesirable behavior without argument, physical contact, or extended negative verbal interaction. These same features make the response-cost procedure a very effective deceleration technique for a number of other problem behaviors. In this section other applications of response cost will be described.

All children have preferred activities and reinforcements which they are willing to work for such as in the HCP, and which they are willing to work to avoid losing, such as in the response-cost procedure. At one time or another most parents learn that by applying this latter principle they can prevent many types of disrupting behavior. However, when a parent imposes penalties in an ad hoc, or strongly punitive manner, they may find that the misbehavior accelerates as the parent and child continuously strive to out-punish one another. This negative cycle usually begins when the parents, frustrated by their lack or loss of control over the child, over-

respond emotionally and impose a penalty that is (1) unreasonable and (2) does not clearly specify how the child can avoid it in the future. The child may also respond emotionally, having learned that by plaintively pointing out the injustice and promising to behave, the punishment is shortened or avoided altogether. In this cycle the behavior of both parent and child will be repeated since the parent is *negatively reinforced* by the termination of their aversive feelings and interaction, and the child's manipulations are *negatively reinforced* by avoiding the punishment.

Another common misuse of response cost occurs when the parents find that by consistently applying penalties they can prevent many disturbances. Again, this technique, although a clear improvement over the previous example, is repeated due to negative reinforcement (the parent successfully terminates aversive behavior) and is thereby often overused.

In systematic parent training the short-term goal of a response-cost procedure (and TO) is to effectively decelerate unwanted behavior, but *only as a means for increasing the likelihood of other, more adaptive behavior.* The following general guidelines describe some of the considerations which should be made in applying a response-cost procedure:

1. If a deceleration program is clearly indicated, the response-cost procedure, like TO, should be carefully studied, planned and rehearsed prior to its application. All the cautions and considerations of using a deceleration technique should be pointed out and discussed with the parents.

2. There are two categories of behavior for which the response-cost method is particularly appropriate. First, as discussed above, resistance to a TO plan can be decreased when contingent penalties are utilized. Second, this method is very effective when applied to problems requiring deceleration which remain after an HCP (via incompatible response training) or TO, or for which an HCP or TO is not indicated. There are no generally accepted rules for including specific problems in these categories since the intervention method chosen depends so much on the treatment context and idiosyncratic difficulties of the family. However, a common class of disrupting behavior for which response cost can be effective is mismanaged or improperly used possessions and activities. These "mismanagement" problems are especially responsive when

the penalty is applied to the item or activity mismanaged. Examples are listed below:

Mismanaged Activity	Penalty
Riding bike in street or damaging bike	No bike use for a stated period
Extreme untidiness	No play until things are put away
Failure to turn off TV when asked	No TV privilege for stated period
Excessive fighting with friends	Friends cannot visit the next day

In many instances, of course, the mismanaged or disrupted activity does not contain a high-rate or preferred activity which can be used as a penalty. In such cases the penalty for infraction can be the removal of any reinforcer, provided that the plan is (a) worked out in advance, (b) has clearly defined contingencies for the penalty, and (c) represents a brief but meaningful punishment for the child. Brief case examples illustrating response cost for the child's mismanagement problems are presented in the following chapter.

As in Intervention III, response cost can also be applied for certain school problems with careful planning and monitoring by the therapist (see Chapter 8). The most common application is for parents to arrange home penalties for school-based behavioral disturbances, although the child's teacher can often develop a classroom intervention with or without the therapist's help. Problems which are responsive to the response-cost method when home penalties are contingently applied are aggressive behavior, excessive talking and moving about the classroom, breaking school rules, and any problems which can be pinpointed, documented, and easily treated by the teacher. Case No. 2, Chapter 14, contains an illustration of the response-cost method for a child's serious school disturbances.

CHARACTERISTICS OF
EFFECTIVE PUNISHMENT PROGRAMS

In this section some of the factors which are present in a successful deceleration program are listed. As has been emphasized, each phase of the application of punishment has a definite rationale and purpose. The therapist's and parents' understanding of these concepts, and how each step functions to minimize negative interaction, is very important for producing the short- and long-term results of Intervention IV.

1. After a successful trial of a punishment procedure, the entire interaction between the child and his disrupted environment is changed in terms of increased structure and expectancies made on him by his parents.

2. The parents' former ineffective, repeated, terminating commands have become more specific and now function as a discriminated cue for the child to terminate some behavior. Similarly, the parents' former threats are now highly meaningful warning signals that are always followed by punishment if ignored, and positive parental attention if the child responds to the signal.

3. Both the terminating commands and the warning signals are usually given with decreased latency as the parent becomes more practiced, which can have the effect of terminating the disruptive behavior earlier in the chain than before, thus preventing much of the behavior from ever occurring and being reinforced.

4. By responding to the terminating command, the child learns to avoid the warning signal; or, by responding to the warning signal, he learns to avoid the punishment. In this way the child not only receives *negative reinforcement* for avoiding the cue for punishment, but *positive reinforcement* for his "self-management"; his parents positively attend to him, and he retains the opportunity to engage in appropriate, reinforcing activity. Thus the child begins to learn a pattern that will tend to be repeated; in the case of TO, he learns (a) how to avoid going in, (b) how to stay out, and (c) that staying out can make other pleasurable activities possible. By this reasoning perhaps the most direct assessment of a punishment procedure is the number of times its use is required. As long as the deceleration procedure is necessary, the child's behavior is being terminated or suppressed by the punishment. Only when the child *avoids* TO or a penalty altogether does his behavior reflect the development of self-management skills.

5. In systematic parent training the therapist attempts to apply the punishment procedure in such a way that it cannot fail. This is accomplished not only by the high degree of structure which characterizes a TO or response-cost technique, but also

by the inclusion of relatively fail-safe backups for use when the child resists the exclusion or penalty for severe aversive behavior. Thus a major reason for the child's deceleration of behavior is his knowledge, in advance, that backups will be used, based on his actual experience of the backup penalty should he choose to test the limits of the program.

6. An additional fail-safe mechanism is the parents' promotion and reinforcement of behaviors which are incompatible with the previous disrupting behavior. If the child has received TO for sibling aggression, for example, his aggressive behavior should gradually be replaced with appropriate sibling interaction and play. This transition can be accomplished when the parents improve the child's compliance to terminating commands (allowing him to avoid TO and continue his interactions with others) and praise the child's appropriate play or positive interaction whenever it does occur. Thus, as in Intervention III, while one class of behaviors is decelerating, another is accelerating. The parents' effective use of punishment requires all the skills emphasized in systematic parent training: understanding social learning principles, basic discrimination ability, and consistently praising desirable behaviors that are incompatible with the punished behavior.

MAINTENANCE TRAINING

In most of the families treated the effect of Intervention IV, by a consensus of reports and judgments, will be a decrease in the presenting problems. In these cases a few sessions of maintenance training should be recommended to help the parents prepare for problems which may arise in the future. As emphasized in previous chapters, the most efficient maintenance skill is *preventive maintenance,* whereby the parents' continued application of consistent, contingent consequences together with structured family interaction makes aversive behavior unlikely.

In the case of punishment procedures it is especially important that the therapist evaluate the parents' judgment and skill for independently utilizing punishment. After the parents have successfully applied the Intervention IV procedures, the therapist can make several suggestions to safeguard their future use of punishment. First, by way of review, it should be pointed out that punishment should only be applied when (a) an acceleration program for incompatible, appropriate behavior cannot be developed, or (b) the child's behavior is so extreme that an immediate deceleration plan is indi-

cated. Second, the parents should be advised to contact the therapist when persistent aversive behavior occurs so that the difficulty can be evaluated and the proposed punishment plan can be reviewed prior to its application. Whenever possible all the concepts, procedures, and cautions emphasized in this chapter should be reviewed carefully each time a punishment program is applied.

Parents who have successfully utilized a TO procedure usually have no trouble adapting it for other punishable offenses, but they may need additional practice and behavioral rehearsal with the response-cost method. For example, TO may not be appropriate for a child over age ten or eleven, but a modified TO procedure, such as a restriction of desired activity, can be very effective. The parents can be encouraged to practice applying a response-cost or penalty procedure for aversive or intolerable behaviors which may occur, and based on their experience with response cost as a backup for TO. When helping the parents rehearse the application of a response-cost procedure, the therapist should reemphasize each of the important ingredients for establishing penalties for unwanted behavior: fairness; family discussion (including the child) and planning of all details of the punishment in advance; relatively brief duration of penalties; posting of rules to specify desirable and undesirable behavior and to forewarn the child; and parental consistency in exacting the penalty. The parents can attempt to anticipate future difficulties and verbally describe how they can most efficiently apply these guidelines to reduce serious undesirable behavior. The therapist's role here should be to provide support and consultation for the parents, helping them with their planning as needed.

ASSESSMENT OF INTERVENTION IV

The assessment of Intervention IV, as with other interventions in systematic parent training, must be made for both the short-term and long-term goals of the treatment.

First, the short-term results will be reflected in the parents' records, reports, and other measures of the intervention effects. These records should be examined regularly to determine whether or not the target behavior is decelerating. There is no special record chart for Intervention IV like the one in the HCP, but the therapist should nevertheless place great emphasis on the child's daily or weekly "chart," however informal, to publicly indicate his progress. Also, no absolute or quantitative significance level is relevant for assessing the outcome of punishment since the important criteria are the parents' perception and the therapist's judgment of the child's progress. Just as the parents and therapist together determined the original degree of seriousness of the child's disrupting behavior, they must also judge after the intervention *if the family environment is disrupted significantly less than before.* The available records should be utilized to clarify judgments. Parents at times disagree with each other, the therapist, and the records about the degree of change occurring in their children, and in these cases the available objective data are important to validate the therapist's assessment.

If problems continue after the application of the punishment procedures suggested here, it may reflect incomplete participation by the parents. The parents may possess inadequate basic discrimination skills or motivation to succeed in Intervention IV. Usually a few sessions of Intervention V (Parent Counseling) will at least clarify for the therapist some of the reasons for the difficulties. If it is then determined that the child's problems cannot be expected to decrease with the parents as the treatment agents, individual treatment of the child or the parents may be indicated.

Second, while the short-term goal of behavior deceleration is essential in Intervention IV, *the most meaningful evaluation of the treatment involves the long-term effects.* Thus, no matter how powerful the deceleration procedures are, the enduring, general influence of the treatment cannot be evaluated until the follow-up assessment is made.

The therapist must carefully examine the entire family interaction during follow-up after using Intervention IV. Initially, the therapist should determine if the treatment gains are maintained, i.e., if the original decelerated target behaviors remain at a low rate. This assessment may require a week or more of parent records, including responses to questionnaires and the therapist's clinic or home observations of the parent-child interaction. Next, assuming that the follow-up data indicate the maintenance of treatment goals, the therapist must determine that the problems are not merely being *suppressed* by the punishment, but that appropriate interaction has become predominant. This can be evaluated by observing *decreases* in the parents' use of punishment and the child's aversive behavior, and *increases* in the child's appropriate play and verbal interaction, and the parents' contingent positive attention for desirable behaviors.

SUGGESTED PROFESSIONAL TIME AND EFFORT

The professional time and effort required for the effective applica-

tion of Intervention IV is quite variable and difficult to anticipate. Even when a structured program of TO is used there is much variation in the way families respond and in the efforts required by the therapist. With cooperative parents, whose only agenda is to decrease some particularly obtrusive or dangerous behavior so that the family can have a more pleasant and enriching environment, the punishment procedures in this chapter are not only effective but *efficient* since minimal professional time and effort (often as little as three to five hours) is necessary. As noted earlier, however, the treatment of many families is complicated by parents who have trouble initiating the parent behaviors that are necessary for the program to be successful, or who misuse the punishment techniques in one way or another. This latter class of parents may have already had problems applying previous interventions (thus contributing to the necessity for Intervention IV) but who have special difficulty using or maintaining a punishment program. In these cases the therapist must exert additional professional time and effort and recommend the procedures described in Chapter 12. The extended application of deceleration procedures often requires ten or more hours of professional time.

It has been emphasized that Intervention IV is technically and clinically the most complex of the interventions yet described in this manual. Accordingly, if clinic staff other than fully trained clinicians are involved in the application of Intervention IV (or Intervention V), they should be well supervised. The regular clinic staff should be available if needed and the families treated should be monitored for any untoward effects or misuse of punishment.

SUMMARY

The application of a punishment procedure in systematic parent training involves considerable therapist skill and professional time and effort. However, when Intervention IV is preceded by and then integrated into Interventions I through III, it can be extremely effective in decelerating unwanted behavior. All the procedures for applying punishment emphasize its transiency and the importance of not only terminating inappropriate behavior but of increasing concomitant appropriate interaction; *punishment is effective when it is used only a few times and helps to develop the child's socialization and self-management skills.*

ELEVEN / PUNISHMENT PROCEDURES: Case Illustrations

INTRODUCTION

The cases in this chapter are presented to further demonstrate the punishment procedures discussed in Chapter 10. As in other case illustrations in this manual, the application of intervention procedures in the families described here allows the reader to observe how the therapist makes decisions about the subtle, unprogrammatic aspects of applying the procedures in parent training. The therapist's *decision-making behavior* is increasingly important as the family problems and required interventions become more complex. The following cases, where the therapist is presenting the TO procedure to parents (the BR and RS families) and helping the parents to devise effective response-cost procedures (the remaining four cases), each require a unique integration of the punishment procedures into their family life.

THE BR FAMILY: INTRODUCING TIME OUT

Mrs. R came to the clinic complaining that her five-year-old, adopted daughter, Brooke, was "very difficult." She whined a lot, was very active and noisy, and occasionally became aggressive with her two-year-old brother. Following Intervention II, Mrs. R's records showed that she was successful in reducing the whining and inappropriate activity, and increasing sustained play. However, Brooke's excessively physical play with her brother was increasing, and Mrs. R said that she could no longer ignore this behavior and asked for help. A week of home records and a clinic observation confirmed the seriousness of the problem: Brooke's "intolerable behavior," defined as "pushing or hitting her brother," was observed more than five times per day at home, as well as frequent rough play in the clinic. The therapist then developed a specific procedure for Mrs. R.

Therapist	Looking at our records for the last week, it appears that Brooke is even more aggressive with her brother than you had guessed. I think that we ought to go ahead with a deceleration program. Did you read the chapter on "Time Out" in Patterson's book?
Mother	Yes. Maybe the Time Out thing will work. You know, I used to take away treats when she hit her brother, but when that stopped working I was about to start spanking her.
Therapist	Now we want to plan very carefully how you can use the procedure. Last week I said that today we would talk about how we use punishment in our parent training programs. (The therapist then discussed the rationale for using punishment, and encouraged Mrs. R to relate her understanding of the chapter she had read. He learned that she and her husband had both read the material and were eager to try the TO procedure.) First we need to find a good place in the house for the Time Out room. We need a room that is easily accessible and free of stimulating toys or fun things to do. What do you think?
Mother	Well, there is her bedroom—but that wouldn't work, and anyway she often is in there when she gets rough. How about the hallway?

Therapist	Is it closed in?
Mother	Only at one end—but I could put up a barrier at the other end.
Therapist	It would be better if there were a small room, completely closed in. But not a closet—we don't want to frighten her.
Mother	How about our small washroom off the hallway? But maybe she would hurt herself in there.
Therapist	How?
Mother	Well, I don't know—but she could run water and mess up the place. I think she would, she'd be so angry at me for putting her in there.
Therapist	We'll come back to the mess-making problem later. But what should you do if she gets angry about being put in?
Mother	Nothing—I would just ignore it.
Therapist	Good. OK, let's think about using the washroom. The next step is to practice the exact procedure you will use. There are several "do's and don'ts" about using Time Out, and we'll cover them as we go. You should make notes of our plan today, then go over the plan with your husband, and then together you can present the plan to Brooke. It's very important that Brooke knows you are both completely together on this plan. Now let's decide how to present the plan to her; you need to remind her that she has been having more of a problem with hitting than before, and that you and her father want to help her stop this since it is dangerous.
Mother	But she'll just start crying and promise to be good—I know she will.
Therapist	Just assure her that you know she wants to stop hitting, and that your new plan will help. When she stops crying, ask her to listen closely so that she will know how it works. Tell her that whenever she is rough with her brother you will let her know that you want her to stop, and that if she continues to be rough, she will earn five minutes in the Time Out room. Take her to the washroom and show her how she should sit in the room and wait for the signal indicating that it is time to come out. Show her your kitchen timer and how you will set it for five minutes. Tell her when the bell rings she can come out if she is quiet. Any questions about how to present the plan before we practice it a bit?
Mother	No, but I'm wondering about something else. You never said what to do if she makes a mess or breaks something.
Therapist	Just look into the room to see that she's all right, then tell her you will have to add one minute to the five minutes for each disturbance in the Time Out room. But she can't come out until all her time is up and the bell rings. Then, if there is a mess at the end of the time, have her clean it up.

Mother	But if I add minutes the first time she starts messing up, she might be in there all afternoon.
Therapist	No, she won't. As soon as she learns that your warning means business, she'll stop her rough behavior.
Mother	That's another thing. I threaten her all the time but it doesn't work.
Therapist	Perhaps you don't always follow through with your threats. A warning should be a specific signal that a particular consequence is about to occur unless the behavior changes; if your warning signal is clear, and you follow through *every* time Brooke ignores the signal, it will soon have a lot of meaning for her. Then when she learns to respond to the warning signals, you won't need to use the Time Out room. Now many children test the TO program when it begins, and try to get things back like they used to be. What should you do if she tests your plan by refusing to go into the room?
Mother	Well, I guess I would add one minute to the timer for every minute she delayed.
Therapist	Very good, But what if she still refused to go? What's your final backup?
Mother	I don't know. I don't want to physically force her.
Therapist	That's right—and you shouldn't. But not following your instruction to go to the TO room is pretty serious. One kind of backup is to restrict the child from some activity she really likes.
Mother	That might work. Brooke's favorite TV shows are in the late afternoon. So if she refuses to go to the Time Out room, she can't watch TV. Is that right?
Therapist	Yes, but only for the day she refuses to go. What if she has a problem after she has already watched TV?
Mother	I suppose if her father's home he could help out—or we could have her go to bed early. But really, I don't think we'll need any of this. She'll go to the Time Out room, I'm sure.
Therapist	You're probably right. Now it sounds like we're ready to rehearse how you and Mr. R will present the plan to Brooke. Let's pretend I'm Brooke, and you are explaining the plan to me. I'll help you if you leave anything out. (Mrs. R then practiced instructing "Brooke" about the new plan until she was very comfortable with it. The therapist and Mrs. R reviewed her written notes of the procedures, which she was to take home to help plan the use of TO with her husband.) Now, next week, can you all come in so we can practice the plan with everyone present?
Mother	Well, my husband will have a very hard time coming in during the day. Besides, I think I can present the plan to them all right.
Therapist	OK. I'll call in a few days to see how you're doing. Also, you should call me if you have any problems.

Comment. In the BR case the mother convinced the therapist that she was capable of communicating the TO procedures to her husband and Brooke, and stated that she wanted to try it for a week without the therapist's direct involvement. In this case Booke responded very well to the TO plan, and no aggression was observed after the second week.

In other cases the therapist may judge that it is important to be present with the entire family, in the clinic or home, to discuss and rehearse the procedures. No proven criteria are available to help the therapist decide how much involvement is necessary when introducing a punishment procedure to the family but, in general, if there are any doubts about the parent's skill or motivation, the therapist can increase the likelihood of success by direct instruction and role playing with the child. Case No. 3, Chapter 14, illustrates the therapist's direct involvement in preparing the family for the TO procedure.

The BR case illustrates a number of the principles for using TO or other punishment of intolerable behavior. Especially emphasized was the importance of carefully specifying and planning each component of the procedural sequence in advance, such as determining the best place for the TO room and establishing the backups for the program.

THE RS FAMILY:
TESTING THE LIMITS

Mrs. S, a single parent, reported that her eight-year-old son, Richard, was continuing to use extremely bad language, even after she had tried for a long time to ignore the behavior. Also, Mrs. S had attempted to give her son points for not swearing, but he usually confronted her when he failed to earn the points (for his allowance) and she would back down or begin yelling vague threats such as "If you get me mad, you've had it." The therapist suggested a retrial of basic discrimination training but Mrs. S complained that she was at "wit's end," and simply could no longer ignore Richard's bad language.

Both the therapist's previous observations and Mrs. S's HCP records on a difficult AM period had indicated that she was capable of consistent, positive attention for many of her son's desirable behaviors, and it was decided to develop a deceleration program for Richard's swearing. The basic plan was to continue the HCP and to introduce a TO procedure initially during the afternoon since Richard's language was usually at its worse when he came home after school. A week of record keeping by the mother indicated that during a two-hour afternoon period Richard used the two words Mrs. S judged to be the most offensive, at a daily average of five times per hour.

The TO procedures were introduced to Mrs. S and rehearsed as described previously for the BR case. Unlike the BR family, Mrs. S lived in a small house with no available washroom or other completely enclosed space. Therefore, the therapist visited the home and worked out a plan with Mrs. S to utilize a closed-off hall space with a door at either end. Although not a room as such, the hall space was referred to as the "Time Out Room," and a chair was placed in the enclosed space.

In the session prior to beginning the TO procedure the therapist met with Richard and his mother and observed Mrs. S introducing the plan and explaining how the TO would work, including the backup of restricted TV use. As part of the plan, Mrs. S named for Richard the two most aversive words he commonly used and stated that the purpose of the program was to help him learn not to use such language so often, and especially at home.

During the interaction sequences below Mrs. S demonstrated her initial application of the procedure for Richard's problem after practicing with the therapist and Richard in the clinic. Commentary is added to illustrate the mother's generally correct use of the principles underlying the deceleration program.

Interaction	*Comment*
Child (Comes in from school, begins complaining that the television does not work and curses it. When he sees his mother approaching, he yells at her, using many swear words)	
Mother Don't use that language in this house. You know I don't like it and I want you to stop it now.	Unlike previous interactions, Mrs. S uses a specific terminating command to clearly communicate her position.

Child	(Again yells a choice epithet, adding "You can't stop me.")	Richard confronts his mother's directive.
Mother	This is a warning. If you use the words f--- or s--- again, you will earn five minutes in the Time Out room.	Mrs. S states her position even more clearly in the form of a warning signal and a specific contingency.
Child	(Repeats his own threat and exclaims with several swear words that he doesn't care if he goes in the TO room)	Richard breaks the rule, testing his mother's warning signal.
Mother	Richard, you have earned five minutes in the Time Out room. Go there at once as we practiced yesterday and sit down. I will set this timer for five minutes. If you are quiet, it will ring in five minutes and you may come out. If not, I will add a minute for each disturbance you make. Now don't say another word and get in there!	Mrs. S follows through just as planned, specifying the exact behavior she wants to see and correctly using the timer. However, she still becomes a bit emotional at a time when she should be trying to be calm and matter-of-fact.
Child	I don't want to go in your stupid Time Out room. Anyway, Johnny (his best friend) doesn't have to do anything when he curses.	Richard indicates his displeasure at going into TO and begins to use diversionary tactics.
Mother	Go on in the room. I just added one minute to your time for delaying.	Mrs. S applies the contingency as practiced by ignoring the diversionary tactic and restating her position.
Child	(Goes into the TO room, and after about a minute yells his favorite profanity)	Richard continues to test the contingency at the same time revealing his discomfort about the isolation. Mrs. S could perhaps have ignored the outburst, but chose to follow through with her stated contingency.
Mother	(Walks to the door of the hallway and informs Richard that his outburst just earned him one additional minute)	
Child	(Begins to sob and moan about being mistreated, calls his mother names, but without yelling or cursing)	Richard may be attempting a new diversionary tactic, but he does terminate the offensive language.
Mother	(Continues her work in the kitchen, makes no response)	Now Mrs. S chooses to ignore Richard's whining.
Child	(Later has several more outbursts, and earns a total of fifteen minutes before the bell rings)	
Mother	(Hears bell, and announces that it is time for Richard to come out)	
Child	(Stomps out of room, says he'll never go back in the room, using f--- and s--- several times)	Richard again tests the new contingency. A number of TO's may be necessary before Richard perceives that the punishment is a consistent, predictable consequence for swearing.
Mother	Okay, you know the rule. Go back to the Time Out room for five minutes.	

Child	(Begins to scream and curse, saying that he will never go back in)
Mother	Go to the Time Out room right now or there'll be no TV for you for the rest of the day.
Child	(Mumbling, goes into the TO room, and is quiet until the timer rings. Hearing the bell, he comes out and is very quiet)
Mother	(Ignores Richard for a few minutes, then asks him what he would like to do)

Mrs. S states the consequence of not complying with her directive to go into the TO room.

Mrs. S could have waited for a praisable behavior after TO ended, but chose to initiate an interaction after a few minutes of quiet.

Comment. In the RS case, the mother correctly and thoughtfully applied TO and a response-cost "backup" to terminate behavior that was very aversive to her and also to help the child control his excessive, limit-testing behavior. This case shows the importance of the parent's assertive skill and absolute consistency in applying punishment.

THE APPLICATION OF RESPONSE COST

Twelve-year-old Sheldon was referred to the clinic for extreme emotional outbursts and destructive behavior. After a very difficult treatment course, involving Interventions I through III and parent counseling for Sheldon's very strict parents, the family interaction improved considerably. Sheldon was able to earn a mini-bike as a result of an HCP focusing on behaviors incompatible with yelling, whining, and destructiveness. Also, his parents were less demanding and more positive toward him. However, shortly after earning his mini-bike, which he was extremely proud of, Sheldon began to abuse his "bike rules" by riding it in the street, letting others ride it, and on one occasion he damaged it in a fall. The parents' initial response was to take the bike away for a month, but after about a week of the penalty Sheldon began to complain bitterly about his "mistreatment" and to scream at his parents as he had before, causing them to argue and fight. Sheldon's father wanted to reduce the penalty, while his mother wanted to double it.

The therapist, on learning of the problem, requested that the entire family come in to systematically plan a program for Sheldon to use his bike. It was learned that no specific contingency was stipulated concerning bike misuse other than the vague rule that

Sheldon would "lose the bike" if he damaged it or rode it in the street.

First, the therapist and parents reviewed earlier discussions about rules, consistency and contingent parent responding. Both parents were very emotional about the bike use, however, and continued to argue about "sending the bike back to the store," and the severity of punishment warranted for rule infractions. The therapist suggested a compromise plan, which included the following:

1. Closer supervision of bike use.

2. Selection and family discussion of penalties for bike mismanagement. It was decided that any rule breaking would result in a one-week loss of bike privileges (the penalty duration was suggested by Sheldon and agreed to by both parents).

3. Posting the bike rules in the garage, which clearly and simply specified the expected behavior concerning bike use, and the penalty for infractions.

Comment. In this case the therapist's efforts at interrupting the deteriorating family interaction, by restructuring the parents' response-cost "plan," was effective. Sheldon was able to understand how he could determine, by his behavior, the penalties associated with bike misuse. If his destructive behavior or other outbursts had continued, the therapist could then have met with Sheldon and his parents to suggest applying the bike-loss penalty as a consequence for other intolerable or severely aversive behavior. However, prior to recommending an extension of the deceleration procedure, the therapist would need to assess all aspects of the disturbing behavior, including possible family interactions which might precede and play a role in Sheldon's outbursts.

A CASE OF
SIBLING RIVALRY

Sandy, age five, began to play very roughly with her toys and dolls shortly after her brother was born. Her mother initially tried to stop the destructiveness by criticism, lectures, using repeated terminating commands, and having long sessions with Sandy to reassure her that her parents loved her as much as they loved the baby. The problem continued, however, and Sandy's mother began screaming at her, perhaps because the result of screaming was usually Sandy's promise to "be good" and not do it again. When the screaming proved ineffective, Sandy's mother decided to take away her playthings when she caught her daughter being destructive. However, Sandy continued to break her toys and to damage her dolls whenever they were available. Finally, the mother requested help for her daughter, feeling certain that it reflected "deep-seated" emotional problems.

Sandy's "rough play with her toys" maintained at a high rate (averaging about three or four episodes a day) during the mother's private record keeping. During this time the mother did well in Interventions I and II, demonstrating much improvement in her ability to appropriately provide differential attention for Sandy's behavior in a contingent fashion. However, neither the record keeping nor Interventions I and II had much effect on Sandy's problem behavior. It was decided to try a deceleration program in conjunction with a modified HCP, whereby Sandy's afternoon "treat" could be earned if no rough play occurred during the day. Thus the cost of a destructive response any time during the day was the loss of Sandy's highly anticipated daily treat, while a perfect day with no rough play was required to earn it. A chart, used to show the number of days with no problem, revealed that over a three-week period Sandy reduced her rough play, and by the fourth week earned her treat every day.

Comment. Sandy's case illustrates the effective use of a combined acceleration-deceleration program for a problem which might ordinarily justify the use of TO. However, the low intensity of the problem, combined with the fact that TO would remove Sandy from the opportunity of reinforcers for appropriate behavior in the presence of her brother, provided the rationale for the therapist to use a less intense deceleration plan.

THE SUNDAY BOX

Mr. and Mrs. O came to the clinic requesting help for themselves, and received treatment for a number of marital difficulties over a six-month period. They began to report progress in improving their relationship, but complained that they recently had become aware of how they argued so much about managing their three children. The children had no serious problems that were apparent, but an issue of some importance to the parents was the reported "chaotic" and "messy" habits of the children. The parents admitted being poor models, but wanted the children to be neater in spite of their own behavior.

The therapist decided to utilize the "Sunday Box" technique devised by Lindsley (unpublished) whereby a clothes hamper would be placed in the hallway to be a depository for stray clothes. The parents were willing to try out the idea, so it was agreed that at the next session the entire family would come in to discuss the plan. During the session the rules were specified; each family member helped to set the plan up with the therapist's assistance. It was decided to post the following rules over the hamper and to try the plan for a month.

1. This hamper is hereby named the Sunday Box.

2. Anyone in the family may place any item of clothes or shoes in the Sunday Box at anytime if the item is found lying anywhere about the house, out of place. Bedrooms will not be included.

3. Items placed in the Sunday Box will remain there until the following Sunday, at which time all items in the box must be claimed by their owners.

Mr. and Mrs. O found the "Sunday Box" plan to be very effective, perhaps because of the unpleasant threat of the "cost" of untidy habits. Modifications of this response-cost procedure can be devised to help decelerate a number of related problems, such as a small child's problem with leaving toys scattered about the house or front yard, or an older child's forgetfulness about putting away skates, other accident-producing objects, or favorite items such as tools or games.

AWAY-FROM-HOME
DISTURBANCES

Five-year-old Danny A was referred for high-rate aggressive behavior. The baseline findings, presented in Chapter 5, supported the need for an intervention program at home, and possibly at school. Following Intervention III, much of Danny's disruptive and aggressive behavior had decreased, and the family interaction with Danny had improved considerably. However, Mrs. A reported that while the interventions were very effective at home, she could not control Danny away from home, and during recent weeks he had caused serious disturbances in the supermarket and once in the car by hitting and provoking his brother. Mrs. A's home records showed that Danny provoked a fight with his brother about twice a day, and several times a week the disruption occurred when she and the children were away from home. Also, Danny's brother was constantly complaining to his mother about Danny's "bugging" him, and had begun to fight back.

In the next session the therapist pointed out that Danny's out-of-home disturbances, especially those occurring in a moving car, were potentially dangerous and should be reduced without delay. The therapist then suggested a response-cost procedure whereby Danny or his brother would be penalized for hitting wherever it occurred, even though the plan was primarily for Danny. The therapist and Mrs. A worked out a plan in which either boy (they both played outside every day until dinner time) would lose the privilege of outside play on the same day he was aggressive in a potentially injurious manner (including hitting, kicking and throwing objects) according to the following procedure:

1. Immediately on observing the first incident of an aggressive act on a given day, Mrs. A should get Danny's (or his brother's) full attention and state a specific terminating command and a warning, such as, "Danny, listen to me. Stop provoking your brother at once. If you continue, you must stay inside the house for the rest of the day. Do you understand?"

2. If away from home when the episode occurs, the penalty should start as soon as Danny arrives home.

3. If both boys are involved in "bugging" each other, they should both be restricted.

Mrs. A was advised to present the entire plan to the boys as a means of helping Danny reduce his "bugging" behavior, and to point out that they would get along much better if there were less fighting between them.

The immediate result was a decline in both the frequency and the intensity of Danny's aggressive behavior and the conflict between the boys. Danny continued to tease his brother, but Mrs. A reported that she found that by ignoring this, instead of criticizing him, Danny usually would stop short of the physical interaction. Mrs. A also felt that the primary difference was the clear rule setting and threat of consequences for both boys since on several occasions in the next few weeks Danny did lose his outside play privilege and was very upset about the penalty. One estimate of the effectiveness of the punishment procedure was the finding that it was applied with decreasing frequency in the first month, and only twice in the following three months.

Comment. In the DA case the response-cost procedure was effective for any one of several reasons, including the restructuring of the mother's expectations by stating the rules, the consistently applied contingency of the penalty, and Danny's cooperation after learning that the plan involved his brother's behavior also. As in the previous cases, the goals were achieved by interventions which produced a number of concomitant desirable changes in the family interaction.

Another consideration concerns the therapist's choice of response cost as the appropriate intervention for the DA case. TO is ordinarily effective for away-from-home sibling aggression simply by instructing the child to go to the TO room when he gets home, as discussed in the previous chapter. However, the effective extension of TO for problems occurring outside the home usually requires that the procedure has first been well established for in-home problems. In the DA case the opportunity was present for a deceleration plan that involved no new elements in the family routine, and thus could be easily integrated into the daily interactions between Mrs. A and her sons. Consequently, the determination of the appropriate intervention was based on the relative parsimony of the response-cost procedure. If the plan had not been successful, then the therapist could still have utilized TO alone or in combination with the afternoon restriction.

TWELVE / INTERVENTION V: Parent Counseling

PURPOSE

The purpose of Intervention V is to provide the parents with an opportunity (1) to discuss current problems which interfere with the treatment progress and, if necessary, to prepare for a retrial of previous interventions, and (2) to continue working on the home interventions when direct child, parent or family treatments are needed.

DESCRIPTION

Parent counseling is necessary in systematic parent training because of the prevalence of families who need and can profit by sessions with the therapist beyond the initial parent training interventions. Parent counseling can be an important aspect of *any* intervention, and is actually being utilized anytime the therapist, judging that the family's progress is slowed or interrupted, attempts to improve the parents' commitment or involvement regarding the treatment. *"Counseling" simply implies that the parent-therapist interaction includes facilitative, corrective, and supportive inputs from the therapist.* This interaction can be initiated any time, by the parent's request or the therapist's suggestion.

In Intervention V, therefore, the term parent counseling does not imply that the modality has a restricted use in the training; rather, it indicates that a time-limited series of regular sessions is set aside for the parents to try to improve their family's progress in the total intervention program.

As will be seen in this chapter, Intervention V includes different applications of parent counseling, from the brief supportive and restructuring contacts to the integration of counseling with intensive therapies.

SUGGESTED APPLICATIONS

In this manual the application of parent counseling will be presented according to the sequence usually followed from the point where the family's progress in systematic parent training is halted or slowed. There are two major steps in this sequence: *(1) recognition and identification of problems,* and *(2) disposition and resolution of the interfering factors.*

IDENTIFICATION OF INTERFERING FACTORS

The initial indication of the need for Intervention V is the recognition of unsatisfactory family progress by the therapist or parent, either informally or in the treatment records. This may occur at any time in systematic parent training. Each intervention makes different demands on the existing family system, and on the therapist, which are intensified as more complex interventions are applied. Thus Interventions I and II often require an *attitudinal and behavioral reorientation* which some parents do not integrate or accept as rapidly as others. Intervention III, the HCP, requires a significant degree of restructuring of the daily family interaction, and the parents' initial acceptance is at times temporary and incomplete for many reasons. In Intervention IV the parents may likewise superficially accept the systematic use of punishment procedures but resist, for various reasons, the correct home application of Time Out or penalties. In some cases, as in Case No. 3, Chapter 14, it is necessary to provide parents with counseling and perhaps individual treatments concomitant with Intervention IV.

Whenever the therapist becomes aware of problems with the family's progress, he should meet with the parents and try to reach a consensus concerning *the identification of the problems encountered.* A good procedure is to use the available records to pinpoint the areas of difficulty, and then to discuss the specific goals which are not being attained as planned. While there are many problems that can interfere with the treatment progress in systematic parent training, most of the difficulties encountered result from (a) situational problems, (b) extreme behavioral disruptions in the family, and (c) inadequate parental responsiveness to the therapist's suggestions, especially in the form of parental inconsistency.

Situational problems often reflect practical scheduling difficulties which have temporarily halted the treatment progress. For example, many single parent families have working mothers who do not effectively implement the procedures at home due to fatigue and concern about their daily schedule. Other practical problems can include a family's excessive distance from the treatment agency (prohibiting regular visits), inability to afford the agency's fees (financial hardship), and unavoidable factors, such as the family's moving from the area or experiencing a serious illness, or loss, of a family member.

Extreme or precipitous behavioral disruptions by the child or other family members can slow or interrupt the treatment. Severe disruptiveness in the child is especially a problem when the behaviors being treated are already intense or at a high rate, such as stealing, fire setting, running away and extreme aggressive behavior. Other family members can also develop crises which disrupt the treatment, as when parents or older siblings have problems resulting from the misuse of drugs and alcohol, or have trouble with the law.

Inadequate parental responsiveness is perhaps the most difficult interference factor to resolve since the parents' behavior of asking for, but resisting, help communicates to the therapist a contradictory message: "Help me but don't expect me to change." Systematic parent training alone is often ineffective and of little benefit for parents who express strong ambivalence about getting help or improving their role as parents. However, parent counseling, used in conjunction with other treatments, may help increase the parents' commitment and responsiveness to their family's treatment.

Parental inconsistency is a very common source of difficulty when parents fail to adequately respond to the therapist's suggestions. *Intraparent inconsistency,* or erratic performance by a single parent, can be a serious problem since the parent demonstrates mastery of the procedures and principles in systematic parent training, but is unstable in the daily performance of the required behaviors. *Interparent inconsistency* can also be troublesome, especially when the parents' response to the interventions indicates their strong unwillingness to work together to implement the home treatment procedures.

These interference factors can impair the progress of any of the interventions described in this manual. Also, several factors may be operating at the same time on different levels. For example, in attempting to deal with one difficulty, such as a practical problem or parental inconsistency, the therapist may discover a more potentially serious factor, such as parental ambivalence about making basic changes in the family interaction.

DISPOSITION

The second step in the sequence of applying parent counseling concerns the *disposition*, or the consideration of available alternatives for problems encountered in treatment, and the attempt to resolve the problem and continue parent training procedures. The therapist should review the cost-efficiency principle in applying systematic parent training: Interventions I through IV are sufficient for most families who come for help, and these procedures should be attempted first. If the response is inadequate or incomplete for any reason, parent counseling should be considered; and if required, interventions such as individual child treatment should be recommended in addition to parent counseling. Thus *the intensive, costly procedures are recommended to the parents only as required,* that is, only after procedures requiring relatively little professional time and effort have been tried.

In the practical application of parent counseling there are three major levels of treatment, each requiring increased professional time and effort for the family to achieve their intervention goals. These levels of expected therapist efforts range from reassurance and support to intensive individual treatment for family members. The following scheme summarizes the relative complexity of treatment involving parent counseling:

Level One: Brief parent counseling (1 to 2 sessions)

Level Two: Intensive parent counseling

Level Three: Parent counseling concomitant with parent and child treatments

Brief Parent Counseling. Brief parent counseling is applied for all families who develop or experience problems which interfere with their treatment progress since usually only a session or two is required to resolve the difficulty or to determine that more intensive work is needed. Throughout the interventions there are opportunities for the therapist to facilitate family progress by helping the parents find a sequence or combination of procedures which they will find productive and satisfying.

Some common problems for which brief parent counseling can be effective are listed below:

1. *"Overwhelmed" parents.* Not infrequently problems arise in the home application of a parent's new management procedures, caused by the simple addition of the demands of the interventions on the parent's already burdensome schedule. This may be especially true in the case of single parents who have both the primary task of providing for the family's existence needs and the responsibility for the child's care and development. Brief parent counseling can help decrease the parent's stress responses by simplifying and restructuring the home interventions. The SP case in Chapter 13 shows how the therapist's supportive counseling improved the mother's and child's response to the HCP.

2. *Minor family "crises."* The therapist often finds in cases where there is a likelihood of extreme or intense behavior that the treatment progress is halted at some point because of a precipitous response by the child. The focus of the parent counseling is to help the parents understand the importance of the *continuity* of intervention procedures despite the disruption in treatment progress. The FJ case in Chapter 13 is an example of the therapist's suggestions to the parents during a major disruption of the home intervention.

3. *The parents' indecision about treatment.* The MG case in Chapter 13 concerns a family for which brief counseling allowed a clarification of the parents' basic resistance to changing their child, which previously had not been apparent.

4. *Negative influences from outside the family.* Parents sometimes report that, despite their best efforts to provide the cues and consequences required to maintain positive family interaction, there are influences arising from outside the immediate family environment which disrupt the intervention progress. Examples are changes which occur in the child's school routine, such as the presence of a new teacher, influences by relatives, and the child's new involvements with people who might not be prepared to maintain the contingencies important during the family's treatment, such as baby sitters or camp counselors. Thus, prior to the child's complete development of the

new social skills emphasized in the parent training, many behaviors are tenuous and depend on a stable environment. In brief parent counseling the therapist should, as noted in No. 2 above, emphasize the importance of continuity of the interventions as much as possible, and in addition help the parents indicate to significant individuals and agencies the ways they can contribute to the child's improvements.

Intensive Parent Counseling. In intensive parent counseling the therapist's purpose is to spend a time-limited number of sessions with the parents dealing with problems and issues which were unresolved after the initial "troubleshooting" discussions in brief parent counseling.

The need for intensive, time-limited parent counseling became evident early in the development of systematic parent training when it was found necessary for the therapist to focus on parent attitudes and behaviors which were counter-productive to the treatment goals. Often the parents' difficulties reflected their inadequate responsiveness and inconsistency in the parent training, coupled with negative attitudes or uncertainty about their children or their marriage. However, the common factor at this level of parent counseling was the family's successful resumption and completion of systematic parent training procedures after a series of meetings to work on their problems with the therapist. Brief case examples are presented in Chapter 13 to demonstrate the application of intensive parent counseling.

Concomitant Parent Counseling. In concomitant parent counseling the therapist provides the parents with the opportunity to begin or to continue working on the interventions in systematic parent training while they or their child are involved in other treatments. While it is not possible to discuss the details of individual child and parent therapies in this manual, examples of available treatment procedures that can facilitate the progress of parent training will be briefly described.

Very often the therapist finds that, when continued disruptions and interferences occur and impede the progress of systematic parent training, there are longstanding parental, marital, or child problems in the family for which the procedures in this manual are not intense enough. Usually in these cases the parents indicate by their response to parent training that either (a) the child's problems are not responsive to parent training, or (b) the primary focus of treatment should not be the child's behavior.

Parent Counseling Concomitant with Child Treatment. In the majority of parent training cases in which the parents are responsive to the therapist's suggestions and correctly apply the interventions, the child's behavioral adjustment problems decrease and are replaced by appropriate interactions with the family. For this reason the parents' responsiveness to the therapist's suggestions is an important element for predicting the outcome of systematic training procedures (see Chapter 15, Issue No. 4). However, there are cases in which the child's problems are not responsive to home-based parent training, indicating the need for treatments that are administered directly to the child outside of the home. As noted in Chapter 2, these individual child treatments have questionable effectiveness; but when applied concomitantly with parent counseling that focuses on the improvement of parent skills, the likelihood of successful treatment may be enhanced. Some examples of problems which require clinic treatment of the child are indicated below:

1. Children with such extreme or dangerous behavior that inpatient treatment is required. Not uncommonly, the therapist is asked to evaluate and help families with self-injurious, severely hyperactive, aggressive, or criminally delinquent children, or children with extreme social withdrawal patterns or retarded development. Often in such cases the immediate disposition is for inpatient treatment where the interventions can be provided in a controlled environment.

2. Children with longstanding, disrupted family interaction whose parents or other significant family members cannot provide the child with necessary relationship and social skills or who are not motivated to change their own disruptive patterns as required in systematic parent training. For example, the parents themselves may have serious disruptive behavior patterns such as drug abuse or aggressive or withdrawn behavior. In these cases effective treatment may require that the child experience a stable, positive and contingent relationship with someone *outside* the family, in the form of social skill-building and self-management training by the professional child clinicians.

In each of these categories of problems requiring clinical or inpatient interventions concomitant parent counseling should be attempted. The therapist can utilize the following informal guidelines for applying parent counseling while the child is receiving treatment.

First, the therapist should recommend to the parents that their regular attendance to the counseling sessions is essential in order to best help their child with individual treatment. If the parents resist coming in and the therapist determines that the parents' home behavior patterns continue to impair the effects of the child's outpatient clinic training, then it may be necessary to make the child's treatment *contingent* upon the parents' attendance. This can be accomplished by having the parents meet with the therapist each week *prior to the child's individual session.* This is an extreme procedure but it can insure that the parents are participating in the treatment plan. Also, as a practical matter, it is often not possible for the same therapist to provide both the individual treatment for the child and also to provide concomitant parent counseling. This division of treatment can reduce the integration of efforts and goals required in the total treatment plan, and the negative effects can be minimized when both therapists communicate with each other regularly and openly about the parents' and child's progress.

Second, it is important from the very beginning for the therapist to specify goals and subgoals for the concomitant parent counseling. Step-like goals that apply to each of the categories of child interventions discussed above are given below:

1. *To introduce the parent counseling sessions in an acceptable way,* which insures that the parents understand the rationale for the meetings.

2. *To determine if the parents are maintaining recent or long-standing negative attitudes and feelings about their child.* If attitudes are verbalized which impede the parents' progress in the counseling or their child's treatment, the therapist should consider applying the procedures discussed later in this chapter for parent interventions.

3. *To have the parents pinpoint and discuss how they can improve family interaction during their child's treatment.* For outpatient children, this process should involve the immediate introduction or reemphasis on social learning concepts and basic discrimination training (Interventions I and II). In this way the parents' attention is constantly focused on their role of maintaining desirable interaction. For inpatient children these procedures can be utilized later, prior to the child's dis-

charge (unless, as in Case No. 4, Chapter 14, the inpatient program includes weekend home visits for the child). The HCP and punishment procedures can be suggested if more structured interventions are necessary and family members are available to apply home treatments.

4. *To prepare the family for the child's termination of individual treatment.* This is by far the most important goal in concomitant parent counseling. Even with intensive, long-term treatment, in most cases the child returns to his family. In successful parent counseling, the home environment is always changed during the child's treatment; parents who already had a positive home environment conducive to desirable interaction learn new skills to improve their child's home adjustment. Also, parents who have experienced family interaction disturbances develop the ability to produce and maintain desirable behavior, and perhaps even develop positive attitudes about their child's place in the family.

By carefully coordinating the child's treatment with the parent counseling, the therapist(s) can optimize the child's posttreatment adjustment. Also, after either inpatient or outpatient child treatment programs, the therapist should plan to continue with the systematic training procedures which were initiated or reapplied during the counseling. This treatment "bridge" can further enhance the treatment effects and, together with *maintenance training* prior to the start of the follow-up period, the parents can be well prepared for family social and developmental problems which may arise later.

Parent Counseling Concomitant with Parent Treatment. In many cases the problems or disruptions in systematic parent training reflect difficulties the parents are having individually or in their relationship with each other. These difficulties can affect the parent training program either by delaying its onset or by interfering with its progress. Often parent counseling, which is concomitant with or integrated into parent or couples treatment, can facilitate the implementation of home intervention programs. The procedure for applying parent counseling concomitantly with parent treatments involves the therapist's attempt to isolate and remediate the disrupting factors in the home intervention programs.

Perhaps the most common parental problem which delays or interferes with parent training procedures, as noted earlier, is *inadequate parental responsiveness* to the therapist's suggestions.

Inadequate parental responsiveness can take the form of failure to cooperate with the therapist in his attempts to implement the intervention procedures, or failure to follow through and maintain the intervention progress once attained.

There are many reasons for the parents' failure to respond to parent training as the therapist would like. However, for most of the cases in which the therapist finds it necessary to recommend parent or couples treatment, the difficulties reflect (a) behavioral instability and inconsistency in one or both parents, or (b) interparental inconsistency in the form of marital difficulties. There are important differences in the two types of parental inconsistency, but both have the same effects on the interventions; namely, there is a retardation of progress and the child's behavior continues to be a source of complaints by the parents.

Intraparent Inconsistency. In the case of unstable parent response to treatment the salient finding is the parent's behavioral demonstration of apparent mastery in the techniques and principles of systematic parent training, but *erratic performance* in the week-to-week assessment. Also, the follow-up period, if reached, has similar difficulties. When extreme erratic behavior is observed in a parent's response to training, one of two major contributing factors is usually evident.

First, there may be the presence of intense personal problems which compete with the demands of the training program for the parent's attention. In those cases the week-to-week assessment of the intervention progress often simply reflects the parent's overreaction to current stresses: he or she may function well until personal and social stress factors increase, and then become frantic and disorganized, angry and aggressive, or withdrawn. In milder forms the parent may work through difficulties by brief parent counseling, as discussed earlier in this chapter. However, the parent may present himself or herself to the parent training therapist as helpless or hopelessly frustrated, and try to dominate several sessions with complaints about life and pleas for relief. Often the supportive, structured and optimistic emphasis in parent counseling can maintain minimal parenting behavior patterns to some degree; but the therapist may eventually decide that the parent's unstable behavior should be an issue in its own right, and recommend additional treatment, to be provided either by the same therapist or by others, to deal with the problems in more intensive therapy.

The second major factor, which can contribute to intraparent erratic behavior, is when the parent communicates ambivalence about the treatment and its implications for the family. Ambivalence occurs when the parent has two contradictory feelings and attitudes about systematic parent training (and other treatments): that it is potentially good and helpful in reducing stress and increasing positive family interaction, but at the same time it threatens to alter a predictable, although painful, family life. Thus there is both an *approach to* and an *avoidance of* treatment which is usually apparent in the parent's discrepant verbal and nonverbal behavior. The parent verbalizes an interest and a commitment, but otherwise the observed behavior is antithetical to the treatment goals and is characterized by excuse-making about missed appointments, forgotten records, and poor implementation of home intervention procedures.

A limited degree of ambivalence about the treatment is natural for parents who participate in highly structured and directive treatments like systematic parent training. Also, in some cases ambivalence is a factor in the parents' initial inadequate response to treatment. However, in most cases the home intervention procedures themselves are the most effective treatment for encouraging the parents' development of positive attitudes and cooperation, and also decreasing their resistance; as they see themselves being effective in producing desirable family interaction, they *feel* and *think* more positively. Social psychologists have often demonstrated this process of positive attitude change following behavior change, even though negative attitudes may have contributed to the original negative interaction (Kelman, 1974; Lieberman, 1956). The TL family on page 39, Chapter 7, illustrates the successful application of behavioral feedback and parent counseling to modify a parent's rigid negative attitudes about her daughter.

When the training, followed by a series of brief parent counseling sessions, is *not* sufficient to promote the parent's positive response to the suggested intervention procedures, the therapist should recommend direct parent interventions. The objectives of individual parent treatment are to help the parent attain at least a minimal level of stability or commitment to the training procedures and to produce or maintain progress in the child's treatment program.

In Chapter 13 four cases are presented to indicate the application of parent counseling concomitant with direct parent treatment. In each case systematic parent training alone was insufficient to improve the parents' consistent utilization of the therapist's suggestions.

Interparent Inconsistency. The parents' contradictory re-

sponses to their children can also be a serious impediment to effective home interventions. As in other cases of parental disturbances, interparent inconsistency can take many forms and varies greatly among families in terms of its implications for successful parent training. In Chapter 7 it was emphasized that a certain degree of varied attitudes and behavioral patterns between parents makes possible the child's development of creative and flexible problem-solving skills. Also, it is likely that even occasional arguments and contradictions between parents have no harmful effect on either the child's development or the progress of an intervention program. However, the concern here is with *parental inconsistency that is pinpointed as the interfering factor in the parent training.*

There are many reasons for the parents' failure to work together in a supportive way. Very frequently, interparental inconsistency reflects problems in the marital relationship. The parents' lack of agreement or cooperation with each other in parent training may indicate the presence of more general negative or ambivalent attitudes about each other which interfere with their response to treatment. Such parents may show intense conflicts about any joint decision involving the family life, and brief parent counseling often can do no more than provide temporary control over the parents' attempts to negate each other's work in the parent training. Thus the problems that occur in the intervention programs can only be successfully dealt with when the therapist is able to improve the parents' daily communication with each other.

One useful technique which the therapist can apply to increase the parents' communication skills is based upon *basic discrimination training.* In Chapter 7 the principles and procedures used to improve the parents' discrimination of appropriate and inappropriate *child* behaviors were presented. Many of these same techniques can be used in marital therapy to help parents learn to respond more positively to each other, which is a skill that can facilitate their consistent application of the home intervention programs.

In the MW family, presented in Chapter 13, page 112, the principles of discrimination training provided the basis of marital counseling with a couple who had made a generally poor response to parent training procedures. In that case, the parents learned to discriminate and respond more appropriately to each other's positive verbal behavior, which was generalized to a degree in their home interactions.

When the parents are trained to use activity, symbolic or tangible reinforcers to improve their rates of *praise,* and to formalize the exchange of these reinforcers in written or unwritten promises, they are utilizing *contingency contracting*. Although the marital counseling in the MW family only involved informal "exchanges" of positive activities, the case does illustrate the essential steps used in contingency contracting and concomitant marital counseling. These steps are as follows:

1. The introduction of a plan which will provide for at least the minimal maintenance of the child's intervention program. While the plan does not offer intensive marital therapy for the parents' inconsistent behaviors and poor relationship, many parents can begin to improve their interaction with such a plan, and continue with treatment if needed after the family routine is more stable and positive.

2. The introduction of the basic mechanism of change in contingency contracting, which is the *quid pro quo* exchange of positive or desirable behaviors. The therapist should structure the parents' positive interaction as much as possible in the clinic by behavioral rehearsal *prior* to suggesting changes in the home. This model of behavioral reciprocity, whereby a parent earns a positive by giving one, has been described in some detail by Stuart (1969). The principles and techniques of applying contingency contracting in marital treatment are described in *How to Make a Bad Marriage Good and a Good Marriage Better* by Stuart and Lederer (in press).

3. The application of the exchange process to the home, especially in areas of interparental inconsistency. After improving the parents' ability to identify and acknowledge desirable behaviors in the clinic, the therapist should help the parents define critical areas of inconsistency which have a negative effect on the child's home intervention programs. Specifically, the therapist can have the parents specify *the minimum desirable behaviors* which, if observed, would facilitate their consistency in responding to their child(ren). In many families, these behaviors can be similar to HCP items. For example:

    a. Increased use of specific positive attention for the child's HCP earnings.

    b. Increased time spent by a parent with a child.

    c. Sharing tasks, such as checking a child's homework, or transporting the children to activities away from home.

    d. No criticism of child's performance in the HCP or other incentive plans.

    e. No yelling at the child.

    f. No criticism of spouse in front of children.

4. The emphasis on the parents' *negotiation* of all behavioral exchanges and rules to be applied in the home. At first, the therapist may find it necessary to be arbitrary in planning the parents' exchange system, caused by the initial limitations in the parents' negotiating skill. However, this skill is necessary if the parents are to develop the ability to satisfactorily solve problems independent of the therapist during the follow-up period. Also, the negotiation of behavioral exchanges in the home insure that each parent experience changes in each other that are *personally meaningful* rather than impositions by the spouse or the therapist.

The intervention model presented here assumes that the parent training problems can result from interparent inconsistency that can result from marital problems, which themselves can have many antecedents. The therapist can focus on any element in this chain in his attempt to help the family and the referred child. However, it is assumed that the most *efficient* treatment *first helps the parents increase their ability to work productively together as parents in their daily interaction with their child(ren).* When this model is used successfully, (a) the parents' increased consistency provides them with the experience of working together which can then become the basis of more intensive marital therapy (if needed), and (b) the child's interactions stabilize and become more positive as the parents improve their response to the therapist's suggestions.

ASSESSMENT OF INTERVENTION V

The effects of parent counseling are assessed by the family's relative achievement of the short-term treatment goal, which is the initiation or resumption of progress in the procedures of systematic parent training, and by the long-term goal of lasting positive family interaction. The following guidelines can facilitate the assessment of the parents' initial response to parent counseling:

1. *The therapist should determine or isolate as precisely as possible the interfering factor to be changed.* This procedure, emphasized throughout this chapter, makes possible the

specification of the goal of parent counseling. There are often primary goals and subgoals in parent counseling and other treatments. Thus, the therapist may find that in order to achieve one goal, such as consistent parental response to the therapist's suggestions, he must first improve the parents' communication.

2. *After the interference factors have been isolated and treated, the therapist should examine the evidence that the problems have decreased.* By assessing the effects of interventions on each specified goal and subgoal, the therapist can best determine the likelihood of reestablishing the home intervention progress. Examples of parent counseling results, which would indicate the attainment of the goal or subgoal in parent counseling, follow:

a. Progress in Interventions I to III, indicated by the therapist's data or parents' home records.

b. The parents' verbal responses indicating reduced dysfunctional anxiety, together with a reduction of previous avoidance behaviors.

c. An increased rate of positive interaction, assessed by the therapist's records in the counseling sessions and, if possible, by the parents' daily records or telephone reports.

Because of the complexity of interference factors which characterize the treatment problems in many families the therapist often must have multiple records available for assessment. Thus, several important changes may occur simultaneously. For example, it often happens that at the same time the parents begin to increase their positive interaction in the clinic, the child's HCP earnings begin to stabilize. In other cases the parents' consistency in the implementation of stable house rules may be followed by the child's increased HCP earnings and decreased negative sibling interaction; or, improved assertion skills in the mother may facilitate the effectiveness of a Time Out procedure.

The long-term results of parent counseling often indicate the overall effectiveness of systematic parent training, and therefore are extremely important. As noted earlier, nearly all cases require, at some time in the training, one or more types of parent counseling. *Families who respond to parent counseling and continue their progress in the home interventions have a good probability of maintaining their gains in follow-up, especially when maintenance training and follow-up contacts are provided.*

The best assessment of the long-term effects of parent counseling, therefore, is the general assessment of the family functioning during the follow-up period. If specific techniques such as anxiety reduction procedures, assertion training, or token exchange games were applied, then the improved skills obtained from the original treatments should also be assessed independently during the follow-up. However, it should be noted that often an original interference factor may again be present during the follow-up but may no longer function to interfere with the maintenance of positive family interaction. For example, parents may resume a degree of their negative interaction during the follow-up period, but may also continue to exhibit sufficient interparental consistency to maintain overall appropriate behavior in their child(ren).

SUGGESTED PROFESSIONAL TIME AND EFFORT

The professional time and effort involved in the application of parent counseling directly varies with the type of counseling being used. By definition, brief parent counseling requires only an hour or two to "troubleshoot" the interference factors and have the parents resume progress in the home contingency programs. More intensive parent counseling may require six hours or more of the therapist's time. Concomitant parent counseling and direct treatments for family members obviously require even greater efforts by the therapist. These efforts may be further extended if two or more therapists are treating the family members for different problems. For example, in a very difficult case it is not unusual for one parent to be involved in individual treatment once a week for six months or more while another therapist is providing parent counseling for both parents to maintain the home intervention progress.

The use of the therapist's efforts in parent counseling also illustrates the natural but unfortunate inverse relationship between the *effectiveness* and the *efficiency* of the treatment. Thus, while increased professional time and effort presumably adds to the likelihood of treatment effectiveness, *each additional hour of professional time decreases the efficiency of the intervention.* This consideration is especially significant in many community child and family guidance centers where the resources are limited or it is likely that parents only come into the clinic a few times. When there is not much professional time and effort to go around *and* a limited commitment from the family, the therapist's goals may change from *resolution* of the interference factors to minimal *maintenance* of acceptable family interaction.

Finally, the "expense" of parent counseling reflects the need for experienced clinicians to provide the treatment, especially in concomitant counseling. The efficiency can be improved somewhat by using experienced paraprofessionals to provide brief parent counseling for minor interference factors. These assistants can also provide ongoing maintenance counseling during follow-up more efficiently than the therapist when they live in the same community or neighborhood as the treated family. However, a full repertoire of clinical skills is often required to deal with the complex interactions and elements of intensive and concomitant parent counseling. As with previously discussed interventions, research is needed to determine more precisely the active ingredients of parent counseling and the kinds of therapist training that are required to maximize both the treatment effectiveness and efficiency.

SUMMARY

In parent counseling the therapist's goal is to isolate and reduce factors which are interfering with the progress of systematic parent training. These interference factors can occur anytime, from the baseline assessment to the follow-up period. Factors of varying disruptive influence can occur and affect any aspect of the family involvement in the home intervention programs. Parent counseling provides the therapist with increasingly complex and costly procedures to help the family initiate or resume their positive response to the treatment procedures. In this regard parent counseling is similar to previously discussed procedures since the therapist intensifies treatments only as needed.

Unlike Interventions I through IV, Intervention V often requires the therapist's full repertoire of clinical skills. When attempting to isolate and reduce the interfering factors in the parent counseling, the therapist is often required to understand the relevance of family *process* variables, including child development principles, child and parent conflicts, and marriage relationship problems.

In the screening process the therapist attempts to differentiate the relative elements in the family system which will function as strengths or liabilities for the parent training procedures. However, it is often not apparent until after the family's progress is interrupted that the parent-child or child disturbances are superficial casualties of parental or marital disturbance. Thus what is initially an interference factor for the parent training program may at some point require treatment in its own right.

For all levels of parent counseling, the emphasis in this chapter is on *active parent participation* in the family's total intervention program, whether it involves a few brief counseling sessions to resolve a minor problem or to maintain a difficult home intervention program while family members are receiving intensive individual treatment. *The therapist should consider parent counseling to be an important contingent intervention to help the parents remain maximally involved in their child's personal and social development while other family problems are being resolved.*

THIRTEEN / PARENT COUNSELING: Case Illustrations

INTRODUCTION

In this chapter cases are presented which demonstrate the application of parent counseling for the three types of counseling used in systematic parent training. At each level there is an increase in (a) the number of sessions required, (b) the complexity of the problems treated, and (c) the degree of skill required of the therapist.

BRIEF PARENT COUNSELING

THE SP FAMILY: SUPPORT FOR THE SINGLE PARENT

The SP case was presented in some detail in Chapter 9 as an example of the development of the HCP. Mrs. P came to the clinic with her seven-year-old daughter, Susan, reporting many problems throughout the day involving Susan's misbehavior and constant negative interaction. After the preliminary procedures and interventions, an HCP was begun first for the morning and then for the evening difficulties. Although Mrs. P made a generally good attempt to begin the home programs, she showed little initiative or consistency in her application of the plan, and at several points Susan made no progress in developing the social behaviors which were contingent on her mother's positive consequences. Then, after the rate of Susan's desirable behavior returned to the baseline level of the private records during the initial test phase, the therapist judged that the meetings with Mrs. P should temporarily focus on her difficulties with the HCP.

During the two parent counseling sessions Mrs. P reported that she felt that part of the problem was Susan's "bad moods," which was the mother's original explanation for the aversive behavior. However, she also pointed out that she had not been able to follow through as well as she should because of increased work responsibilities and night-school exams. The therapist acknowledged Mrs. P's difficulties, and suggested that they spend some time trying to find ways for Mrs. P to get more out of the treatment and at the same time to simplify the procedural aspects of the HCP. First, the therapist helped Mrs. P redefine the goals of the treatment *in terms of her own needs,* which were to develop Susan's independent, age-appropriate skills so that Mrs. P could accomplish her daily goals without disruption, and to continue her own program in school. The therapist strongly supported Mrs. P's desire to improve herself and her family, and pointed out that her two goals were really one and the same: as she and Susan learned more positive and productive ways of interacting, she would feel more relaxed and also accomplish more in her work. The therapist advised Mrs. P to seek ways to simplify and better organize her schedule, and suggested changes which would improve the treatment program. The steps used to increase the efficiency of the HCP, together with the results of the treatment, are presented in Chapter 8.

Comment. The application of brief parent counseling in the SP case illustrates the importance of providing *support* for the parents and *individualization* of the treatment plan. It is difficult and probably unnecessary to isolate which of these or additional variables contributed to Mrs. P's successful application of the HCP after counseling. In parent counseling the therapist utilizes all of his clinical experience and skill in the most effective manner possible, and tries to follow the same guidelines in helping the parent that are used by successful parents to help their children. The therapist always encourages the parent to find personally meaningful experiences in the treatment, and to organize and simplify the required procedures as much as possible.

The SP case also indicates how the therapist often makes assumptions about the parents' motivation. In the counseling sessions, Mrs. P projected the responsibility for the problems onto Susan's "bad moods" and made excuses for her own inability to follow through. However, the therapist chose to respond only to the positive aspect of their communication, namely that Mrs. P had her own rights and needs which, if properly acknowledged and expressed, could benefit the entire family. Thus the therapist *assumed* that Mrs. P would be motivated to "follow through" if the treatment and its procedures were presented to her in a personally meaningful way. This assumption is important in brief parent counseling since the therapist is able to focus entirely on tailoring the treatment procedures to the parents' individual needs so that the parents will maximally participate in their child's improvement. When this assumption is not supported by the parents' behavior, more intensive counseling is indicated, as will be seen in other case examples in this chapter.

Finally, the SP case illustrates how brief parent counseling is applied for the majority of families treated in systematic parent counseling. In most cases the interventions begin, then at some point problems arise, and then the therapist steps in to provide a "boost" to the parents' responsiveness in the form of parent counseling which usually results in continued family progress.

THE FJ FAMILY:
REGAINING PROGRESS AFTER A CRISIS

The FJ case was presented as an example of introducing the screening process to the parents in Chapter 4. The referred child, thirteen-year-old Fred, had a prior history of delinquent behavior and extremely negative interaction with his parents, siblings and peers. The initial effect of the interventions was to stabilize and restructure the entire family interaction which previously had been very chaotic and negative. The parents' records and observations during a series of home visits showed a marked decrease in Fred's daily disruptive behavior at home and an increased level of appropriate, responsible behaviors. The intervention plan involved all of Mr. and Mrs. J's children, and they reported much more pleasant family interaction as the daily family activities became more routine and positive. These initial positive results of the treatment occurred during eight sessions when the parents met weekly with the therapist.

In the week prior to the ninth parent training session, when the therapist was planning to discuss maintenance training, Fred committed several acts of vandalism which threatened the existence of the HCP and the entire treatment plan. One afternoon the police escorted Fred home after he damaged several automobiles parked along the street. The police indicated that the owners of the cars had been notified, and would not press charges if all damages were paid. Mr. J, whose relationship with Fred had improved markedly during the treatment, became very angry and critical of Fred, and told him he would have to pay for the damages out of his earnings from the HCP. Fred complained bitterly about this since he had been saving his earned money to buy a bicycle. In the following days Fred's behavior became very disruptive and he stopped doing his daily chores, claiming the HCP was unfair and that he wanted nothing more to do with it. Mr. and Mrs. J then came in to see the therapist, fearful that the treatment wasn't working, and that Fred was "going to become a juvenile delinquent."

The therapist acknowledged the seriousness of Fred's disruption of the family treatment plan and decided to focus the next family session on two important issues: how to deal with the current crisis so that the family program could continue, and how to respond in the future when similar problems arose which threatened the progress made in treatment.

First, regarding the vandalism, the therapist attempted to help the parents formulate a fair plan for Fred to pay for the damages. Mrs. J argued that Fred should pay half and his father the other half, but Mr. J angrily refused, saying that even if the entire treatment program ended, Fred would have to pay for all damages. After some discussion, a plan was worked out whereby Fred could earn money from his father for yard and house chores without involving the HCP. The therapist helped to plan the specific items and payment, to insure that Fred's interaction with his father concerning the penalty would not further jeopardize the HCP. The parents then informed Fred of the plan, and encouraged him by saying that they were pleased with his progress in the HCP and that it would continue.

The second issue, dealing with the parents' response to extreme disruptions which might yet occur, was also discussed in the same session and in subsequent meetings. Basically, the therapist emphasized the following points: (1) the successful HCP should continue if at all possible in spite of occasional severe disruptions by Fred, and (2) the parents should not respond to Fred's extreme behavior in a precipitous manner that would create a confrontation with him. The parents were advised to try to remain calm if possible and to phone the therapist if other crises should arise which they could not handle.

Comment. When the therapist intervened in the FJ family crisis, the brief parent counseling focused on the *perspective* and the *process* of the family's dilemma, as well as the immediate problem. There was no way of knowing in advance the effect of the crisis intervention, but the therapist reasoned that the probability of successful resolution was increased by emphasizing *general* techniques and attitudes which would be appropriate in crisis situations. In Fred's case the program continued with excellent results throughout follow-up for the home intervention plan without a further serious disruption.

THE MG FAMILY:
THE MISLABELED PROBLEM

Five-year-old Maureen G was brought to the clinic by her parents who had been advised by the kindergarten teacher that she was not learning as she should due to her "short attention span." The screening process, which included complete physical, psychological and educational examinations, showed that Maureen had no problem with her learning ability, but did have a high rate of noncompliance, poor self-control, and general social immaturity. During a playroom observation Maureen was very bossy and demanding with her parents and older brother, and extremely noncompliant. For example, the therapist requested the parents to have Maureen pick up her toys prior to leaving, but the parents instead provided much attention for her diversionary tactics such as "I'm the boss, you pick them up" and picked up the toys for her. The therapist and other observers all agreed that parent training was indicated and should focus on helping the parents teach Maureen age-appropriate self-management skills, including compliance.

During the disposition session which followed the screening the therapist communicated his findings and recommendations to the parents and asked them to consider a trial of parent training. Mr. and Mrs. G agreed to participate although they appeared primarily concerned with the "good news" that their daughter was not a "slow learner." However, in the following weeks the therapist found it very difficult to meet with the family. The parents usually reported that someone in the family was ill, or Mr. G couldn't get off work to come to the clinic. When the parents did come in, their home records, although incomplete, showed high rates of tantrums and aggressive behavior.

After several weeks, the therapist still had made little progress in establishing a regular meeting time with the family and only minimal parent records or baseline measures were available. Finally, the therapist judged that although there was a clear need, the parents were perhaps not interested in pursuing treatment, and he notified them that they should make every effort to come in to discuss their involvement with the clinic. The parents agreed, but only Mrs. G came to the meeting. She indicated to the therapist that bringing the family to the clinic for Maureen's treatment was not so important anymore, especially since Maureen's teacher had noted an "improvement" in her school behavior. Also, she pointed out for the first time that she had not come to the clinic for family treatment, but rather she was interested in having Maureen's school problem evaluated. The meeting ended with the therapist expressing his concern about Maureen's social problems, and informing Mrs. G of the clinic's continued availability if her family needed help in the future.

Comment. In the MG case brief parent counseling served the important function of giving the parents and therapist an opportunity to clarify and restate the goals of treatment, even though the outcome was to temporarily discontinue the parent training. It became apparent in the discussion with Mrs. G that once the likelihood of a learning handicap was ruled out for Maureen, the parents lost interest in the clinic. Thus what initially appeared to be an excellent treatment case proved, in brief parent counseling, inappropriate at that time for the continuation of parent training procedures. The therapist feared that the observed disrupting parent-child interaction would become even more serious without parent training, but in the absence of parental involvement, no treatment was possible.

INTENSIVE PARENT COUNSELING

THE BR FAMILY:
WHEN ADOPTION IS AN ISSUE

The BR case was presented in Chapter 11 as an example of helping the parents prepare for the Time Out procedure. Brooke, age five, responded very well to Time Out and other home intervention procedures, and Mrs. R rapidly attained her initial intervention goals.

In the original screening procedures Mrs. R had been concerned about what Brooke's response might be when she learned that she was adopted, and had asked for help and advice about this. Specifically, Mrs. R was very unsure about how to answer Brooke's persistent questions, such as "Did I come from your tummy?"

Usually Mrs. R became very anxious, feeling that Brooke was concerned about adoption, and responded with a true but diversionary remark such as "all babies come from their mommy's tummies." In a preintervention session devoted to the topic of Mrs. R's concerns about adoption the therapist guessed that Brooke might be concerned with where babies came from, rather than adoption. Then, after Mr. and Mrs. R discussed the birth process with Brooke, she stopped her questions for a while. However, about two months later, when Mrs. R was preparing to begin the follow-up period, Brooke again began to question her mother about where she came from, and this time the mother's answers were met with angry demands to know if Mrs. R was her "real mommy" and questions like "Why won't you just say I came from your tummy?" At that point the therapist reasoned that further delays would result in increased anxiety for the whole family and recommended a series of sessions in which the parents could prepare themselves for discussion of adoption with Brooke.

In the BR case parent counseling involved meeting with the parents and focusing on their anxiety reduction and increased confidence and competence in dealing with the problems of adoption. Using the popular book *The Adopted Family* (Rondell and Michaels, 1965), and the technique of behavioral rehearsal, the therapist and parents role played and discussed the communication of important adoption facts to Brooke. At first the parents, especially Mrs. R, were quite anxious, but after three sessions they became very competent in presenting the adoption process in simple terms. Finally, they reported that they were ready to discuss the subject with Brooke. Later, while meeting with the therapist prior to beginning follow-up, the parents reported that the discussion with Brooke had gone very well, and that they felt very confident about helping Brooke gradually integrate the new information in a supportive but matter-of-fact manner. No further problems concerning adoption arose during the follow-up period, although Brooke occasionally asked for clarification about some aspect of adoption.

Comment. The BR case illustrates how parent counseling becomes more intense as process variables like the parents' anxieties and informational and skill-building issues are dealt with. In this case the problems were successfully treated in a relatively brief period. However, if necessary, the therapist could have applied even more complex interventions to help reduce the parents' anxieties, such as *systematic desensitization, progressive relaxation training,* or *systematic assertion training* in addition to parent counseling.

THE BL FAMILY: UNRESOLVED MARITAL CONFLICT

The BL case was presented in Chapter 5 as a demonstration of how baseline procedures are applied. Bob was referred by his mother, who was very concerned about his delayed development, tantrums, and poor social skills. The baseline observations and records indicated the seriousness of Bob's problems, and revealed that Mr. and Mrs. L were motivated to help their son, but that they were extremely inconsistent in their attempts to manage Bob, and often provided positive attention for his aversive behavior.

During the first phase of the treatment, Mr. L was separated from Mrs. L and did not participate, although the therapist emphasized the importance of his involvement. Mrs. L, however, was very responsive to the intervention programs, and after ten hours of training she was able to improve Bob's compliance from zero to about eighty-five per cent. Also, a Time Out procedure was effective for Bob's aggressive and tantrum behaviors.

At about the time Mrs. L was beginning to express confidence in her parenting skills, and to show evidence of Bob's increased self-management, Mr. L moved back in with the family. Almost immediately Bob's behavior became worse, and within two weeks virtually returned to the baseline levels of disruptiveness at home. At that point the therapist met with both parents to discuss Bob's renewed problems.

During a session with both parents present the therapist immediately observed a change in Mrs. L; she was extremely reticent and tense in the presence of her husband and, as noted in the baseline, Mr. L attempted to dominate their interaction. According to him Bob's present disturbances were due to his problem adjusting to his father's return, but otherwise Mr. L was reluctant to acknowledge that he played a significant role in the recent exacerbation of his son's behavior. He did, however, agree to try to support his wife's involvement with the clinic.

The initial brief parent counseling only indicated the complexity and seriousness of the BL family's problems. It was clear to the therapist that the success of systematic parent training at that time depended to a great extent on either (a) Mr. L's active participation, or (b) his supportive nonparticipation. In the interview excerpt presented below the therapist communicated his concerns to both parents and explored their attitudes about working together in a treatment plan that would involve intensive parent counseling.

Therapist: As we discussed last week, I'm concerned that Bob's problems have gotten much worse recently. Perhaps we should spend some time today planning how we can help Bob improve his behavior. What do you each think about that?

Mr. L: Well, like I said before, the boy is still getting used to my being back in the house. He'll be OK.

Mrs. L: (to Mr. L) It's been three weeks and he's worse now than when you first moved back in.

Mr. L: (to Mrs. L) Now, look, he had all these problems before I ever left. You can't blame me for what he's going through.

Therapist: I don't think it's a question of blame. What we want to do today is decide what we can do for the immediate future. Mrs. L, what do you think would be a good first step?

Mrs. L: I don't know. Mr. L and I disagree about everything when it comes to Bob. I wish somehow we could begin to work together more.

Therapist (to Mrs. L) I think that's very important. We've spent much time talking about how you need to be consistent in applying what you've learned here. And when you both are present, you need to be consistent with each other in the way you relate to Bob. Perhaps Bob is a bit confused about what's expected of him if you disagree with each other a lot about how to manage him.

Mr. L Well, I don't know what else I can do. I don't put up with any of his resistance. He knows I mean business.

Therapist (to Mr. L) Does your approach seem to work?

Mr. L It used to. Now my wife gets so upset when I discipline Bob that *he* gets upset and becomes worse. If she would just let me handle him, we'd be all right.

Mrs. L (to Mr. L) But what do I do when you're not there? You don't want me to use the Time Out room.

Therapist (to Mrs. L) You don't use the Time Out room any more?

Mr. L I know you told her to send him to his room when he's bad. But I think she should just teach him to stop his bad behavior on the spot. Then he'll respect her.

Therapist How?

Mr. L By spanking him. He has to learn that you mean business.

Therapist I agree—although I think we can teach him to improve his behavior and that you mean business without physical punishment.

Mr. L But that's the way I learned. It'll work for Bob, too, if, like you say, we can start working together.

Therapist	It seems that you both want many of the same things from Bob, but disagree on how to get them. The first step is just as you both have suggested: for you to become more consistent.
Mrs. L	But how can we do that when we argue so much?
Therapist	What I'd like to do is suggest a plan that will reduce the arguing between you and help Bob at the same time. In order to give the plan a good trial, we will need to meet together for six to eight sessions, once a week. The best way I know how to help you and Bob is to see you both together regularly.
Mr. L	I'm not sure I can come regularly. Besides, I don't have the problems with Bob that my wife does. I would like to work out some of the problems we have between us, though.
Therapist	I'd like to hear more about that.
Mr. L	Well, I just mean this whole business of us always fighting about everything.
Therapist	Things other than Bob's problems?
Mr. L	I don't know. I guess not because we always end up arguing about Bob.
Therapist	The reason I asked is that I was wondering if your separation involved problems besides your difficulties with Bob.
Mrs. L	Bob's problems are my main worry. Before I came here, I couldn't handle him alone, and now I can't handle him even with my husband home.
Therapist	Let me suggest this. We have two things to do here, and they both have the same goal. Let's meet every week for six weeks. Each session we'll spend half the time talking about Bob's home management plan, and give you, Mr. L, a chance to find out more about the procedures your wife has found successful in helping Bob. We'll spend the other half of our time looking at some effective ways we've found at our clinic to help parents become more consistent. In the second half of each session we can discuss anything you think is important about your marriage or your relationship with Bob. After six sessions we'll have a good idea how useful this plan will be for your family, and can add more sessions if necessary. How does this sound to each of you?
Mr. L	Do I have to come each time? It will be difficult.
Therapist	Well, we've agreed that one of the main problems is how you interact with your wife concerning Bob. I would like to meet only when you both can come.
Mr. L	I'll see what I can do.
Mrs. L	When can we start? Bob's behavior gets worse every day.
Therapist	(to Mrs. L) We can start now. In our remaining time today, let's summarize for your husband what you've learned about helping Bob. Then each week when you come in I would like you to bring Bob with you so you both can practice working together.

The therapist's primary goal in meeting with Mr. and Mrs. L was to develop a plan that could reestablish the progress made earlier in the parent training with Mrs. L alone. Thus a plan was arranged which would focus on the parents' inconsistency and also provide an opportunity for marital counseling. To insure the father's active involvement in the plan, the therapist specified that both parents should come to the sessions and that the parents' consistent application of the home intervention plan be reviewed in the sessions prior to discussing other issues.

In each of the sessions which followed the therapist encouraged Mr. L to try out the techniques and procedures which Mrs. L had found successful. Both parents were, in general, quite responsive, perhaps due to the need for relief from Bob's extreme behavior. The major problem which arose concerned the week-to-week maintenance of Bob's appropriate behavior; the parents developed a consistent style of responding to Bob in the clinic, but both reported that they continued to argue at home. Thus, after the third week of parent counseling, the sessions consisted largely of role playing exercises to develop skills that could generalize to the home setting.

First, the parents carefully planned how each of Bob's disruptive behaviors could best be dealt with at home, and then role played the implementation of the procedures by supporting each other's interaction with Bob. Also, on two occasions the therapist met with the family in their home and, with Bob present, demonstrated additional ways to consistently praise Bob's appropriate behavior and to terminate undesirable behavior.

After six clinic visits, the parents' records showed increases in Bob's compliance nearly to the level attained while the therapist was working only with Mrs. L. Also, the parents reported that they were using much more positive attention for Bob's desirable behavior than before. The therapist suggested that another series of sessions might be useful if spent discussing other issues in their marriage, but Mr. L rejected the idea, and indicated that they would be able to work out their own problems from that point on.

During the follow-up period Bob's parents reported that they still argued quite a bit, but had tried to work out disagreements about how to handle Bob outside of his presence.

Comment. The parent counseling in the BL case dealt with long-standing marital and parent-child relationship problems that would likely require additional treatment in the future. However, the dis-

ruption in the mother's progress in systematic parent training after Mr. L returned was regained at least for a short-term follow-up period. The time-limited series of meetings helped to focus the treatment goals and procedures, and to provide an acceptable treatment goal for Mr. L, who was very reluctant to participate in long-term therapy.

CONCOMITANT PARENT COUNSELING

The following case examples illustrate the kinds of problems for which systematic parent training procedures were insufficient to improve intra- and interparent inconsistency, thus necessitating direct parent or child treatments.

THE TB FAMILY:
THE UNSTABLE PARENT

Tom B, a five-year-old boy, was first seen by the therapist as the result of a school referral. It was quickly learned that the child had an extremely high rate of aggressive and physical activity, and neither the teacher nor his mother, a single parent with a younger daughter, could control him. After a brief trial of school interventions, during which Mrs. B indicated that she was "unable to cope" with Tom, a trial period of inpatient hospitalization was recommended and initiated. A comprehensive behavior management plan was begun on the ward, emphasizing a modified HCP for increasing prosocial skills in the morning, a Time Out procedure for aggressive behavior, and an all-day token program for improving self-management skills along with weekly parent counseling. After introducing home intervention procedures to Mrs. P, Tom began to spend the weekends at home with his mother and three-year-old sister. Tom made a delayed but very favorable response to the contingencies set up and enforced by the ward staff. He was a bright and charming child, and initially staff members were manipulated by his diversionary skills and were often inconsistent. As the staff became more consistent in their application of the procedures, however, they gained increased control over Tom's behavior, and after about six months he was functioning well in all phases of his hospital adjustment, including his school activities. He continued to be a very physical, imaginative child, but learned to manage his behavior within acceptable limits.

While Tom's hospital treatment response was gradual (but eventually very stable and effective), the home treatment was just the opposite. Mrs. B, a bright but immature and easily frustrated person, quickly mastered the necessary skills to help Tom improve his behavior, but the week-to-week status of Tom's progress was almost totally unpredictable. For example, she would report excellent results in the HCP and punishment procedures for two or three weeks, and then become mildly ill, or have problems with her job, and suddenly stop all her work with Tom, complaining that he was too much for her even on the weekend. However, the overall changes in Tom's behavior in the hospital and at home led to his discharge and return home. The therapist, ward staff, and Tom's new school staff then attempted to maximize the structure of his activities and behavioral contingencies both at home and at school.

For the first month Mrs. B kept careful records and her data and reports indicated a surprisingly good adjustment for Tom. About a month after he went home his mother developed a mild illness, and at the same time it became necessary for her to increase her work hours. She came to the next session without her records, and complained that the home programs "fell apart" and that she couldn't stand Tom anymore. Most of the session was spent calming Mrs. B to the point where she could discuss the factors that produced the deterioration in Tom's behavior and how additional problems could be prevented. The basic difficulty in that particular instance began by Tom's losing his earned money and stealing a few coins from his mother's purse. Mrs. B responded by screaming at him, making a number of "doomsday" threats, and then ignoring all programs for a few days while returning to her old pattern of scream-control. Tom's behavior would briefly terminate following a threatening scream, and thus both Tom and his mother were negatively reinforced by this interaction. Also, Tom's sister was beginning to respond to her mother in a manner similar to Tom's, and Mrs. B had begun to scream at her also.

After two weeks of reestablished, successful home intervention, Mrs. B's mother became very ill and the collapse of the home program was repeated. Afterward, the therapist attempted to develop a crisis plan for Mrs. B in which she would call the therapist at "the first sign of trouble," but she continued to function in an extremely reactive manner to all stresses, which produced an unstable, unpredictable system of interaction and management in her home. Throughout this entire posthospital period, Tom's behavior was generally quite stable and appropriate. He continued his manipulative, impulsive habits, but even Mrs. B noted that he was maintaining his recently learned good behavior whenever she consistently applied the home contingencies; she agreed that her precipitous overreaction to difficulties was the family's major problem.

The therapist indicated to Mrs. B that she might profit from more intensive treatment than the weekly counseling, which primarily focused on the home intervention program. It was pointed out that the home intervention program and the weekly counseling must also continue in order to maintain the highly structured management plans still required for Tom. Mrs. B agreed and began visiting another therapist to work on her overreaction to stress and other problems, and continued to come for her parent counseling sessions. As was her pattern, for about a month there was a very stable period and she reported her improved feelings of reduced anxieties and optimism about Tom. The other therapist was treating her basically by supportive methods and antidepressive medication.

During this period Tom's behavior was generally appropriate, and he earned most of the points in his HCP. However, Mrs. B reported that she still had problems with the Time Out procedure since she found it so difficult to keep from just screaming at Tom when he was aggressive or noncompliant. Neither the parent counseling nor Mrs. B's other therapy helped her to decrease her verbal punishment of Tom's misbehavior.

Mrs. B began to talk about the possibility of being unable to deal with Tom at home even with his improvement since she and her other therapist agreed that she needed to work more on her own problems for a while. The parent training therapist agreed that a foster home placement could be considered if she found she couldn't handle Tom any longer.

A few weeks later, after a missed appointment, Mrs. B called the therapist from a local hospital and reported that she had become very agitated during a bad week with Tom, had taken some of her medication, which made her worse, and finally had gone to the hospital. She said that she "just gave up" and that she thought it was no longer possible for her to take care of Tom's problems while she was so upset by his behavior. By the time she spoke with the therapist she had already contacted a family who agreed to take Tom on a trial basis. With the assistance of the therapist and local social service agency Tom was legally placed in a foster home where there were very pleasant but firm parents. After a two-month follow-up, Tom was adjusting well with no major disruptive behavior at the home or at school. Mrs. B returned home, continued in her individual therapy, and reported that she was a "different person" and was doing fine with her daughter.

Comment. In the TB case many of the procedures described in this manual were applied, with varying results. Although Tom was a very difficult child, the hospital treatment, parent training, and concomitant counseling initially appeared, according to both the records and informal reports, to be successful. However, Mrs. B's intense personal problems, often stimulated by Tom's behavior, produced an unstable, erratic home program.

The TB case shows how parent counseling was utilized concomitantly with direct child and parent treatments in a very difficult family. While the results were judged unsuccessful by the original goals of treatment, the combined treatments functioned to help the parent determine how she could best work on her own problems and at the same time provide what was best for her children.

THE TR FAMILY:
THE AMBIVALENT PARENT

Mrs. R came to the clinic with her six-year-old daughter, Tracy, anxiously complaining of her inability to manage her or get her to "behave herself." Mrs. R, a recent divorcee, was distressed by the confusion and fighting in her home between herself, Tracy, and another daughter seven years old. The treatment progress in the TR case was similar to that in the TB case discussed above since the mother made a rapid initial response, gained very good control over the child's high-rate aversive behavior using an HCP and Time Out, but then on a week-to-week basis had difficulty following through with the home interventions. However, even more so than Mrs. B, Mrs. R was "crisis oriented" and each week the sessions were increasingly concerned with her current worries about herself, her children, her job, and her very disturbing ex-husband. When it became apparent that the home programs were no longer enforced or effective, and that the brief parent counseling only seemed to reinforce her complaining, the therapist recommended more intensive treatment.

In her treatment sessions with another therapist Mrs. R verbalized her general feelings of inadequacy about managing her affairs alone, while demonstrating an extremely intense anger at her husband, her employer, and others who "manipulated" her. The therapist combined assertion training, insight building, and parent counseling to try to help Mrs. R develop increased feelings of adequacy in her relationships with others.

Another major issue in the treatment was the manner in which Mrs. R expressed her feelings toward her children and especially Tracy. She convincingly described her primarily positive attitudes and feelings about Tracy, but reported that she became enraged at Tracy to the point of using the home intervention procedures in a punitive way whenever she felt "manipulated" by her daughter. For example, after several instances of noncompliance, Mrs. R reported that she would often take away points that Tracy had already earned. As assessed by her verbal response to the therapist, the treatment gradually helped her gain a better awareness of Tracy's needs as a six-year-old and how Mrs. R was misusing the relationship to punish Tracy in a nonobjective, excessive manner. Gradually Mrs. R was able to regain a more stable and less intense interaction with both her children concerning her daily expectations, and exchanges with them concerning the home interventions. However, she continued to receive treatment for her more general problems of interacting ineffectively with others and responding to threats with angry, impulsive outbursts.

THE JF FAMILY:
THE ANXIOUS MOTHER

In case No. 3, Chapter 14, John F's mother had particular difficulty with punishment procedures since she was terrified about the imagined consequences of a confrontation with her six-year-old son. Also, she worried constantly about John having a seizure, and had developed a number of obsessive fears and avoidance behaviors. The therapist treated this problem, which directly interfered with the family's progress in parent training, by applying systematic relaxation and desensitization to reduce the fears. After six sessions in which Mrs. F learned to relax in the presence of stimuli which previously had produced high arousal and avoidance behavior, together with ten more counseling sessions with Mr. and Mrs. F both present, she gradually became comfortable and effective in terminating John's high-rate aversive behavior in the home. Systematic desensitization was chosen as the treatment for Mrs. F's fears based on their irrationality and specificity, and because a rapid reduction of the factors interfering with parent training was needed.

Comment. In other cases where parents experience fears, anxieties, and general inadequacies about their ability to assert themselves appropriately in the parent-child relationship the therapist can use *assertion training* procedures. The therapist can utilize *personal effectiveness training* for parents who feel inadequate in their family and general interpersonal relationships. The techniques and principles for applying these various procedures are described in several sources, including *Progressive Relaxation Training* (Bernstein and Borkovec, 1973), *Behavior Therapy: Techniques and Empirical Findings* (Rimm and Masters, 1974), and *Personal Effectiveness: Guiding People To Assert Themselves and Improve Their Social Skills* (Liberman, et al., 1975). Whenever these specific techniques are used to facilitate a parent's progress in systematic parent training, the therapist should arrange an additional series of sessions to insure that the parents have adequately integrated the new personal and social skills into their behavioral repertoire. Also, as in the JF case, it is important that, when a fear or anxiety reduction procedure is used, the therapist take great care not only to decrease the avoidance behaviors, but also to help the parent acquire new skills which will receive positive reinforcement from the environment.

THE MW FAMILY: IMPROVING PARENTAL CONSISTENCY WITH DIFFICULT PARENTS

Mr. and Mrs. W originally came to the clinic for an evaluation of their seven-year-old son, Maury. The screening procedures documented Maury's low average intelligence, very poor school achievement, and extreme immaturity and withdrawal. He was a fearful child with no friends, and at home often had screaming tantrums whenever he was reprimanded or asked to do something. His parents also had problems: Mr. W was very passive and dominated by Mrs. W, who was an anxious and complaining person. Baseline observation of the family interaction at home and in the clinic revealed disrupted parent and parent-child interaction. The parents rarely agreed on anything, and used almost no positive attention with each other or with Maury. Usually Maury received negative attention for noncompliance and whining, both of which were at a high rate.

The treatment of the MW family included the following:

1. Recommendations for systematic parent training and parent counseling, which the parents initially rejected.

2. Recommendation for educational therapy, which the mother accepted and followed exactly, even to the point of following through and taking Maury when he refused to go.

3. The return of the parents to the clinic, after about a year, with increased complaints about Maury's disruptive behavior at home, although he was then functioning much better at school.

4. Combined individual and group applications of systematic parent training, in which the parents improved Maury's compliance somewhat, but continued to show extreme interparental inconsistency and negative interaction in Maury's presence.

5. The therapist's renewed recommendation for parent counseling based on Maury's continued problems and the parents' inconsistent manner of applying the home intervention procedures necessary to maintain positive family interaction.

In the next session with the therapist Mr. and Mrs. W reluctantly accepted the recommendation for a treatment plan focusing on their negative interaction with each other. The therapist pointed out that after the previous parent training program the parents had demonstrated their ability to manage Maury in a productive way, and that the current problems with Maury reflected their own poor communication and inconsistency.

When the concomitant parent counseling was initiated, the parents had been involved with the clinic for over a year. Maury's school achievement and self-management skills were considerably better, but he was still socially immature and was involved almost daily in the parent's fights and arguments. The therapist determined that a great deal of professional time and effort (over thirty hours) had already been expended on the MW case, but feared that *even the modest achievements at that time would be lost if the interparental inconsistency was not directly treated.* An initial series of eight sessions was proposed for Mr. and Mrs. W to work with the therapist on developing a consistently applied maintenance program for Maury. During the first session the therapist discussed the new treatment plan with the parents.

Therapist   Last week we decided to meet together for eight visits to try to work out some of the difficulties you have with each other which affect Maury's adjustment at home. Today I'd like us to plan our goals carefully so that we will be able to evaluate our progress from week to week.

Mrs. W	Well, as I said last time, I think it's a hopeless case between us. Maybe it would be best for you to see Maury without us being involved at all.
Therapist	Yes, you mentioned that before. I want to be sure we've tried everything we can with our family interventions before we think seriously about individual treatment for Maury. You've done a lot of good things for Maury. I'd like to see what more we can do to help you work together with him.
Mrs. W	We've never agreed on how to handle Maury and I don't see how coming here can help. Mr. W turns Maury against me by giving him everything he wants. Then Maury runs all over him and, when he can't stand it any more, he demands that I punish Maury and he leaves. Then I'm the big bad mother and Maury says he hates me. You know all this, we've been over and over it. Nothing will change him.
Therapist	Mr. W, what do you think about this problem you have with your wife about Maury?
Mr. W	He's not that bad.
Therapist	Do you think our meetings can help you and your wife work together better?
Mr. W	I don't know; maybe. What do you want us to do?
Therapist	Mrs. W feels very strongly that you turn her into the bad guy at home. What do you think?
Mr. W	Maury needs somebody to love him. My wife only hollers at him.
Mrs. W	Well, we also argue about other things than Maury. He's not our only problem.
Therapist	What are some of the other problems?
Mrs. W	We fight about everything. My husband is lazy and never does anything to help.
Mr. W	I work, don't I?
Mrs. W	Yes, but what about your family? You undercut everything I do with Maury. And you never show me any affection. Doctor, we don't even sleep together any more.
Mr. W	You know I have trouble sleeping. I have to get my sleep. That's no problem. (Mrs. W stares at her husband and says nothing.)
Therapist	Is this argument what it's like at home?
Mrs. W	Yes, only louder.
Therapist	How loud?
Mrs. W	Very loud. I have to scream at him or he won't listen.
Therapist	Does Maury hear all this?
Mrs. W	Sure. We have a small house. He's always there.

Therapist   OK. Let me describe what I have in mind for our meetings so we can begin to work on some of these problems. I think that my observations of your family in the past and today give me a good picture of some of the difficulties you are having with each other and with Maury. What we want to do here is try to develop some guidelines for your family which will provide Maury with the structure he needs to improve his adjustment at home. He's doing better at school now. Also, we know he can respond very well to you both as we can see from our observations of his improved compliance to your directives. (Therapist shows Mr. and Mrs. W the graphs of Maury's increased compliance during the earlier parent training interventions.) So the plan I have in mind will do two things for your family: first, it will allow Maury to continue to improve at home; second, many families find during the interventions that by being more consistent with their child they begin to agree more on other things as well. These goals are important right now, for Maury's sake. I think we should be prepared to work on other problems in your marriage after things are more settled down in your family. What do each of you think about this plan?

Mrs. W   Well, we have to do something—but I don't know exactly what you have in mind.

Mr. W   I'll go along, I guess.

Therapist   Fine. Before we stop today, let me give you a brief overview of the procedures we'll use. For each of the coming weeks I want you to keep the home contingency program going on as best you can. Keep Maury's charts filled in and bring them in each week. Also, tell me each week if there are new problems you need help with. Next week we'll try to pinpoint a few things each of you can do for each other in the coming weeks that will help both Maury and you. Then each week we will spend part of our time discussing ways to improve your communication with each other, and part of the time finding ways to improve Maury's behavior. If you like, we can start today by each of you listing several things you would like each other to do which, if accomplished, might also help Maury.

During the remainder of the session the therapist attempted, with some difficulty, to have Mr. and Mrs. W name behaviors they wanted to see increase. Each time the therapist allowed them to communicate freely the parents began to criticize each other: Mrs. W listed Mr. W's faults in terms of negative traits and generalities; he tried to defend himself by denying all accusations.

At the next session the therapist began by pointing out the parents' well-practiced style of communicating in only negative ways, and by indicating the need for rules of interaction at home and in the clinic that would protect Maury from the negative effects of arguing and would help structure their communication as well.

After some discussion, Mr. and Mrs. W and the therapist agreed on the following "house rules":

1. No arguing or criticizing each other in front of the children.

2. If the rule is not followed, the criticized parent should try to ignore the remark by turning and walking away. One of the parents should make a note of the instance to bring into the next session for discussion.

Then, to help the parents utilize the rules, the therapist had them recount several ways in which criticism and arguments were likely to occur in Maury's presence. First, the therapist role played the criticized parent, demonstrating how to turn away and leave the room if necessary. Then each parent was asked to practice "nonresponding" to negative statements while in the imagined presence of Maury. At first the parents were reluctant to role play, but with the therapist's demonstrations and the brevity of the interaction, both Mr. and Mrs. W were soon able to "ignore" each other's negative remarks with no trouble.

The therapist acknowledged the parents' success, pointing out their convincing and excellent response to the suggestions. Then the therapist described several guidelines which would facilitate the parents' use of the time spent in the clinic each week. First, the primary focus each week would be to increase the parents' ability to identify positive attributes and statements about each other. The therapist would help by initially pointing out each instance of improved positive communication, and then helping the parents learn to *label* behaviors they observed that they liked and wanted to see more of.

Second, arguing and criticism would be permitted in the session, but on each occasion the therapist would use the argument as the basis of a practice exercise in which each parent would learn alternative ways to respond that could terminate the argument.

In the third session the parents brought in the HCP records, but only Mr. W brought notes about infractions of the rule about arguing. The therapist praised Mr. W who, both parents agreed, had not responded to his wife's criticism in the past week. It was learned that most of the negative interaction was initiated by Mrs. W, who admitted to her "nagging" Mr. W about his inadequacies. Thus it became clear that in order to reduce the negative interaction it would be necessary to develop a *contingency contract* which would specify that, in return for receiving reduced criticism, Mr. W would perform some of the activities which Mrs. W found it necessary to nag about.

The therapist suggested an informal contract be tried initially, based on a simple exchange whereby each day Mr. W would spend more time with Maury, helping him with homework and playing with him outside, and in return Mrs. W would refrain from criticizing her husband in front of Maury. As before, infractions of the agreement were to be discussed in the following session.

As a result of the need for rules, guidelines and the informal contingency contract, the first four sessions with Mr. and Mrs. W were taken up with *deceleration* procedures. Thus it was found that until the negative interaction was minimized there was no motivation and little time available to identify or engage in positive interaction. Also, it was found that for Mr. and Mrs. W, positive interaction was perceived as the *absence* of arguing and fighting.

In general, the parents responded well to the therapist's sug-

gestions, and each week improved in their practice of both ignoring negative statements and decreasing the frequency of the arguments. Also, as the parents began to follow through with their *responsibility* in the contract, it was possible to help the parents *identify, label, and respond positively* to each other's improved behavior.

During the fifth and sixth sessions the therapist was able to focus almost entirely on the parents' practice of using praise more frequently. At first, only the targeted items on the "contract" were used in the practice: Mrs. W was asked to practice ways of acknowledging her husband's increased efforts with Maury, and Mr. W was encouraged to find ways to thank his wife for decreased criticism and nagging.

During the seventh session the therapist noted the parents' considerable improvement in their communication skill concerning the simple exchanges required so far, and suggested that other areas could also be improved using the same procedure. Mr. W noted that Mrs. W still criticized Maury a lot, even in the morning when he failed to earn a particular HCP item. Also, he was concerned that his wife was rarely "pleasant" with Maury. Mrs. W said the same was true of Mr. W's remarks to her; that she fixed him his lunch every day, but he only commented when he didn't like something.

On the basis of this discussion the therapist proposed that the two items be added to the contingency contract. Mr. W would make a positive comment each day on his lunch, and Mrs. W would comment each morning on Maury's earnings and not respond to him about any lack of earnings. During the last part of the session each parent rehearsed positive statements that could be made daily that would satisfy each other. It was suggested that each parent keep a daily record of each other's successes in fulfilling their responsibility in the agreement, and discuss their results with each other prior to coming in the following week.

At the eighth meeting the parents reported that each had improved in positive verbal statements as agreed upon, although neither one kept records as suggested. Also, although they agreed that it had been a good week, with no criticism or fighting, they had not discussed their progress prior to coming in. In fact, both parents said that they had never discussed the treatment outside of the session, and didn't want to work on improving their discussion at home.

The therapist suggested a new series of meetings since the eight planned sessions were completed, but both parents again indicated that they didn't want to continue coming together to see the therapist to work on their own problems. They were strongly urged to consider, as an alternative, coming in weekly to discuss Maury's progress and to plan better ways to help him, and they agreed to try to come in regularly if the focus would be on Maury. Mrs. W said that she continued to worry about Maury's social immaturity and his lack of friends; the therapist proposed a plan whereby the parents would work on maintaining three positive activities for him. First, they would continue Maury's morning HCP. Second, they would continue to refrain from negative interaction in his presence. Third, they would develop a plan whereby they would encourage Maury to attend weekly scout meetings, see to it that he was taken to the meetings, and discuss his progress in scouts each week in a positive way.

During the following four weeks the parents continued to report that their interaction at home, while still needing improvement, was considerably more positive than previously reported to the therapist. They also continued to show agreement and increased pleasant interaction at the meetings. They seemed to be willing to reduce their fighting, but not to work seriously on improving their positive exchanges any further. As promised, the therapist maintained the focus of the interaction on Maury's progress at home, school, and the scout meetings, and Mr. and Mrs. W continued to follow through on the three areas agreed upon. They were especially dutiful in keeping Maury's schedule regular for his weekly attendance at scouts. In the first three-month period after the therapist stopped seeing the parents they reported continued progress in Maury's social development and that he had even brought a friend home from scouts. Also, his public HCP earnings stabilized during the same period.

Comment. In the MW case, the therapist attempted to have the parents begin a minimal level of cooperative interaction which would at least insure that Maury's social and personal development were not further jeopardized. By the therapist's observations and the parents' reports, the concomitant parent counseling and informal contingency contracting were in general successful. The treatments, however, were not a solution for Mr. and Mrs. W's relationship difficulties. Nonetheless, they did offer the parents a view of what they might accomplish by working together more with Maury. That they did not pursue marital counseling when recommended was unfortunate, but perhaps it was not essential to certain aspects of Maury's progress. For example, the parents did show progress in their interaction with each other, and did maintain the HCP and improve their verbal interaction with Maury. Also, they were especially consistent and dutiful about promoting Maury's social and educational development outside of the home.

Perhaps more than anything else, this case demonstrates the therapist's flexible use of available procedures and increased structured interventions when the parents do not respond adequately. Using the procedures of basic discrimination training and behavioral rehearsal, the parents successfully learned to identify and respond to each other's behavior in ways that could be beneficial to Maury. Although the preferred treatment would have been to increase the positive interaction first, the MW case shows that, with some families, there is no time or incentive to be pleasant while the current interactions are predominantly negative.

SUMMARY

The cases presented in this chapter describe families who had problems that were significant enough to interfere with the parents' response to systematic parent training. It has been emphasized that in most cases where the procedures in the manual are correctly applied the family makes a favorable response to the interventions. Two examples of such successful families are the JM and GW cases presented in Chapter 14. However, the fact remains that many families do fail to respond as desired to the therapist's suggestions, and that parent counseling procedures are often necessary. The cases presented here demonstrate how therapists can use their skills to resolve the interfering factors or, if necessary, integrate systematic parent training into more intensive, complex treatments.

FOURTEEN /   CASES IN SYSTEMATIC PARENT TRAINING

INTRODUCTION

Individual differences in families, therapists, and settings require the flexible use of parent training as an effective modality for child, parent and family intervention. In this chapter four cases are presented to further illustrate the total treatment of families, and the necessity of individualizing the treatment programs for maximum effectiveness and efficiency. Each case was selected for inclusion to demonstrate the different kinds of problems the therapist may encounter when applying the procedures in systematic parent training. These cases were also selected to show that different assessment and treatment procedures can be effectively applied within the general flo-chart model of systematic parent training. The cases are necessarily described in an oversimplified form; it is not possible to provide in this chapter a full, detailed picture of the families' problems and qualitative responses to the interventions. The four cases presented, like all others described in this manual, were treated at the Neuropsychiatric Institute, UCLA, by the author and his colleagues.

CASE NO. 1: THE DISCOVERY OF PARENTAL INITIATIVE*

Background. John M was brought to the clinic by his parents when he was nine years and eight months old. He was the second of three children with an older and younger sister (eleven and two years old). The primary referral reason was a reported extreme degree of increasingly hyperactive and aggressive behavior in the home and in the classroom. The parents complained that living with John had

become an "unbearable stress," and that they were considering placing him in a residential center for disturbed children.

John's parents reported that his birth and early development were normal. There was no history of serious illness or injury, and all developmental milestones were within normal limits. The first problems appeared in the form of hyperactivity and a short attention span when John entered nursery school, and these difficulties continued into kindergarten. At the age of seven John was evaluated by a psychiatrist who concluded that he had all the symptoms of minimal brain damage, including hyperactivity, short attention span, perceptual deficits, and an abnormal EEG; he prescribed Mellaril and biphetamine. After receiving the medical treatment, John appeared to concentrate more on his schoolwork and was reported to have "calmed down" somewhat at home. However, when he started the fourth grade at the age of nine, John again became disruptive at home and at school. The parents and teachers felt that his schoolwork was too difficult and was causing the problems so he was moved to a lower grade. However, his behavior continued to deteriorate.

Socially, John was not a popular child and had few friends. At home he had special difficulty with his older sister. Although she had been told by her parents to ignore him, he persisted in teasing and hitting her and any friends she might have visiting her.

Screening. When John was first seen at the clinic, he appeared to be a very nervous, agitated child, but otherwise his outward appearance was that of a normal boy. The physical examination and a new EEG revealed no abnormalities. Based on the negative medical findings, John was taken off his medication for a trial period during the intervention program. A psychological examination indicated that John had above average intelligence and normal perception, but was

* The therapists for this case were P. Guilbert and W. H. Miller. The treatment details are reproduced from Guilbert and Miller (1973) with permission from the publisher.

underachieving in school in all areas. Other psychological tests showed that he had largely negative attitudes and feelings toward his family members. The screening process also included psychological tests and behavior checklists completed by John's parents. The parents' MMPI's were judged to be well within normal limits, although Mrs. M's profile contained indications of anxiety and negative self-evaluation. The results of the Missouri Child Behavior Checklist were consistent for both parents and supported their earlier reports that John was extremely aggressive and hyperactive and had difficulty sleeping, but that he also had periods of generally appropriate social behavior. Finally, a playroom and videotape assessment of the entire family interaction was made to observe John and to assess his parents' basic discrimination skills. Analysis of the videotape indicated that John was noncompliant (less than a third of his parents' directives were obeyed), and was verbally aggressive, especially when his parents directed attention toward his older sister. Mr. and Mrs. M were consistent in their responses to their children, although Mrs. M was more critical of John's whining and complaining. Both parents attended in a positive or nonpunitive way to more than half of John's negative behaviors.

After examining the available screening material, the therapists judged that systematic parent training would be appropriate for the M family's problems. The parents were ostensibly motivated. And while John had several areas of difficulty, his primary adjustment problems appeared to reflect inappropriately applied contingencies by his parents.

Baseline. The therapist's baseline assessment of John's problems and behavioral deficits included the following:

1. The results of the initial behavior checklist ratings by John's parents.

2. The analysis of the videotape made of the family interaction in a clinic playroom.

3. The preintervention portions of Figure 7, representing the mother's daily home ratings. Figure 7 is based on the occurrence of John's aversive behavior rated by his mother for a two-hour period in the morning and a two-hour period in the afternoon. In this procedure Mrs. M was asked to keep hourly tallies of each occurrence of observed aversive behavior. Included in the composite score were daily totals of John's teas-

ing and aggressive interaction with his older sister or any neighborhood child who was visiting. For the total four hours observed John averaged more than thirty-five instances of aversive, disrupting behaviors for each of the first three weeks of records (Figure 7).

4. John's private HCP earnings, shown in Figure 8. His parents had previously specified three daily disrupted periods which would constitute the initial intervention areas, including many disruptions in the morning, the aggressive "wild" behavior in the period after school, and the dinner time to bedtime disruptions. Dinner time was reported to be especially difficult, with John often throwing food and displaying very messy eating habits. The morning period was chosen as the first period for intervention, with the following items:

   a. Out of bed when called.

   b. Putting on pants and shirt.

   c. Putting on socks and shoes.

   d. Brushing teeth.

   e. Combing hair.

All items except the first were to be earned only when the behaviors occurred without any verbal prompt. This procedure was instituted so that when the contingency program began, John would be rewarded for developing independent personal management skills. A high frequency item, "combing hair," was included to insure that John would have some initial earnings. Figure 8 shows that John earned, on the average, less than two of the five items possible for each day during the three-week baseline period.

Taken together, the parents' records and questionnaires and the therapists' ratings of the family interaction provided a reasonably objective documentation of the problems in the M family concerning John. The information gave a consistent picture of John as a very angry, impulsive child with a high rate of socially disruptive behavior and few prosocial habits. The parents' excellent initial cooperation and participation encouraged the therapists to develop an intervention that would utilize the interparental consistency and the mother's apparent responsiveness.

Figure 7 Results of Mrs. M's Daily Home Ratings

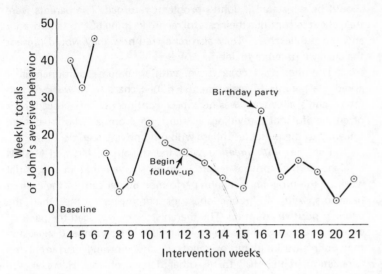

Figure 8 John M's Progress in the Home Contingency Program

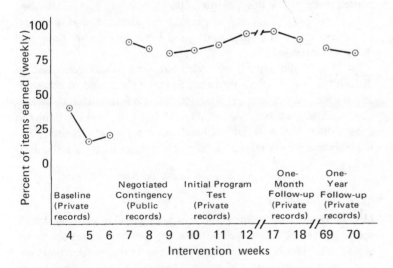

INTERVENTIONS FOR CASE NO. 1

The following treatment overview briefly characterizes the interventions applied in the JM family and the initial results.

INTERVENTIONS I AND II

During the *fifth meeting* the therapists discussed social learning principles and had the parents purchase a copy of *Living With Children*. Also, the therapists and parents reviewed the initial home records and the videotape made earlier. The parents were quite insightful about discussing the importance of parental consequences. Both Mr. and Mrs. M correctly pinpointed several instances of John's aversive behaviors on the tape which they should have ignored, and desirable behaviors, such as John's approximate compliance, which they could praise more often. Both parents expressed a strong desire to alter their own behavior in any way that would help John. However, Mrs. M verbalized her fear that John's problems were caused by his "brain damage" and that he would not be able to respond to the treatment. The therapists reassured her that while there were no guarantees of successful outcome, other children with problems similar to John's often responded well when the parents did their part to improve the family interaction.

The therapists suggested that the home intervention program should begin the following week, and that the parents should bring John in with them to participate in the discussion.

INTERVENTION III

During the *sixth session* the parents reported that John's behavior the previous week was worse than ever. Mrs. M noted that he was extremely agitated all week, had played hooky from school for one day, and was extremely negative to his older sister. The parents' home records supported their report (see the third weekly data point in Figure 7). Because of the severe disruptiveness of John's behavior, the therapists decided to institute a *negotiated contingency* for the morning HCP as the next step in the intervention program, and to bypass the social contingency phase which usually would follow the private records.

Most of the sixth session involved a discussion of the negotiated contingency plan. Mr. and Mrs. M agreed that the item John would most likely work for was his allowance of one dollar a week since he needed gas money for his minibike.

The plan was constructed so that the five daily points earned would be worth a nickel each. A box with the weekly maximum number of nickels was to be placed on the parents' dresser at the start of the week. The goal would then be for John to have the nickels in his box by the end of the week. Each morning prior to leaving for school he would receive his earned nickels for that day.

The parents were instructed to post his HCP chart in a conspicuous place for the coming weeks, and to register his earnings each morning. The therapists stressed the importance of providing profuse positive attention to John when he earned points daily, since it would be the natural application of praise, rather than his allowance, that would maintain his good behavior later on.

John was then invited to join the meeting, and his parents explained all the details of the program to him very clearly, and answered his questions about the plan as well. He said he thought the plan was a good idea and, at the end of the session, said he was looking forward to earning his allowance.

"Payday" was to be on Saturday morning and was to include a special treat or bonus if John earned a daily average of four out of the possible five points. Mrs. M was initially concerned that John's behavior would become even worse if he had a bad week and did not earn gas money for his bike, but when it was explained that even earnings equivalent to John's baseline average (five points of twenty-five cents weekly) would keep him "gassed up," Mrs. M agreed to the plan.

For the *seventh session* the parents brought their records from the first week of the public negotiated earnings. As shown in Figures 7 and 8, there was a dramatic decrease in John's aversive behavior in the mother's records, and an increase in his HCP earnings. Both parents reported that they were completely surprised by the reversal in John's behavior. By the end of the week they had also noted that his dinner-time behavior was much improved. John responded to the program on the first day with enthusiasm, and consistently earned the points necessary for the HCP bonus. However, Mr. and Mrs. M noted that their main concern was that the improvements would be temporary. The therapist again emphasized the importance of contingent praise as well as contingent allowance earnings, and the parents said that their own behavior toward John had become much more positive in the last week.

In the *eighth session* the parents' records again were very encouraging. John continued to earn nearly all of the available points and had shown no disruptive behavior for the two-week period of the negotiated contingency. Both Mr. and Mrs. M wanted to try the program without the public chart and said that, on the basis of John's excellent response to their increased praise, they felt they should no longer require him to earn his allowance.

The therapists, although preferring to extend the public negotiated contingency for another week, agreed to test the durability of the changes, but cautioned the parents that the contingency should be reinstated if John's problems returned. The parents were then asked to continue their careful record keeping but to temporarily end the public chart. They also rehearsed how they would present the changed program to John.

The therapists could have, with minimum additional time, asked the parents to maintain the public chart for a week or two after John's allowance was no longer contingent. This procedure is often helpful for providing a transition from a negotiated contingency to the initial test phase with only private records.

For the *ninth meeting* with the therapists, Mr. and Mrs. M brought in their private records, which showed that in the initial week of the program test John performed 80 per cent of the desired behaviors, with no public chart or contingency other than the parents' positive attention. The therapists acknowledged the parents' excellent response to the home intervention program, and suggested that John's striking improvements in the morning warranted the application of the HCP to his other daily problems. However, the parents reported that John no longer had any serious disruptive behaviors at dinner or bedtime. The parents accounted for the change as a consequence of the positive interaction which had been established in the morning program, although they admitted that their expectancies and praise for John's good behavior at other times had definitely increased.

Mrs. M did report, however, two areas which continued to disturb her about John's behavior. First, he continued to occasionally hit his older sister, and although the rate was much less, he also continued to tease her. Second, Mrs. M felt that John continued to show evidence of a perceptual handicap; his writing was nearly unreadable and all her efforts to help him practice better graphic skills had failed.

INTERVENTION IV

Mrs. M continued to keep her four-hour daily records on John's aggressive verbal and physical behavior, and her record sheets revealed that John was hitting his sister about three or four times per day during the observed period. The therapists had only asked her to keep these records during the three-week period of the HCP baseline, but Mrs. M said that the regular observation periods helped her attend more closely to John, and that she had wanted to continue. Thus, with a baseline for John's hitting already available, the therapists instructed the parents in the use of the Time Out procedure. Mr. and Mrs. M again responded very well to the therapists' suggestions, and with very little practice demonstrated their ability and confidence in applying Time Out for John's aggressive behavior. While there was no dramatic cessation of the aggression, John gradually decreased his hitting during the following weeks. The parents did not feel that John's teasing was serious enough to warrant Time Out, but they reported that ignoring the teasing was generally effective. Regarding the poor penmanship, Mrs. M was asked to bring in samples of John's writing for the following session.

During the *tenth meeting* Mrs. M reported that, although it was her own idea, she applied small monetary contingencies for John's improved handwriting during his homework sessions. She showed samples of his writing before and after the contingency, and the therapists were very impressed by the improvements. Mrs. M also said that for the first time she was beginning to see how John could control his behavior if he knew what was expected of him and that there would be a positive consequence for good behavior.

Maintenance Training. On the basis of the parents' excellent response to the therapists' suggestions, and especially Mrs. M's very appropriate initiative, the therapists decided to discuss maintenance skills in the next two sessions and then to begin the follow-up period. In the discussions that followed the therapists reviewed the details of the program and emphasized the effectiveness of the treatment, especially in terms of the severity of John's presenting problems. The therapists indicated their continuing availability to help the parents if needed, but suggested that whenever possible they should attempt to apply the procedures they had learned when new or old problems arose in any of their children. Potential problems and alternative interventions were discussed, and both Mr. and Mrs. M said that they were satisfied with John's progress and confident that they could deal with most of the problems they would encounter.

Follow-Up. The intervention program for the JM family covered twelve weeks, including the intake and screening interviews. Although the period between the last family meeting and the one-year follow-up was without serious disruption, the therapist had two significant contacts with the family shortly after follow-up began.

First, Figure 7 shows that about one month after treatment ended Mrs. M recorded a large number of aggressive behaviors. By phone Mrs. M reported that John's sister had had a Saturday birth-day party and John became very upset, nearly wrecking the party and disrupting the weekend for the whole family. John went to the Time Out room six times over the weekend, and lost play privileges in addition. However, on Monday, when Mrs. M called, John had settled down and, as week No. 17 shows, he had relatively few problems, as observed by his mother, in the following weeks.

Also, a school program was initiated in the week following the disrupted weekend. John had been increasingly active in his classroom, and had begun to disturb the teacher and other children by his constant out-of-seat behavior. Perhaps as a result his work productivity decreased. After a school visit, the therapists arranged a simple plan whereby John would take home a card each day indicating how many of the following items he had achieved during a one-hour afternoon period:

1. Sitting in chair.

2. Completion of assignment.

3. Good social behavior.

4. Independent work at desk.

A chart was kept showing John's earnings, and at the end of the week an average of three out of four items earned each day was rewarded by a brief shopping trip so that John could buy a toy with his allowance and, at the suggestion of Mrs. M, a small bonus from his parents. The program was started, even though there were only six weeks left in the school year, with the rationale that John needed to learn without delay that he could control himself in the class just as he had at home. Also, it was important that the teachers' and school's attitudes were positive if at all possible at the end of the year since he would be returning there in the fall.

Although John had several days initially with zero earnings, he gradually earned enough points to be reflected in improved classroom behavior and in regular shopping trips with his parents.

In the one-year follow-up interview, the therapists met with Mr. and Mrs. M to discuss John's adjustment to date. They were extremely pleased with his progress, and reported that he had developed a positive relationship with his sister. Many of Mrs. M's comments are presented below in the Parent's Assessment of Therapy, which she completed during the follow-up period.

Parent's Assessment of Therapy

1. Describe very briefly your child's problem prior to involvement in the UCLA Home Intervention Program.

    John was very aggressive, destructive, made noises almost constantly, and was super-sensitive. He refused to dress in the morning and didn't function well in school.

2. Describe the essential details of the Intervention Program in which you were involved.

    Through a reward system that was set up on an hourly basis, while at home, John was disciplined and encouraged to accomplish and perform daily duties.

3. List the three most important changes which occurred as a direct result of the Intervention Program.

    1. Friendly towards family and friends.
    2. Improvement in school.
    3. Happy with himself.

4. Describe very briefly the child's behavior since the most recent Intervention.

    Behavior has been easily handled, and the change has been for the better.

5. Describe very briefly the single most important factor which led to the changes you observed.

    The token program was the thing that changed John and us (our family) for the better.

6. Please compare the effects of the Home Intervention Program with other therapeutic techniques attempted for your child's problem.

    John was on medication which, after a while, increased his negative symptoms.

7. Are there any additional comments you would like to make about the program? Be critical.

    I can't say enough for the program. How it has changed all of us for the better!

8. Please compare the relative contributions by the child's mother and father to the program's outcome.

I implemented the program. My husband backed it up and at times assisted me.

The parents were also requested to keep private HCP records for two weeks on the original morning items, and to complete post-treatment behavior checklists as well. Figure 8 shows the maintenance of the morning behaviors for the two-week follow-up after one year as well as the earlier six-week follow-up.

The parents' HCP records and verbal reports were supported by the results of the checklist comparisons. All the categories reflecting initial disturbances showed decreased scores on the follow-up tests. Mrs. M's scores were especially indicative of her changed perception of John's behavior, as shown below:

Behavior Checklist Category	Screening: % items answered "yes"	Follow-up: % items answered "yes"
Aggression	63	42
Inhibition	21	7
Hyperactivity	70	10
Sleep Disturbance	67	0
Somatic Disturbance	0	0
Social Maturity	50	70

Although specific interventions were applied only to decrease aggressive behavior, Mrs. M's checklist results also contained decreases in other categories of problem behaviors.

John and his family moved out of the area after the one-year follow-up was made. However, based on telephone and letter reports over an additional two-year period, John continued to show progress in his social maturity and stopped all aggressive behavior. His parents also reported that John's learning difficulties in school persisted, and that he was receiving tutoring in several subject areas.

Comment. The JM case illustrates the successful and efficient application of systematic parent training procedures. A total of eighteen hours of professional time and effort were applied, and this total includes the presence of two therapists for many of the treatment sessions.

Using the flo-chart on page 10 as a treatment guideline, it can be seen that the JM family proceeded successfully through the first four interventions and then began follow-up. There were no significant interruptions in John's or his parents' response to the interventions, and all the stated original and additional intervention goals were achieved.

Many factors were concomitantly operating which contributed to the successful outcome in this case, but some of the salient, observable features are listed below:

1. The parents were responsive to the therapists' suggestions and consistent in their application of the procedures throughout the treatment.

2. The home interventions allowed John and his parents to correctly discriminate each other's behavior so that they were able to learn new predictable means of producing mutually gratifying interactions between them.

3. According to Mrs. M the "turning point" for her was the discovery that John could control his behavior once he learned how, and that he was responsive to her attempts to help him.

4. The onset of positive change correlated in time with the onset of the interventions, at least as based on the parent records and verbal reports. Thus, the positive changes appeared to be functionally related to the parents' application of the interventions.

Finally, there were two features of the JM case which may be atypical for families in systematic parent training, both of which are implied in the title of the case, "The Discovery of Parental Initiative."

First, in the majority of cases in systematic parent training the therapist must discover reinforcers that will maintain the parents' *cooperation* with the therapist's suggestions. In the JM case the parents displayed not only complete cooperation, but *initiative,* or appropriate, timely inputs of their own based upon the intervention procedures. For example, Mrs. M continued her daily home ratings of aversive behavior on her own, saying that the procedure helped her to attend to John's behavior. Also, she and her husband were active in managing the HCP procedures and even correctly judged that their increased social praise for John's earnings would sustain his good behavior after only two weeks of the negotiated contingency. Most important, the parents themselves, at least by their verbal report, undertook to apply contingent social praise for improvements in the other, previously disrupted daily periods, which

was a probable factor in the reported reduction of John's other problems. At several other times John's parents, and Mrs. M in particular, made useful contributions to the production and maintenance of the effective home intervention programs. The apparent effect of these parent-initiated inputs was to accelerate the treatment response as well as to increase its efficiency by reducing the therapists' involvement.

Second, while the main treatment data in terms of the family's weekly response were in the form of the parents' records, Mr. and Mrs. M's home records and questionnaire results were extremely consistent and were supported by the therapists' direct observation of the family interaction. For this reason Mrs. M's weekly behavioral frequency counts are presented here graphically, in Figure 7 (p. 119). Except for the usually well-specified items in the HCP, it is not recommended that the parents' ratings of daily occurring behaviors be utilized as an indication of treatment response unless some independent estimate of their reliability is available, such as home or videotape observations.

CASE NO. 2: MAINTAINING GOOD BEHAVIOR*

Background. Mrs. W, a young, single parent, brought her son George into the clinic just after his ninth birthday. Her primary initial complaint was George's "defiance"; he resisted all authority and rules in the home and at school. George was popular among his friends but constantly teased and provoked his ten-year-old brother, Lee, at home. He also frequently took money from his mother's purse and then denied it. Mrs. W complained that she had no control over George and usually screamed extreme threats at him when he confronted her. Occasionally she sent him to his room, but he would scream and bang on the wall, and Mrs. W would make him promise to "be good" and then let him out.

Mrs. W also complained of her own problems. She said she felt she should do whatever she could for her boys, but that it was very difficult without a husband. Mrs. W began working as a laboratory technician when George was two years old, and was still at that job, in addition to being enrolled in college evening classes. She described the current home life as "one big hassle" and wondered at times if she was the one with the problem.

---

* The therapist for this case was W. H. Miller.

According to Mrs. W, George had been very active and aggressive since infancy. She said he was an early walker and talker and had "never liked rules"; also, his earliest sentences, when George was only eighteen months, were often demands for attention from his parents. George was reportedly a very healthy child throughout his development.

Although he was always somewhat of a problem, after his parents' divorce one year prior to the clinic referral, George became increasingly disruptive at home and at school. Mr. W visited with the boys infrequently, and provided no financial support for the family. However, Mrs. W said that although she needed more money, she didn't want to confront him about his lack of support since he had "enough problems already." She also revealed that she and Mr. W had always fought a lot and had never consistently disciplined the boys.

Screening. The screening procedures included a physical examination, a psychoeducational evaluation, behavior checklists, and a personality inventory completed by Mrs. W. The physical examination showed no abnormalities, but psychological testing revealed several problems. First, George was underachieving in school by about one year, although he was functioning in the above-average range of intelligence. Also, his drawings, sentence completions, and stories were those of a very angry boy who had little impulse control. On the Family Relations Test (Binet-Anthony, 1965) he showed positive feelings only for his father, and largely negative feelings toward his mother and brother. On the behavior checklists, Mrs. W revealed a striking difference in her perception of her two sons' behaviors. While no problems were noted for Lee, she scored an extremely high number of serious aggressive behaviors for George, even for the clinic population. The pre- and postintervention behavior checklist ratings for both boys are presented on page 129.

Mrs. W's MMPI profile was that of a practical minded and generally adequate person who might tend to become easily agitated and angered about family conflicts, and who tried to present herself in a socially acceptable way.

The screening results indicated that while many of George's adjustment problems might reflect the longstanding difficulties of Mr. and Mrs. W, his current daily difficulties appeared to relate to Mrs. W's inadequate management skills. It was decided to accept the case for parent training, and then to determine if more intensive or individualized treatments would be needed later.

Baseline. The baseline procedures consisted of Mrs. W's initial behavior checklist ratings, and four weeks of home ratings. First, Mrs. W kept tallies of aversive behaviors for both boys to document the level of disruptions in the home. The four-week records were consistent with the mother's behavior checklist scores: during the three-hour period of observations made each evening that Mrs. W was home George averaged about ten instances of hitting and teasing his brother per hour. Second, a morning HCP baseline was constructed so that the initial intervention could restructure the family interaction early in the day. The details of the HCP, including a discussion of the items selected initially for the AM and then the PM Programs (which were included in the second two weeks of private records) are presented in Chapter 9. Briefly, as shown in Figure 9, over the four-week baseline both boys earned on the average about 60%, or three of the five items in the AM Program. In the last two weeks of the HCP baseline both George and Lee earned fewer PM than AM items during the private records, but they still performed much better than was expected by the inclusion of one "free" item for each boy. Thus, instead of earning only 20% of the PM items, based on the expected achievement of one of the five items, George earned over 30% and Lee about 45%. As discussed in Chapter 9, Mrs. W probably increased her expectancy for the baseline items to occur and also restructured several of the observed activities.

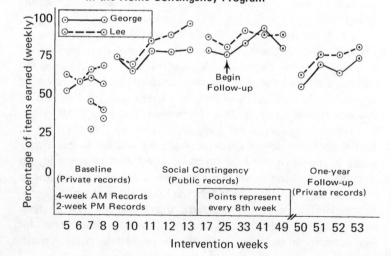

Figure 9 George and Lee W's Progress
in the Home Contingency Program

The results of the baseline assessment were challenging in that they documented the severity of George's problems, but were also promising in that the private HCP records suggested that Mrs. W would be responsive and follow the therapist's suggestions.

INTERVENTIONS FOR CASE NO. 2

INTERVENTIONS I AND II

For the *fifth meeting* Mrs. W brought in her first week of HCP private records. As is often the case when using the HCP, only the first week of private records constitute a "pure" baseline since Intervention I usually begins after one week of record keeping. After reviewing the records, Mrs. W was presented with a copy of *Living With Children* and the application of social learning principles was discussed. The major concepts of basic discrimination training were introduced (see Chapter 7) and special emphasis was placed on the recognition of George's praisable behavior. To facilitate the development of Mrs. W's parenting skills, a playroom setting was used to observe the family interaction.

First, the therapist watched from behind a two-way mirror and recorded the mother's directives, the boys' compliance, appropriate play and verbal interaction, and then the mother's response to the children's behavior. The boys played generally well during the thirty-minute period, although George was constantly criticizing and teasing Lee. Also, George tended to ignore his mother's directives. The most revealing aspect of the session was Mrs. W's response to the boys, and especially George. After the session, the therapist's records showed that Mrs. W ignored nearly all positive interaction, appropriate play, and compliance. Usually the only attention the boys received was criticism or a terminating command.

Second, after observing the interaction for about a half hour, the therapist asked Mrs. W to come out of the room for a few minutes while the boys continued to play. While observing the boys together, the therapist pointed out instances of the boys' appropriate behaviors and rehearsed with Mrs. W how she could begin to attend positively to the behavior she liked and wanted to see more of. Also, the therapist emphasized that her rate of ignoring behavior was much too great, and that she should look for positive features of the children's behavior to praise. She was also asked to continue to ignore behavior she didn't like when possible. After about five minutes, Mrs. W was asked to return to the room and practice the changes discussed. (In other cases, such as Case No. 4 in this chapter,

the electronic "bug-in-the-ear" communication device can be used with considerable effectiveness to facilitate the feedback training in the clinic.)

During the fifteen-minute session that followed, Mrs. W increased her praise rate for both boys' behavior. However, she continued to attend to their arguments and George's teasing. At the end of the session, with the boys in the waiting room, the therapist praised Mrs. W for her improvements, specifying both her increased use of praise and the resulting increases in George's behavior, as well as the areas which needed improvement. It was decided that this procedure would be repeated the following week, and that Mrs. W should add to her evening records instances of her own positive attention for George's behavior. She was given a wrist counter, and asked to record each of her praise responses so that she could simply record the totals later.

At the *sixth session* Mrs. W's records showed that she praised George ten, five, and eight times in each of the three-hour blocks observed on the evenings she was home. She noted that this was a considerable improvement over her usual rate of praise.

The playroom observation and feedback procedure used for the previous week was repeated. Mrs. W continued to show improvement in the timing and frequency of her praising appropriate behavior, and began to ignore instances of George's whining at her and teasing his brother. Mrs. W was asked to use her wrist-counting procedure to record her rate of praising George for one more week.

During the second part of the session Mrs. W showed the records of her observations for the previous week. The HCP morning items continued to be stable at about 60% for both boys, and private records were also begun for the evening period. The therapist reasoned that since the boys were doing so well in the AM private records, a few weeks of assessment of an HCP during the difficult evening period might later allow the intervention program to begin with a *composite* AM-PM public intervention.

INTERVENTION III

During the *seventh* and *eighth sessions* the therapist continued to focus on improving Mrs. W's ability to rapidly identify and respond to George's appropriate and inappropriate behavior. Also, in the eighth session it was decided that her improved parenting skills, together with the continued high rate of HCP earnings, indicated the need for beginning the public intervention. *Thus the home intervention was not begun until Mrs. W had mastered the basic social learn-*

ing concepts and skills. The delay also allowed the therapist to further document, by the mother's records and the clinic observations, the problems in the family interaction.

As planned, the therapist suggested that Mrs. W apply a public HCP which would combine certain behaviors of the AM and PM Programs. Together with Mrs. W, the therapist selected six behaviors for each of the boys from the two private charts. There were no AM items which were consistently unearned, so three of the less frequent behaviors were chosen. However, there were three PM items which were rarely achieved by either boy. Mrs. W suggested using a single chart for both boys, by drawing diagonals through the boxes and marking the upper half with a blue pen for George and the lower half with a red pen for Lee. She also asked if she could get a number of charts typed with the items duplicated "so they will be neat and look official." The therapist welcomed these suggestions, and in fact adopted them for use in later cases.

During the last part of session eight the therapist and Mrs. W briefly role played the procedure of explaining the public chart system to the boys. Mrs. W was worried that George would want to know what the checks were worth, and that without a tangible reward the children would "turn off" to the program. The therapist suggested she tell them the truth; namely, that she wanted to see how well the boys could do with the chart, and that she would be extremely proud of their ability to take care of themselves and help her out with some of the chores.

Mrs. W brought in her records for the *ninth session,* and reported that the family had a very good week. After a brief percentage count, the therapist pointed out (see Figure 9, p. 124) that she should be pleased, since both boys earned nearly 75% of the available items on the composite public chart. Mrs. W added that both boys really liked having the chart, and they were careful that each of their earnings was duly registered. There was also a competitive aspect to the boys' behavior since they were reported to be very verbal about seeing who could earn the most checks on the public charts. Mrs. W noted that this was nothing new, but that previous competition had involved fighting and much anger, whereas these negative aspects of their competition were missing in the past week.

After some discussion, Mrs. W said that she had not been praising them as much as she should have for their improvements, but that it was still difficult for her to thank them for something they "should" be doing already. She further explained that part of the problem was her parents' and boyfriend's reaction to the plan.

On several occasions they had visited Mrs. W and the boys; when they saw the chart they ridiculed Mrs. W for "having to go to the doctor to make the children behave." They recommended using "the stick" which was "what all little boys needed." The therapist sympathized with her, knowing that in her particular neighborhood and subculture it was unrealistic for her to suddenly change her child-rearing habits. Mrs. W said that her conflict was between doing what she had always done and using the new procedures given her, which seemed to be reducing her problems as well as George's. Mrs. W agreed that the HCP should continue and that the family problems, as well as George's, would be dealt with as they emerged.

INTERVENTION V

From the *tenth* through the *thirteenth sessions* the therapist continued to meet with Mrs. W weekly to review her records and discuss the week's activities and problems. Usually the meetings lasted about one-half hour. During this period Mrs. W reported that as family life became more routine, she was able to relax more. Also, the therapist praised Mrs. W's efforts each week, emphasizing that as she praised the children's improvements they would learn better self-management and maintain their progress later when the formal program ended. Figure 9 shows the continued improvements of both boys in the initial weeks of the composite public HCP.

There were no records kept or meetings in the month following the thirteenth session, as both the therapist and the GW family were on vacation prior to the start of the new school year. It was agreed that the treatment plan for the fall would be to stabilize the HCP for both boys at the start of school, and then to begin fading out the treatment.

For the *seventeenth program week* Mrs. W brought in the HCP records for the first week of school. Both boys showed decreased earnings, but were still at or above the 80 per cent level. Thus nearly five out of the six items were being performed regularly by George and Lee. Mrs. W also noted that there was less fighting between the boys, and that they had started to volunteer to help her with her household chores for the first time.

Figure 9, beginning with the HCP data points of the *seventeenth week,* shows the home intervention progress at eight-week intervals, although Mrs. W kept continuous records in this period. The therapist continued to meet with Mrs. W for weekly half-hour sessions through the *twenty-fifth week* of the program, after which the follow-up period was started. These sessions were concerned primarily with the boys' weekly progress in the home program, although several one-hour sessions dealt with Mrs. W's occasional periods of agitation and concern about her progress in night school and continuing financial problems. Also, on two separate occasions these parent counseling sessions focused on Mrs. W's extreme agitation and anger toward George.

The School Intervention. The first problem occurred in the *eighteenth week* when, after only two weeks of school, Mrs. W complained that George had returned to his previous habit of provoking and fighting in school. On several occasions George had nearly seriously injured other children by testing out his new array of karate blows, and by sticking nearby children in the classroom with sharp objects. At the time Mrs. W reported this problem George was suspended for a five-day period for sticking a girl with a sharp pin.

The therapist developed a simple strategy to try prior to visiting the school. First, George's principal and teacher were phoned, and the plan presented to them. George's teacher was willing to try the procedure if it didn't disrupt her teaching responsibilities, and the principal, although preferring to suspend George indefinitely, agreed to back up the plan.

Each day George was to have a small index card marked off into half-hour periods placed on his desk. For every half hour, including playground time, when George managed a half hour without "any behavior that might injure someone," he was awarded a check. Any instance of the intolerable behavior was noted by an "X." Immediately after earning the second "X," George was to go to the principal's office for the rest of the day and then to miss the following day of school. He was to stay in the house all day, monitored by Mrs. W's friend next door.

While planning to present the punishment plan to George, Mrs. W rehearsed the procedure in the therapist's office. The following points were emphasized:

1. George should first be told (again) of the serious nature of his behavior, and that since he had difficulty controlling himself, a plan would be started at school to help him.

2. Mrs. W was to emphasize that attending school was a privilege, and that by hurting other kids George would lose that privilege. On the other hand, he could earn the right to stay in school by not hurting others.

3. The exact details of the punishment were to be explained to George, and then he was to verbalize the details back to his mother as best he could.

4. Each day George was to bring his card home with him, and Mrs. W was to praise him for one or less "Xs." If he had two "Xs" when he arrived home, he was to go to his room immediately and miss all play and TV privileges that day and the next.

5. George's teacher was also asked to present the plan to George on the first day he returned to school after his suspension period was over. She too was to praise George whenever he reduced his dangerous behavior.

The school program was in effect for five weeks. George never lost the "privilege" of attending school although he had three "Xs," on different days, the first week. The teacher called the therapist and requested that any two "Xs" in a given week be made the new criterion for punishment, and this new criterion was instituted the next week after the teacher explained it to George.

During the next two weeks there was one "X" for each week, and afterward no more instances of aggressive behavior at school. After the third week, the teacher changed George's card from thirty-minute to one-hour periods, and the following week to morning and afternoon periods. The therapist never discussed the problem directly with George, although a school or clinic meeting could have been arranged if the suggested plan had not been effective, or to make a more thorough study of the problem.

The Stealing Incident. The second problem which Mrs. W brought up in her sessions with the therapist concerned an incident in the twentieth week, less than two weeks after the school program had begun. Reportedly, George had taken money from Mrs. W's purse for the first time since the treatment began. According to Mrs. W, she found George with large quantities of candy in his room one evening, and when he refused to tell her how he got the money for his purchases, she became enraged. After a lot of screams and threats from his mother, George admitted taking the money the night before, which caused Mrs. W to become even more upset. She punished him by restricting him to his room with no play or TV privileges for a week.

Mrs. W was still angry when she met with the therapist. It appeared by her account that, except for her tirade, Mrs. W handled the problem well, especially since she said that a year previously she would have "beat him, for sure." Her main concern was that several young delinquent boys lived in the neighborhood and she worried a lot that George would become like them. Fortunately, George accepted his punishment well, and the therapist's only suggestion was that Mrs. W meet with both boys to discuss the seriousness and consequencess of stealing. There were no more instances of stealing throughout the program.

As Mrs. W began to express more confidence in her ability to maintain her son's good behavior with praise, with the public HCP, and by ignoring aversive behavior, the therapist raised the issue of termination. Already the professional time and effort in this case had exceeded twenty hours, but Mrs. W had indicated on several occasions that the brief meetings were very helpful. When the therapist suggested, in the twenty-fourth week, that a trial period of private records be started, Mrs. W reacted strongly against this plan. In a positive but firm manner she asked why she should take the charts down *anytime* in the near future. She said that she needed help in organizing the children's interactions and chores on a daily basis, and that she didn't want to end a plan that worked so well.

Mrs. W convincingly argued that the HCP provided her with a daily structure that was indispensable for her at that time, and the therapist agreed that a test of the program would be more appropriate later. Thus the onset of follow-up noted in Figure 9 was atypical since, although there were no more weekly meetings, the public HCP continued.

Maintenance Training. During the *twenty-fifth week* the therapist and Mrs. W met for the last regular time. The entire focus of the meeting was on her maintenance of George's excellent response to all of the programs and procedures used to that date. Several potential problem areas were discussed, including George's school and home disruptions. It was suggested that if problems arose Mrs. W should use the following steps: first, to try to use the HCP by substituting the desired behavior for a high-rate behavior on the chart; second, to discuss the problem with George and mutually agree on a period of lost privileges of playing outside or TV time; and third, to call the therapist if problems arose that she couldn't handle.

The therapist also suggested that, if Mrs. W wanted to discuss any problems of her own, the therapist could see her a few times or arrange for a longer period of meetings. However, she noted that

recently she had felt much more at ease in her work and studies since she was able to trust George to manage himself when she was not at home.

Follow-Up. During the *forty-ninth week* of the program Mrs. W was contacted and asked to come in for a brief assessment of the program. She brought in her records for the six-month follow-up period, which showed excellent maintenance of the selected behaviors. During this period she had changed two of George's items, both of which involved new household chores, and were 100 per cent on her recent charts. Mrs. W reported that George had continued to improve his behavior at home and school, although he did miss one day of school for fighting in the playground.

The absence of any reported problems in the six months was unexpected by the therapist. However, Mrs. W said that her boyfriend had proposed marriage, and that he had been involved with the boys during the six-month period; she felt that having a man around helped them to "shape up." Recalling her boyfriend's philosophy of child rearing, the therapist was concerned that George's progress might be partly caused by a fear of punishment. However, Mrs. W noted that her boyfriend had become impressed by George's improvements at home and in school, and was supporting the program completely.

As part of the follow-up assessment, Mrs. W was asked to keep private HCP records. She said that since the boys' behavior appeared to be so consistently appropriate, she would now be willing to test the program without the public chart. Thus, to get a good estimate of George's level of functioning without the chart, Mrs. W kept private records for four weeks. She was also asked to keep her evening ratings of George's aggressive behavior for two weeks, and to complete posttreatment behavior checklists and the Parent's Assessment of Therapy.

In general, the six-month follow-up ratings of George's behavior all showed considerable improvement over the baseline levels. The HCP results are shown in Figure 9 (p. 124). It can be seen that during the first week of follow-up (week No. 50), the boys were functioning near the baseline level. However, during the next three weeks the intervention level of eighty per cent was nearly regained. Mrs. W was concerned about the relative losses, and announced her intention to return to the public records when the follow-up assessments were over. By her report, the old posttreatment levels of behavior were later completely recovered by both boys, and she maintained the public chart for nearly four more months before successfully removing it. She was supported in her wish to return to the public procedure whenever she needed an extra "boost" in the boys' good behavior.

Mrs. W's evening ratings of George's aggression were also important because, while she had originally counted about ten instances of George's hitting and teasing Lee for each three-hour period observed, there was only one recorded hitting episode and no teasing for the two weeks of follow-up observations.

The mother's behavior checklist ratings showed that her perception of George after treatment had greatly changed. The pre- and posttest ratings for both boys, for each of the six categories, are presented below.

Behavior Checklist Category	Screening: % items answered "yes" George	Lee	Follow-up: % items answered "yes" George	Lee
Aggression	89	5	21	5
Inhibition	7	14	0	7
Hyperactivity	40	10	0	0
Sleep Disturbances	56	11	33	22
Somatic Disturbances	13	38	0	13
Social Maturity	30	100	70	70

As was noted in the baseline assessment, Mrs. W originally reported that George was extremely aggressive, and that the two boys were very different in their behavior. After treatment, however, her scores for both boys were well within the normal range. Especially significant was Mrs. W's decrease in aggression items answered "yes" (89 to 21 per cent) and increase in items reflecting social maturity (30 to 70 per cent). Finally, Mrs. W's responses on the Parent's Assessment of Therapy are presented below.

Parent's Assessment of Therapy

1. Describe very briefly your child's problem prior to involvement in the UCLA Home Intervention Program.

   George was always fighting, disrupting the classroom, disobedient, and would sometimes take things that didn't belong to him.

2. Describe the essential details of the Intervention Program in which you were involved.

   Reorganizing myself first so that I was able to deal with the situations in a more positive manner.

3. List the three most important changes which occurred as a direct result of the Intervention Program.

   1. I became more patient with my children.
   2. George became more cooperative at school and at home.
   3. We are now able to communicate with each other.

4. Describe very briefly the child's behavior since the most recent Intervention.

   He's learned to control his temper most of the time. And he's not so eager to create a disturbance.

5. Describe very briefly the single most important factor which led to the changes you observed.

   The reorganization of our lives to the point where we could communicate.

6. Please compare the effects of the Home Intervention Program with other therapeutic techniques attempted for your child's problem.

   There really hadn't been any type of program, and verbally and physically punishing him was only making things worse.

7. Are there any additional comments you would like to make about the program? Be critical.

   I would like to know more about my children's test results.

8. Please compare the relative contributions by the child's mother and father to the program's outcome.

   Not applicable.

9. Please describe briefly your overall opinion of the Intervention Program you were involved in at UCLA. Were you in general satisfied with the treatment your family received? Is this the kind of family Intervention Program you would recommend to other families with similar needs to your own?

   The program played an extremely important part in our lives. I only wish I had known about it sooner. It would have made life so much easier for me and my children. I was very satisfied with the treatment we got. And I recommend this type of program very highly to families with similar problems.

Comment. The GW case was judged to be a success in terms of the achievement of the original intervention goals. By the flo-chart model, the GW case involved the application of social learning concepts, an intensive use of basic discrimination training, a complex and lengthy HCP, and parent counseling, which at two points required a school intervention plan and a brief response-cost punishment procedure. Over twenty-two hours of professional time were required to attain a level of desirable behavior in the referred child that was maintained in the follow-up assessment.

As a result of the interventions, Mrs. W learned to manage her children by positive reinforcement for desirable behavior rather than threats and punishment for undesirable behavior. No claim could be made for a change in Mrs. W's basic child-rearing *attitudes,* but she did change the way she responded to her children, and directly influenced the way her boyfriend (who later became George's stepfather) related to the referred child.

The GW case illustrates several important features of successfully applied parent training procedures. First, in a family where the mother needed additional structure and support to carry out the home intervention, the therapist judged the role of full sibling participation as extremely important. Lee's involvement (a) prevented George, originally a very resentful child, from being isolated as the person responsible for the family problems; (b) prevented Lee from being left out of a plan that involved much of Mrs. W's time and attention; and (c) allowed for the development of positive, friendly competition and thus increased motivation for George to engage in appropriate behavior.

Second, the case shows how, for some families, the HCP provides an increased level of structured family interactions that can be effective without the need for negotiated contingencies and rewards. The therapist fully expected to have to introduce rewards for the children at some point, but their excellent response to the public chart suggested that performing their tasks and earning contingent chart points were their rewards.

Third, a very important feature of this case was Mrs. W's suggestion about the simplified construction of the actual HCP chart, as well as her insistence that the charts remain up during the follow-up period. By remaining open to her requests, the therapist was able to further individualize the intervention as well as learn new important variations in applying the HCP.

Although considerable planning and effort were devoted to the *modification* of George's interaction at home and at school, the real issue in this case was clearly that of behavior *maintenance*. Usually when maintenance is a major issue the case involves much parent counseling and possibly intensive treatments for family members in addition to systematic parent training. In this case the goal of "maintaining good behavior" was achieved, but not without the continuing daily structure provided by the HCP. While the long-term implications of *chart-maintained behaviors* are uncertain, it is notable that since working with Mrs. W other single working mothers involved in parent training at the UCLA clinic have also requested the use of long-term HCP public charts.

CASE NO. 3: WHEN PRAISE IS NOT ENOUGH*

Background. Tommy F, age five and a half, was brought to the clinic by his parents after being referred from another child treatment agency. During the initial interview it was learned that Mr. and Mrs. F's primary concerns were (a) that Tommy would not be able to adjust to first grade placement because of his extreme temper tantrums whenever limits were placed on his behavior, and (b) Mrs. F's "total inability" to manage Tommy at home. Mr. F indicated that he had always been able to control Tommy by being firm and consistent, but that his wife was thoroughly intimidated by the boy. Tommy was said to ignore nearly all of Mrs. F's requests and to be very aggressive with both her and his four-year-old brother, Jerry.

Mrs. F admitted that when Tommy's behavior became so bad that she couldn't stand it anymore she would usually give in to his demands to have his own way. She was extremely distressed as she described the problems at home, and worried about what would become of Tommy if his "wild" behavior continued.

Both parents agreed that Tommy had always been a difficult child since his adoption when he was one month old. The parents had unsuccessfully tried for five years to have a child, and although they both wanted a girl, only male children were available at the adoption agency and they decided not to wait any longer. From the beginning Tommy was "a screamer and a kicker." Mrs. F had much

* The therapists for this case were D. Auerbach and W.H. Miller.

trouble diapering him and often was up most of the night with the child.

Tommy had various medical problems including allergies and infections, and Mrs. F had to take him to the doctor quite often. By the age of nine months he was jumping out of his crib and banging his head; already, by that time, Mrs. F reported that she did not enjoy Tommy's presence and that he was aversive to her.

When Tommy was nine months old, Mrs. F became pregnant with Jerry. Again she reported disappointment when Jerry was born a boy, especially since she was afraid Jerry would be like Tommy. However, Jerry's development and behavior were very normal, and even at the time of referral Mrs. F reported no problems managing her younger son.

When Tommy made a very poor adjustment in nursery school at the age of three and a half due to his excessively careless, rough play, and high activity level, Mrs. F took him to a clinic for hyperkinetic children. However, trials of amphetamines, Ritalin, and Tofranil had no effect on his behavior. No other treatments were attempted.

When Tommy was four, he had a grand mal seizure; the event had an extremely adverse effect on his mother. The seizure occurred while on a shopping trip, and Mrs. F was terrified and took him to the hospital. There were no other seizures, but a neurologist interpreted Tommy's EEG as abnormal, and Mrs. F became convinced from that point on that Tommy's difficulties were due to "brain damage." This belief played a major role in the family's later delayed response to treatment, although the therapists, other doctors, and even Mr. F repeatedly assured her that Tommy's seizure disorder was not responsible for his behavior problems.

Mr. F said that, as a result of the seizure, Mrs. F found a solution to many of her own worries. For example, Mr. F and his parents had been extremely and openly critical of Mrs. F, saying that if she were a good mother, Tommy would be normal. She had previously accepted this onus, but after the seizure she "no longer felt guilty about being a bad mother," and became convinced that neither she nor Tommy could control his organically driven behavior.

Screening. In the screening procedure a medical examination revealed that at the time of referral Tommy was a large, normal child in good health, except for a mildly abnormal EEG. Testing showed that he had above average intelligence and good school-related learning skills. Questionnaires completed by Tommy's parents revealed that, while they differed in their attitudes about him, they were very consistent in their perception of his behavior problems. Thus both parents generally saw him as moderately aggressive and extremely hyperactive and socially unskilled, although on specific items Mrs. F noted that her main concern was Tommy's noncompliance. The pre- and posttreatment scores on the behavior checklists are presented on page 138.

Finally, the parents' MMPI's showed that Mr. F was an extremely sensitive and honest person who would probably contribute as much as he could to Tommy's treatment program. Mrs. F's profile revealed a tense, fearful person with very low self-esteem and a tendency to become quite depressed. However, her mild distress and sensitive, introspective characteristics had been seen in other mothers who were highly motivated to improve their problems and had made good, long-term response to parent training.

In summary, the TF family members showed many disturbed interaction and behavior patterns. It was estimated by the therapists that systematic parent training was appropriate and much needed in this case to improve Tommy's behavior and to thereby provide Mrs. F with positive feedback that could help change her negative, counter productive attitudes toward her son.

At the time of the referral, the therapists were involved in a research program to assess the home observation data system used for families in the UCLA child outpatient clinic, and it was decided to include the TF family in this study. This meant that while the family was involved in the regular procedures of systematic parent training, home observations by trained observers would be systematically made throughout the baseline, interventions, and follow-up phases of the treatment. Also, videotapes of the family would be made at intervals to compare the home data system results of clinic and home observations.

Baseline. First, the parents' initial behavior checklist scores further documented their reports of Tommy's behavior problems in the home. Second, Mrs. F kept hourly records for a three-hour after-school period, which she described as the worst part of the day for her and Tommy. Over the relatively long (four-week) preintervention period, she noted that even on "a relatively good day" Tommy engaged in several instances of hitting Jerry and "excessively rough play." On many days the records showed that Jerry was victimized five or more times per hour.

Third, a videotape of the family interaction with all members present was made and reduced (scored) using the home observation data system. Figure 10 (below) shows the baseline levels for Tommy's "obey" and "aggressive behavior," and Mrs. F's "praised obey." Aggressive behavior included Tommy's hitting, yelling, and verbal defiance.

The 45-minute session involved (a) free play with everyone participating, (b) instructions for the boys to play while the parents read quietly, and (c) an instructed "pick up the toys" time. Mr. F was asked to leave the room for the first portion of the "pick up" time so that the therapists could observe the mother-child interaction in a compliance test situation. While Tommy complied at a very low rate, confirming Mrs. F's earlier complaint, she praised none of his obeys, but attended to his noncompliance by repeating her commands. Also, Tommy showed a very high rate of aversive behavior, with nearly a fifth of the scoring intervals containing an instance of verbal or physical aggression, which was responded to by Mrs. F's mild correction or criticism. As reported earlier, Jerry showed no significant problems, and when Mr. F returned to the room he had no problem getting both boys to pick up their toys.

Fourth, home visits were made in the baseline period, each lasting about one hour. The raters were previously trained to score chains of behavioral interaction in the home with better than 80% interrater reliability, using repeated fifteen-second scoring intervals

and a time-sampling procedure. Thus components of "compliance," "aversive behavior," "verbal interaction" and "appropriate play" chains were scored only once for each of the fifteen-second observation intervals. Figures 11, 12, and 13 (below) show the average values obtained for the compliance chain, appropriate play, and aversive behavior for each group of home visits made. All points except the baseline values (for four visits) represent three-visit averages. The visits were made to Tommy's home three times per week at monthly intervals.

Since all the visits were made in the troublesome after-school period, with Tommy, Jerry and Mrs. F present, the results allowed the therapists to carefully examine the problem areas in the relationship between Tommy and his mother. Figures 11 and 12 provide further baseline documentation for these problems. Figure 11 shows a normal (for the clinic population) average percentage of commands given per home visit; about ten per cent of the fifteen-second intervals contained a command. However, Tommy's percentage of "obeys" and his mother's "obeys praised" (Figure 12) were quite low even for the clinic population. As observed previously, Mrs. F's typical response to Tommy's few obeys was to ignore the behavior (Figure 12).

Figure 10 Videotape Analysis of Tommy's Obeys and Aversive Behavior and Mrs. F's Praise for Obeys

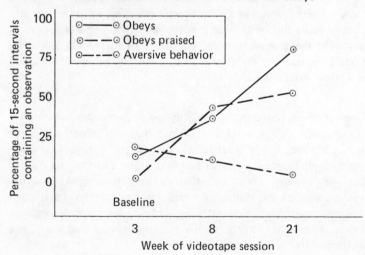

Figure 11 Home Observation of Tommy's rate of Compliance for Baseline (BL), Interventions (I-V), and Follow-up (FU)

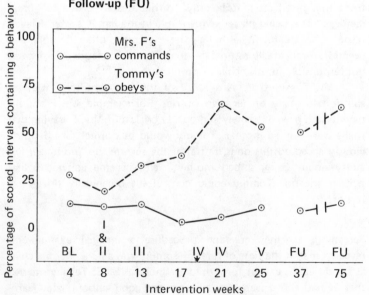

132

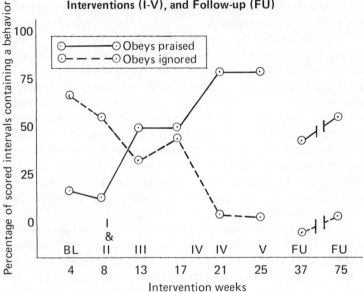

Figure 12 Home Observation of Mrs. F's Response to Tommy's Compliance for Baseline (BL), Interventions (I-V), and Follow-up (FU)

Percentage of scored intervals containing a behavior

○——○ Obeys praised
○- - -○ Obeys ignored

BL | I & II | III | IV | IV | V | FU | FU
4 | 8 | 13 | 17 | 21 | 25 | 37 | 75

Intervention weeks

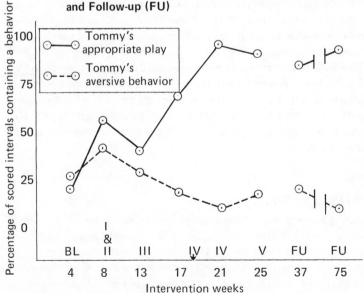

Figure 13 Home Observation of Tommy's Appropriate Play and Aversive Behavior for Baseline (BL), Interventions (I-V), and Follow-up (FU)

Percentage of scored intervals containing a behavior

○——○ Tommy's appropriate play
○- - -○ Tommy's aversive behavior

BL | I & II | III | IV | IV | V | FU | FU
4 | 8 | 13 | 17 | 21 | 25 | 37 | 75

Intervention weeks

Figure 13 shows the initial very low rate for Tommy's "appropriate play," which referred to a period of constructive play in which there was no negative interaction. Also shown is Tommy's preintervention rate of aversive behavior, which at 30% was even higher than the rate observed on the clinic videotape.

With the available baseline information, especially augmented by the home observation results, the therapists were able to conceptualize the TF family's problems and to specify the short-term goals of intervention in a relatively precise manner. The primary goals were to develop Mrs. F's discrimination and differential response skills so that Tommy could begin to predict the appropriate consequences of his desirable and undesirable behaviors. Thus Mrs. F would have to improve the timing, frequency, and quality of her responses to Tommy. Also, she would need to learn the importance of her own stimulus control of Tommy's disruptive behavior, and that Tommy usually misbehaved in her presence only. Other goals were to restructure the difficult after-school period with an HCP, and then to apply a Time Out procedure if the disruptive behavior continued. Other individualized treatments for Mrs. F or Tommy would be applied only as indicated by the family's response to the planned procedures.

The treatment plan was presented to the parents, and there was some discussion of the roles each parent would have in the program. Both parents were very supportive of the plan, and agreed to participate fully. Mrs. F predicted that she would have a difficult time but said that she "needed relief" and would try her best. Also, Mr. F agreed to come to the meetings and to support his wife's efforts in every way possible.

INTERVENTIONS FOR CASE NO. 3

INTERVENTION I

For their *fifth meeting* the parents came in to discuss social learning concepts. Especially emphasized were the importance of understanding the current interaction between Tommy and his mother without dwelling on the past, and the concepts of reinforcement through praise for small increments in Tommy's desirable behavior. Also discussed were the steps necessary to improve Tommy's compliance, including not only discrimination and shaping, but parent consistency in the home application of the procedures discussed in the clinic. Mr. and Mrs. F then purchased a copy of *Living With Children* and agreed to write out the answers and bring them in the following week.

During the *sixth week* both parents brought in their written responses to the book. In the first part of the meeting the therapists asked Mr. and Mrs. F to discuss their reactions to the book. Both parents named several chapters that contained information they could relate to Tommy's problems. Mrs. F in particular said that she could see how Tommy's behavior had become disruptive since she had been giving him a lot of attention for tantrums and hitting. However, Mr. F, an accountant, reacted somewhat negatively to the book, feeling that it "insulted his intelligence" and was "too easy." He did complete all the blanks correctly, and the therapists encouraged him to read Patterson's *Families,* which is somewhat more sophisticated and specific in its coverage of social learning concepts.

INTERVENTION II

Based on the parents' responses in the previous discussions, the therapists decided to begin basic discrimination training the following week. The plan would include working first with Mrs. F, using the initial family videotape for discrimination and feedback training.

During the *seventh session* Mrs. F was brought into a small room where she and the therapist could view the playback together. Mrs. F was asked to watch the tape closely and to point out examples of Tommy's behavior that she liked and would like to increase. During the first part of the playback she only identified things that she liked about Tommy's brother, and complained about Tommy's misbehavior, such as disobeying her and hitting Jerry. However, when the therapist began stopping the video playback and emphasizing each instance of Tommy's approximate obeys, and moments of appropriate play, Mrs. F showed that she could also identify many of Tommy's desirable behaviors. Then, using the guideline "if you see something you like, praise it," Mrs. F was able to indicate, by the therapist's judgment, almost every instance of praisable behavior.

The therapist then rehearsed with Mrs. F several ways to praise Tommy for desirable behavior. It was decided that the following week she and the therapist would again view the videotape and practice new ways to identify and respond to Tommy's behavior.

During the *eighth session* Mrs. F continued to show progress in identifying Tommy's praisable, ignorable, and punishable behaviors. Also, each time Mrs. F made the appropriate discrimination, the therapist stopped the tape and helped her to practice various styles of praising and ignoring Tommy's behavior. It became apparent early

in the basic discrimination training that Mrs. F was not comfortable with discussions involving punishing or confronting Tommy, so the topic of negative attention was delayed until she was competent in praising and ignoring behavior.

In preparation for the third session of basic discrimination training Mrs. F was asked to bring Tommy and Jerry into the clinic with her so that a videotape could be made of her interaction with the boys. In this way a systematic assessment could be made of her discrimination skills, and the results compared with the previous videotape. Figure 10 (p. 132) shows Mrs. F's progress after Intervention II, as assessed in the second videotape, during the ninth treatment session. Although Tommy's rate of compliance increased from the first videotape session, the most significant change occurred in Mrs. F's rate of praising Tommy's obeys; during the second videotaping session she was praising Tommy for nearly every other instance of compliance.

A new series of home visits made in the eighth week, however, showed mixed results concerning the generalization of the clinic training. In Figures 11 (p. 132) and 13 (p. 133) it can be seen that Tommy's behavior was generally worse: he was obeying less, and there was an increase in aversive behavior. On the other hand, closer scrutiny of the home-visit results did indicate some promising changes.

First, Figure 13 shows a large increase in Tommy's appropriate, nondisturbing play. Second, analysis of Tommy's obeys by the type of command given revealed that Tommy had actually *increased his compliance* to *initiating* commands, which required that he begin some new behavior (see page 49, Chapter 7). The decrease in Tommy's compliance (Figure 11) reflected his poor response to Mrs. F's *terminating* commands. Third, Mrs. F showed a higher rate of *specific* directives. These changes indicated that while basic discrimination training was not sufficient to significantly improve the home interaction, it could facilitate the application of more structured interventions.

INTERVENTION III

During the *tenth session* the baseline for the HCP was planned. Mrs. F noted that her daily difficulties with Tommy began when she picked him up from school. He usually refused to come to the car and then was very aversive in the car on the way home. Thus, the initial home intervention program was based on private records of

Tommy's problem behaviors immediately after school, which were the following:

1. Getting his lunch box and sweater from his classroom after one reminder.

2. Leaving the playground to accompany his mother to the car after one request.

3. Getting into the car after one request.

4. Playing quietly in the car on the way home.

5. Going into the house with one request after arriving home.

6. Putting away his lunch box and sweater in the proper place when he arrives home.

After two weeks of baseline records, in which Tommy earned about two out of the six items daily, or about 30 per cent, the public program was started. Tommy's HCP baseline earnings are shown in Figure 14.

Figure 14   Tommy's Progress in the Home Contingency Program

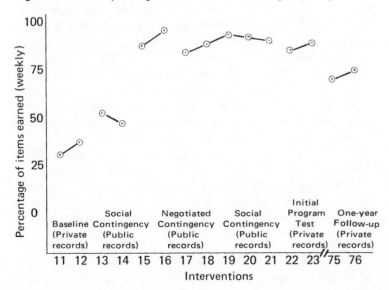

According to the social contingency plan, Tommy would have a happy face drawn on his chart and be praised by his mother each day after school for each item achieved. It was also agreed that Mr. F would give Tommy as much positive attention as possible each evening for his daily earnings. After two weeks of the public HCP, Tommy's earnings had improved by approximately one daily item and he was achieving about three items each day. More importantly, the primary items involving Tommy's refusal to come to the car and get in when requested, and to refrain from aversive behavior in the car, were still not being earned.

During the *fourteenth session* the therapist suggested a trial period of negotiated rewards for Tommy's earnings, in an attempt to provide Tommy with additional incentive to improve his very disrupting behavior. Each day Tommy would receive a token for each happy face, and Mrs. F would continue to praise Tommy's earnings. On Saturday Mr. F would take Tommy on a short trip or let him purchase a small toy if an average of four of the six tokens were earned each day.

As shown in Figure 14, in the first week of the negotiated contingency program, Tommy earned 90% of the tokens, far more than the daily quota required to earn his weekend reward. However, Mrs. F noted that she had not been praising Tommy often enough, and once had used his tokens as a threat to coerce him into complying. She said that she was glad to see him do the items on the chart, but that there was no carry-over to the other times of the day when Tommy misbehaved.

Interestingly, the home visit results after the first week of the public HCP contrasted strongly with Mrs. F's verbal report since, as shown after week No. 13 in Figure 12 (p. 133), she was praising Tommy's obeys at a much higher rate. In fact, for the first time her dominant response to Tommy's compliance was to *praise* rather than to *ignore* the behavior. Also, Figure 13 (p. 133) shows a mild decline in aversive behavior for the same period.

During the *fifteenth session* the therapist discussed the new encouraging home visit results with the parents. They both acknowledged that they had a good week with Tommy and for the first time Mrs. F said that she was becoming aware of his attempts to control himself.

After one more week of the negotiated contingency program, in which Tommy's earnings were again very high, the therapist suggested that the parents again try the social contingency program. Accordingly, they would announce to Tommy that his weekly treat or reward would continue, and that the charts would stay up so that he would still know how well he was doing each day, but that he would not have to earn his reward.

In the *sixteenth session* Mr. and Mrs. F's records showed that Tommy was maintaining the progress he had made in the reward condition. However, they both reported that, in general, Tommy had a bad week and was very aggressive toward his brother and his mother. Mrs. F agreed that Tommy's after-school behavior was better, and said that she was trying her best to praise him for his good behavior, but that Tommy's fighting with Jerry and his angry defiance of her had generally continued. The recent home observations also supported her concerns; Tommy's rate of observed aversive behavior in the home had not diminished significantly since the baseline period.

On the basis of the poor generalization from the HCP program to other behaviors, and the continuing reports of Tommy's extreme disturbing behavior, the therapists decided to deal directly with the problem with a *deceleration plan* and to introduce the Time Out procedure to the parents in the following session.

INTERVENTION IV

During the *seventeenth meeting* the therapists outlined the TO plan. First, TO was explained as a procedure which was especially appropriate in cases where children like Tommy had difficulty complying with their parents' *terminating* commands. The most commonly reported examples by Mrs. F involved Tommy's excessively rough play and aggression at and away from home. It was emphasized that TO would allow Mrs. F to help Tommy learn to control himself without having to confront him physically.

The details of the plan closely approximated those described in the BR and RS cases in Chapter 8. Based on Mrs. F's discomfort using negative attention in basic discrimination training, the therapists had learned that she would resist any plan that involved her confronting Tommy directly. Therefore, Mr. F was asked to play a major role in the plan, according to the following steps:

1. Mrs. F would first learn to effectively give Tommy a terminating command and warning, and finally instruct him to go to the TO room contingent upon repeated aversive behavior.

2. If Tommy refused to go into the TO room, Mrs. F was to say: "Tommy, if you do not go into the Time Out room right now, you will have to go in when your father comes home." If

Tommy went in, she was to thank him for complying and point this out publicly when Mr. F arrived home. If Tommy continued to resist, Mrs. F was to state the consequences again and turn away from him.

3. Immediately upon arriving home each day Mr. F was to go to Mrs. F and ask her to report on her interaction with Tommy. If he had refused to go into the TO room, Mr. F would place him in the TO room for fifteen minutes and remind him of the importance of doing what his mother asked during the day. Coincidentally, Mr. F had an established play period with the boys after work, so that Tommy not only had an extended TO period but missed the play period with his father and Jerry.

During the following week the therapists went to Tommy's home and role played the TO procedure with Tommy, Jerry, and their mother. Mrs. F was hesitant at first, but finally explained and demonstrated the procedure to both boys quite well. The therapists suggested that when Mr. F came home she should reemphasize the details and have Mr. F point out his role to the boys.

During the same week a new series of home visits was made by the observers. In their informal notes, the observers reported that Mrs. F said that she didn't think TO would work for her since "Tommy only went into the room when the therapists were there because they were men." There were no significant changes in any of the behaviors observed, except for a large increase in Tommy's appropriate play. Figure 14 (p. 135) shows that Tommy continued to earn his HCP points at a high rate.

In the next two weeks the therapists attempted to help Mrs. F apply TO by calling her each night and encouraging her to use the procedure more often. However, Mrs. F's usual pattern was to complain about Tommy's behavior, and to report that she had given him many warnings, but that she had not used TO enough.

After two weeks of observing Mrs. F's difficulty with TO, it became apparent that her anxiety about confronting Tommy would require direct attention. Thus, it was decided that one of the therapists would meet individually with her for several sessions and, using relaxation training and systematic desensitization, try to reduce her irrational fears about the consequences of her being firm with Tommy.

The desensitization procedure for Mrs. F involved items relating to Tommy's having a seizure, to his attacking her and Jerry, and to his defiance when she tried to use the TO procedure. After learning to completely relax her muscles, first on cue from the therapist and then by herself, she practiced relaxing while imagining the feared consequences of interacting firmly with Tommy. The relaxation and desensitization training continued for six weeks, from the *twentieth* to the *twenty-sixth week* of the intervention program.

By the sixth desensitization session, Mrs. F reported that she felt less tense and more confident about applying TO and in general was less anxious in relating to Tommy. Also, one of the therapists called her twice weekly in the evening to discuss the ongoing problems, and Mrs. F indicated that, as she had increased her use of TO, Tommy was beginning to respond to her instructions to go into TO with less resistance.

Shortly after beginning the individual treatments for Mrs. F, another series of home visits were made by the observers in the *twenty-first week*. Tommy was making and maintaining progress in all areas assessed. Most significantly, the large increase in Tommy's general compliance rate shown in Figure 11 (p. 132) reflected his improved compliance to *terminating* commands for the first time in the treatment.

A videotape made of Tommy, Jerry, and Mrs. F in the twenty-first week of the program also reflected the treatment progress. Figure 10 (p. 132) shows an increase in Tommy's compliance rate to 80%, and a decrease in aversive behavior to nearly 5%.

Thus, while Mrs. F continued to be concerned about Tommy, she was increasingly effective in producing Tommy's appropriate behavior as well as reducing his disruptions. Also, the final regular series of home visits was made in the *twenty-fourth week*, at about the end of the desensitization treatment, and showed that the recent improvements in Tommy's interaction with his mother were stable over the four-week period.

Maintenance Training. Because of the lengthy and difficult course of treatment in the TF case, the therapists placed considerable emphasis on helping the parents learn to maintain the progress that had been achieved. The basic two-part plan for maintenance was (a) to meet with Mrs. F for a few sessions to help her integrate her new parenting skills, and then (b) to meet with both parents, and explore new ways Mrs. F could use her husband to support her efforts with Tommy.

In the ten maintenance and parent counseling sessions that followed, Mrs. F expressed concern about the role of Tommy's

earlier neurological problems. The therapists and Mr. F emphasized the irrelevance of organicity as an important factor in Tommy's development, and pointed to the significance of his excellent school adjustment in the first grade, which had been Mrs. F's major worry, and his excellent recent response to adults, including Mrs. F, when firmness and consistency were applied. Mr. F indicated in one session that he didn't care if his wife continued to worry about Tommy's problems as long as she was consistent and maintained Tommy's good behaviors at home. Mrs. F responded that she would continue to try her best in applying the methods she had learned. The therapists agreed with Mr. F's appraisal, and the remaining sessions were spent discussing new applications of the procedures emphasized in the parent training.

Follow-Up. The first follow-up home visits were made in week *thirty-seven* of the program, two-and-a-half months after the last home visits. However, since the maintenance training occurred during the first part of this period, the two-and-a-half-month assessment was not a "true" follow-up. Perhaps the only significant change reflected in the data from these home visits was a decrease in Mrs. F's positive attention for Tommy's compliance. Also, the observers reported in the first of the three visits that Mrs. F "became tense when Tommy approached her," although "there was little actual negative interaction."

One year after terminating treatment with the TF family the therapists contacted the parents and made arrangements for the new follow-up procedures.

Figures 11-13 (pp. 132-133) show the results of the three home visits conducted in the *seventy-fifth* week. Tommy continued to comply with his mother's directives at a fairly high level (61%), and she praised him for roughly every other instance of his compliance. The analysis of compliance by type of command showed that while Mrs. F previously had used terminating commands predominantly with very little compliance, at follow-up less than a fifth of her commands were of the terminating type, and most were obeyed.

Figure 12 shows Mrs. F's reduced rate of praising Tommy's obeys, possibly reflecting her ability to utilize praise more effectively and thus more efficiently. This interpretation of Mrs. F's increased efficiency in developing Tommy's compliance was supported by the results of the last videotape session. Thus, the large increase in Tommy's obey rate from session two to session three in

Figure 10 (p. 132) occurred even though only half as many commands were given in session three; Mrs. F was working less and getting better results. It appeared that this trend of Mrs. F's successful thinning out the frequency of praise for Tommy's obeys was being maintained in the follow-up home visits.

Figure 13 reflects Tommy's stable, appropriate behavior and absence of aversive behavior. There were almost no observed instances of hitting or aggressive play in the follow-up, although the raters' notes indicated that Tommy's general behavior was that of "a loud, active, but generally pleasant child." They also noted that Mrs. F appeared to be at ease with the boys, and that Tommy and Jerry were more relaxed and played well together.

Figure 14 (p. 135) shows, in general, the maintenance of the HCP items. Mrs. F's procedure of picking Tommy up after school had continued when he went to the second grade, and the records showed that the slight decrease in earnings was largely due to his old problem, rough play in the car. However, Mrs. F noted that his disturbances were less intense, and that she occasionally used TO when Tommy's car behavior became excessive. The therapists pointed out that she could consider reinstating the public HCP anytime she felt it would be useful for improving Tommy's car behavior, or any of the old items.

Other sources of information collected during the follow-up were behavior checklists from both parents and the Parent's Assessment of Therapy from Mrs. F. The pre- and postscores of the behavior checklists are presented below.

Behavior Checklist Category	Baseline: % items answered "yes"		Follow-Up: % items answered "yes"	
	Mrs. F	Mr. F	Mrs. F	Mr. F
Aggression	32	26	26	16
Inhibition	21	35	29	29
Hyperactivity	80	80	70	60
Somatic Disturbance	22	33	11	22
Sleep Disturbance	0	13	13	0
Social Maturity	10	10	30	50

Perhaps the most significant finding in the follow-up besides Tommy's maintenance of improved behavior was his mother's only partial acknowledgment of the changes. Her scores on the follow-up behavior checklist reflected only slight improvements in Tommy, and overall were still descriptive of an active, immature child. Mr. F,

on the other hand, noted several improvements in Tommy's behavior, especially in social maturity. Mrs. F's feelings about Tommy and the effects of the treatment were also reflected in her responses on the Parent's Assessment of Therapy.

Parent's Assessment of Therapy

1. Describe very briefly your child's problem prior to involvement in the UCLA Home Intervention Program.

   Very difficult to control. Defiant. Angry. Overactive. Would not comply to parents' requests.

2. Describe the essential details of the Intervention Program in which you were involved.

   Charting specific behavior problems. Terminating specific behavior problems through use of Time Out, reward program, etc.

3. List the three most important changes which occurred as a direct result of the Intervention Program.

   1. The reward program helped greatly with Tommy.
   2. Child's response to Time Out program.
   3. My ability to terminate difficult behavior through the use of Time Out.

4. Describe very briefly the child's behavior since the most recent intervention.

   Child responds to Time Out program. This has been most useful in terminating behavior problems.

5. Describe very briefly the single most important factor which led to the changes you observed.

   Time Out program and reward program have been equally useful in changing Tommy's behavior problems.

6. Please compare the effects of the Home Intervention Program with other therapeutic techniques attempted for your child's problem.

   No other techniques were tried except medication, which did not seem to have any effect.

7. Are there any additional comments you would like to make about the program? Be critical.

Tommy continues to be a difficult child at times. He has made improvement and I look forward to more improvement.

8. Please compare the relative contributions by the child's mother and father to the program's outcome.

   This program was a great deal of hard work on the part of my husband and myself. However, I feel that the rewards of the program in terms of helping our child and our family were worth every minute of time and effort on our part.

Comment. The follow-up records generally showed that the TF family made significant progress in systematic parent training, and that their gains were maintained through at least the first year of follow-up. Using a rough cost-efficiency estimate, most of the intervention goals were achieved with a moderate amount of professional time and effort. Without the home visits and added time for data reduction, about thirty-five hours were required for the actual treatment time. This total included the six desensitization sessions and the ten maintenance and parent counseling meetings; thus, the actual parent training time was only about twenty hours. However, the total time required for the full applied research project in the TF case was over sixty-nine hours which, while not excessive in terms of research, does show the prohibitive aspect of using home observers in usual clinic practice, especially in difficult cases.

The added professional time and effort which were required to help Mrs. F improve Tommy's behavior became the major issue in the TF case. As Mrs. F noted in her follow-up responses, both parents worked hard and still Tommy was at times a "difficult child." An additional factor which extended the treatment was Mrs. F's own excessive anxiety.

The therapists assumed that Mrs. F was *motivated* to change; i.e., she would be reinforced by Tommy's improvements. This assumption was found to be largely true based on her responsiveness to the majority of the therapists' suggestions, but in itself was insufficient to achieve significant attitude change. It appeared that her negative attitudes about Tommy resulted from her long-term, intense fears of Tommy hurting himself, Jerry, and even herself in some uncontrollable fashion. This fear presumably prevented her from confronting Tommy, and delayed her ability to apply the basic program requirements, such as the delivery of terminating commands and the utilization of TO.

Mrs. F began to show significant progress in her management of Tommy's aggressive behavior only after receiving individual treatment for her anxiety and after experiencing the gradual success of the TO procedure. She later said that the significant factors in her improvement were her reduced fears about Tommy and the security of her husband's support in the application of punishment. The treatments provided were all seen by the therapists as necessary to help Tommy *by first helping his mother.* Both the behavioral and emotional changes which Mrs. F experienced in the total treatment program were important in the production and maintenance of Tommy's progress.

A final observation about the TF case concerns the therapists' rationale for the intervention sequence. An alternative to the selected flo-chart sequence would have been to begin treatment with a deceleration procedure. This approach might have not only slowed down Tommy's excessive aversive behavior, but also might have given Mrs. F positive feedback much sooner about her ability to significantly influence Tommy. However, the flo-chart sequence used was based on the observed need to carefully prepare Mrs. F for any intervention involving a confrontation with Tommy. As will be seen in Case No. 4, the intervention program can begin with an initial deceleration procedure, but in all such cases the need remains for *acceleration* programs to develop the child's positive, adaptive behavior.

CASE NO. 4:
WHEN PARENT TRAINING IS NOT ENOUGH*

Background. Kathy C was referred to UCLA by the community service for retarded children shortly after her sixth birthday. At the intake interview both Mr. and Mrs. C reported that Kathy had previously been diagnosed as moderately retarded, but that her major problem concerned her "uncontrollable" hitting, pinching, biting and kicking her mother and her two-and-a-half-year-old adopted brother. At the community service center, the staff had unsuccessfully attempted to develop a home-based behavior modification plan to stop Kathy's extreme aggressive behavior. After several months of home interventions with no improvement, the family was advised to seek inpatient care for her at UCLA.

---

* This case was treated by N. Brown, J. Abbott, and the staff of Ward 4-West, Neuropsychiatric Institute, UCLA.

An additional reason for the referral concerned the parents' longstanding questions about Kathy's developmental potential, especially in the area of educational abilities. The parents reported that Kathy had always had problems, and never seemed to develop appropriate social skills. According to Mrs. C, Kathy's very poor communication skills, together with her tantrums and seemingly vicious aggressive behavior, often frightened her and made her wonder if Kathy should continue to live at home. However, she was especially distressed by her own inability to control Kathy and by Mr. C's verbalized conviction that Kathy's problems were largely due to his wife's "inadequacy" as a mother. Mrs. C noted that her husband, a full-time student who worked at night, left her with the "total burden" of raising Kathy. Mr. C reported that he had very few problems controlling Kathy's behavior, and he felt strongly that Kathy should return to the home following an inpatient evaluation.

Screening. The screening procedure consisted of a series of interviews and questionnaires for the parents by the hospital ward staff and consultation with a pediatrician and psychologist. The MMPI profiles of Mr. and Mrs. C were both generally within the normal range. However, Mrs. C showed considerable shyness and minor difficulty asserting herself, while Mr. C's response indicated that he was a very competent, success-oriented person.

Kathy's examinations were very difficult to administer and thus were incomplete because she physically attacked both doctors and refused to cooperate. However, enough information was obtained to confirm tentatively a diagnosis of mild retardation, and to support Mrs. C's observation that Kathy showed a very high rate of aggressive behavior. The staff recommended admitting Kathy without delay based on her obvious need for a completely structured and controlled environment. Hospitalization would also allow the staff additional opportunities to clarify Kathy's developmental potential. At the next meeting with the parents the therapist presented a two-part treatment plan.

First, a period of hospitalization for Kathy was suggested on a ward for children with similar problems. Kathy would be in the hospital four days a week and would be at home with her parents for three days each weekend. While on the ward the staff would develop procedures that would attempt to reduce Kathy's intolerable behavior and to develop her self-management and social skills. It was pointed out to the parents that similar treatment programs for other children lasted three to six months.

Second, the therapist emphasized that the hospital treatment could only be helpful for Kathy's long-term adjustment if her parents were involved and learned to maintain Kathy's improved behavior at home. Accordingly, it was proposed that Mr. and Mrs. C meet regularly with the therapist and with the nursing staff. The sessions would focus on teaching the parents the same procedures found to be effective on the ward by the staff working directly with Kathy.

In summary, the treatment program would consist of concomitant hospital and home interventions for Kathy and her parents.

Mr. and Mrs. C responded differently to the presentation of the treatment plan. Mrs. C was extremely relieved that her daughter would be treated in the hospital and that she would be given some training about how to manage Kathy at home. She said again that, without some help with Kathy, she could not keep her at home. Mr. C, on the other hand, while not against the treatment plan, again said that his wife's mismanagement of Kathy was the real problem, and that he did not think it would be necessary for him to participate in a parent training program, and that his schedule would make it difficult for him to take part in the weekend home management plan. The therapist and staff decided to begin the treatment with Kathy and her mother, and attempt to elicit Mr. C's participation later.

Baseline. The baseline assessment was made in both the home and in the hospital since the problems and the treatments occurred in both settings. The urgent aspect of Kathy's aggressive behavior precluded the usual multidimensional assessment of behavior and the family interaction. Thus, since a deceleration plan was to be applied first, an abbreviated preintervention estimate was made of Kathy's ward and home rates of aversive behavior, and then the treatment of this problem followed. After the acute disturbances were diminished, baselines on Kathy's other problems were made prior to further interventions.

As was the usual procedure for new admissions, the ward staff first observed Kathy informally and kept records on the relevant target behaviors. Accordingly, the staff made hourly tallies of Kathy's biting, pinching, hitting, and kicking, whether directed toward the staff or her peers. Meanwhile, Mrs. C kept weekly three-day records at home on the same behaviors. At the end of the two-week period the records showed that Kathy averaged over eleven aggressive behaviors per day on the ward, and nearly four per day at home.

INTERVENTIONS FOR CASE NO. 4

THE DECELERATION PROGRAM

The treatment program for Kathy's aggressive behavior consisted of setting up a modified Time Out *corner restriction* procedure for Kathy contingent upon each occurrence of aggressive behavior. The ward staff had previously used the corner restriction with considerable success for problems usually treated with Time Out. Kathy's deceleration program followed the same sequence as all punishment procedures used in systematic parent training:

1. The delivery of a sharply worded terminating command immediately after Kathy was observed to begin an aggressive behavior.

2. The presentation of a warning signal, which was an exact statement of the intolerable behavior and the consequence if it continued.

3. Placement of Kathy on a chair in an isolated corner if she persisted.

The punishment duration was three minutes, a period found by the staff to be effective. The staff avoided giving Kathy any attention during the punishment period. When the time was up, Kathy was encouraged to engage in some appropriate play and the staff then praised all approximations of her desirable behavior that followed.

The punishment procedure began in the third week of Kathy's hospitalization. In the same week Mrs. C came in for two sessions with the therapist to begin the parent training. During the first session the therapist introduced the important social learning concepts and presented Mrs. C with a copy of *Living With Children,* and the details of Kathy's ward deceleration plan were then discussed. Special attention was given to the exact procedure Mrs. C would use when the corner restriction punishment began at home. Prior to the *second session* Mrs. C met with the ward staff to observe several instances of the nurses' application of the punishment. After each visit to the ward, the therapist met with Mrs. C and again rehearsed the procedure, in preparation for beginning the corner restriction at home the following week.

There was an almost immediate decrease in Kathy's aggressive behaviors following the institution of the home and hospital interventions for aggressive behavior. On the ward the total daily average of the behaviors decreased from the baseline level of 11 per day to 4 per day after the first week, 1.6 after the first month, 1.8 after the second month, and 1.4 after four months, just prior to Kathy's discharge from the ward. In the home, there were equally good results and the total daily average of Kathy's aggressive behavior decreased from 3.5 during the baseline to 1.5 by the second week, 1.0 a month later, and by discharge there were no occurrences of biting, kicking and pinching, and less than one occasion of hitting per day.

THREE ACCELERATION PROGRAMS

The results of the first intervention program were very encouraging for the ward staff and Mrs. C, and made possible the planning and implementation of interventions designed to increase Kathy's appropriate social behavior. Thus, after about one month on the ward, Kathy no longer exhibited dangerous or aggressive behavior, but continued to show a number of behavioral deficits that warranted intervention. For example, her rate of compliance, as judged by the parents and the ward staff, was very low. Also, Kathy was observed at home and on the ward to have an extremely poor attention span and virtually no sustained appropriate or constructive play. An additional longstanding problem for Mrs. C, and also for the staff, concerned Kathy's very poor verbalization. She almost never used more than one word to express herself and her verbalizations were usually inaudible; her major means of communication was pointing and gesturing.

1. *Sustained Appropriate Play.* At the beginning of the second month of Kathy's hospitalization the therapist met with Mrs. C and the ward staff and first developed a program to improve Kathy's compliance to directives and her sustained appropriate play. During a one-week baseline assessment the maximum time Kathy spent on any task or play activity on the ward or at home was found to be less than thirty seconds. The training program for Mrs. C consisted of six weeks of clinic visits, in which a structured interaction activity lasting about one-half hour was videotaped each week. During the second part of each session the tape was used to provide videotape feedback training for Mrs. C.

Since one of Mrs. C's primary complaints was her inability to talk on the phone or engage in conversation at home with another adult without being interrupted by Kathy's demands for attention, the structured activity was arranged to maximize Kathy's independent play. Each training session consisted of the following steps:

a. Mrs. C and one of the ward staff members went into the videotape studio room with Kathy and started a discussion of some interesting topic.

b. At the beginning of the discussion Mrs. C instructed Kathy to play with the toys by her side. For each ten seconds of appropriate play Mrs. C gave Kathy a small edible treat and praised her.

c. If there were minor disruptions, Mrs. C ignored them.

d. If there were serious disruptions or if Kathy engaged in any of her previous behaviors such as hitting, grabbing, or pinching her mother, the corner restriction procedure was utilized in the studio room.

e. After about a half hour of interaction, the staff member and Kathy returned to the ward and the therapist met with Mrs. C to review the videotape. During the feedback sessions Mrs. C pinpointed important aspects of Kathy's behavior and of her own interaction with Kathy and then was asked to evaluate her own delivery of positive, neutral, and negative consequences for Kathy's behavior. The therapist frequently praised Mrs. C for her increasingly appropriate responses for Kathy's behavior, and emphasized all the available opportunities for Mrs. C to increase her recognition of Kathy's improved attention span and independent play.

During the second and third sessions a bug-in-the-ear device was utilized to facilitate Mrs. C's progress in delivering reinforcement for approximations of appropriate play, and to give Mrs. C immediate feedback for her positive responses to Kathy. After the second week of training, in the *tenth week* of the treatment program, the therapist suggested that Mrs. C begin to reduce her use of the candy treats and to rely more on *social praise* for sustained appropriate play. Also, beginning in the second week, Mrs. C was encouraged to practice maintaining these desirable behaviors with Kathy at home. Specifically, it was suggested that she arrange a specific time, several times a weekend, when she could have a friend or

neighbor come and sit with her while she practiced the same procedures that were used in the clinic. Usually, then, there were three practice sessions for Mrs. C during each week: once a week with the therapist and nurse in the hospital using the videotape feedback training, and twice a week on her own at home with a neighbor.

After about three weeks of training, the therapist's records began to show gradual increases in the duration of Kathy's sustained play, and after six weeks of training, Kathy's play usually continued for more than twenty minutes at a time with a single toy or play activity. Even greater increases in independent play were observed by the mother on the weekends, and for the first time Mrs. C noted long periods of Kathy's appropriate play outdoors in the yard as well as in her room with her toys.

2. *Compliance.* An additional area of primary concern by the ward staff and Mrs. C was Kathy's very low rate of compliance. In the initial weeks of the hospitalization Kathy ignored nearly all staff commands. After the punishment program, she responded much better to terminating commands, especially those directing her to stop aggressive behavior, but she continued to ignore many *initiating* commands, such as "brush your teeth" and "come to breakfast." Consequently, the staff had to repeat their requests many times to get Kathy to engage in the minimal daily self-help behaviors.

A two-week baseline, which was made in the last two weeks of the acceleration program for appropriate play, supported the staff's observations. During two daily observation periods Kathy complied with less than 47 percent of all directives given.

In the ward program, to increase compliance, each staff member was asked to carefully observe his or her interaction with Kathy each day and to reinforce each instance of compliance. The reinforcement initially consisted of positive attention in the form of a smile, a hug, and verbal praise, together with a small edible treat. In the event of noncompliance the staff first repeated the command and then, if necessary, physically intervened if the task were a necessary one. Otherwise the staff would simply turn away from Kathy and readminister the command a short time later. Then, following the procedure applied for shaping Kathy's appropriate play, the staff reduced their use of edible rewards in the second week and by the third week were using only social praise for compliance. After four weeks of the program, Kathy's compliance had increased from 47% to 80%, and one month later was maintained at 73%.

The staff's procedures for improving Kathy's compliance were also added to Mrs. C's homework and although no systematic observations were made, she reported that Kathy was responding to most of her directives.

3. *Audible Speech.* During the third month of Kathy's hospitalization the staff began to work systematically on her very low rate of audible verbalizations. This program, which began shortly after the compliance treatment was started, used the same shaping procedure that had previously been successfully applied. The ward staff was instructed that on each occasion of a poorly verbalized response by Kathy they should immediately call her attention to it by giving her a highly specific initiating command to speak more clearly, and then if she complied, to reward her with attention. The staff was to ignore Kathy if she repeated her poorly verbalized response, or if within ten seconds there was no response to the initiating command. While no daily numerical records were kept, examination of the nurses' notes indicated that each week Kathy's speech quality improved and that at the time of discharge she was speaking in a clearly audible manner and using three-word phrases for the first time.

PARENT COUNSELING

After about three months of the treatment program, Kathy's nonaggressive, appropriate play and general compliance were greatly improved, both on the ward and at home. However, although Mrs. C was making considerable progress with Kathy, she continued to be extremely anxious about her role as a mother and was also concerned about her husband's lack of support. Mr. C indeed had participated only minimally in the treatment program. In the second month of hospitalization the therapist had urged both parents to come in for weekly meetings to prepare for Kathy's return home, but the joint parent counseling was short-lived. Mr. C came for the first three sessions, stated that he was happy that his wife was improving, but that he didn't have time to attend any more meetings.

His lack of participation intensified Mrs. C's distress, and she again expressed doubts about her ability to manage Kathy alone. During the next few weeks the therapist spent several sessions attempting, with some success, to show Mrs. C all the progress she had made and how she was very capable of managing Kathy. However, the therapist reemphasized that at some point the therapy should focus on Mr. C's lack of support for Mrs. C's efforts.

In the third month of treatment a parents' group was organized for the parents of children on Kathy's ward. All parents were required to attend; the goal was to facilitate the generalization of each child's improved behavior at home. Unexpectedly, Mr. C became very involved in the parent group, and not only quickly learned what his role in the posttreatment period should be, but also contributed a great deal to the group. He later revealed that he found it easier to become active in his daughter's treatment when he could relate with other parents whose children had problems like Kathy's.

Eight weeks later, after the parent group ended, Mr. C agreed to attend the parent counseling sessions again. The most notable outcome of these meetings was Mrs. C's verbalization of her changed self-perception and attitude about Kathy. For example, she pointed out that her perceived failure as a mother had been the source of many of her arguments and problems with her husband, and that, as she was becoming more confident, Mr. C had begun to support her weekend projects with Kathy. For the first time Mrs. C said that she was able to observe Kathy's positive response to her management procedures, and as a result she had decided to try to keep Kathy at home.

Maintenance Training. The application of maintenance training in the KC case was atypical, like many of the other procedures used. In one sense the entire application of systematic parent training was to maintain the progress made in the hospital. It was also true that Mr. and Mrs. C were both competent and confident in carrying out the procedures begun on the ward only after they had several meetings with the therapist. Prior to Kathy's discharge from the hospital, the parent counseling sessions focused on the problems they might encounter once Kathy was home again, and on the procedures which the ward had found to be effective. Also, there were other ward deceleration programs (for spitting and throwing food) and acceleration programs (for increasing peer interaction and sharing) to which Mrs. C had not yet been exposed. To facilitate Mrs. C's development of more general problem solving skills, she spent several hours on the ward in the weeks prior to Kathy's discharge in order to observe and participate in the new socialization and self-control programs.

Special emphasis was placed on ways to deal with Kathy's *limit-testing* behavior. In every deceleration program attempted Kathy made a good initial response and then, according to the ward staff, found very inventive ways to misbehave to a point just short of the criterion for punishment. These diversionary tactics had the effect of maintaining Kathy's high level of low-intensity aversive behavior on the ward. However, by the therapist's efforts in helping the staff respond consistently as a unit in applying the rehearsed contingencies, this general behavior problem was reduced. In her ward visits, the staff demonstrated for Mrs. C the importance of consistent and contingent management skills in the reduction of limit testing. Also, in the maintenance training sessions, the ward staff's experiences concerning the importance of consistency were emphasized for Mr. C. Finally, after Kathy's discharge, her parents continued to meet with the therapist for four sessions to discuss the family adjustment with Kathy in the home again.

Follow-up. After Kathy's discharge from the hospital, there were follow-up contacts, usually by phone, with Mrs. C every two weeks for three months by the hospital staff. The follow-up contacts were largely informal, but they did indicate that no serious new or old problems existed, and that the family was capable of solving many problems as they arose.

One year after Kathy's discharge Mr. and Mrs. C were contacted and asked to participate in the follow-up assessment. In general, the parents reported excellent progress in Kathy's behavior and development. Mrs. C indicated that she had continued to use her new management procedures after the hospitalization, and that Kathy had no major disruptions in her behavior.

In the two week follow-up period, Mrs. C was asked to keep records on the original target behaviors, including aggressive behaviors, appropriate play, and audible speech. Also, she was asked to write a daily summary of Kathy's general behavior and complete the Parent's Assessment of Therapy. After the two-week period, Mrs. C's records provided estimates of Kathy's behaviors one year after the hospital and home treatment.

First, the daily tallies of Kathy's aggressive behavior showed that on four occasions Kathy hit her mother. On two occasions,

when the behavior was repeated after a warning, Mrs. C applied the three-minute punishment using the corner restriction. No biting, pinching, or spitting was observed and Kathy showed no aggressive or rough play with her brother.

Second, to estimate Kathy's appropriate play, each day Mrs. C observed Kathy during an afternoon period in which she usually played inside or in the backyard. Mrs. C structured her observation by timing Kathy's self-initiated play or instructed play with her brother. On her own initiative Mrs. C also asked a friend to come over each afternoon since Kathy's pretreatment aversive behavior was at a maximum whenever Mrs. C attempted to converse with someone else while Kathy was in the room. Thus, Mrs. C observed Kathy's play with and without her friend present, alone and with her brother, and by instruction and by self-initiation.

The two-week records showed that Kathy's total "appropriate play" time ranged from one to four hours each day, as opposed to the pretreatment estimate of less than thirty seconds of sustained play. Most importantly, for the one-hour period each day when Kathy was observed while Mrs. C talked with a friend, there was no period in which Kathy played less than thirty minutes continuously, either alone or with her brother. On one occasion Mrs. C's friend brought over a one-year-old child and Kathy behaved to her mother's satisfaction while playing next to the baby and her own brother. Mrs. C estimated that approximately half of Kathy's play was self-initiated, and pointed out that she no longer had to closely supervise Kathy's activities.

Third, Mrs. C reported that Kathy's speech quality had continued to improve. Four months after the discharge from the hospital Kathy had started school and, although she was only speaking in two-word phrases, her speech was clearly understandable. By the end of the school year she was communicating in four-word sentences and, as indicated in Mrs. C's notes, could answer questions directly and completely. The treatment had involved only Kathy's speech fluency and audibility, but it appeared that the hospital and home training had facilitated her ability to develop more complex communication abilities. Mrs. C's responses on the Parent's Assessment of Therapy are presented below.

Parent's Assessment of Therapy

1.   Describe very briefly your child's problem prior to involvement in the UCLA Intervention Program.

Mostly a behavior problem. Kathy wouldn't mind—was very frustrated—would take everything out mostly on her mother by kicking, hitting, pinching, biting and spitting. We couldn't control her while we were away from home. She did very little talking, and mostly motioned or used signs to tell us what she wanted. She wouldn't play by herself at all. Required complete attention of her mother—if she didn't get it, she would hit, etc.

2. Describe the essential details of the Intervention Program in which you were involved.

    She was put on Time Out when she kicked, hit, bit or pinched. Videotape sessions with Kathy's nurse and mother to develop her playtime by herself while mother was busy. When she used her hands to talk, we ignored.

3. List the three most important changes which occurred as a direct result of the Intervention Program.

    1. Kathy very seldom uses aggressive actions towards people to show her displeasure or frustrations.

    2. She plays by herself for long periods of time without coming to mother and also plays well with others.

    3. She can talk and communicate with others now.

    4. She has a good relationship with her mother now!!!

4. Describe very briefly the child's behavior since the most recent intervention.

    She accepts the intervention and goes back to being "Mommy's Good Girl."

5. Describe very briefly the single most important factor which led to the changes you observed.

    Helping us, as parents, to be more consistent in our discipline.

6. Please compare the effects of this Intervention Program with other therapeutic techniques attempted for your child's problems.

    The difference between the other programs and the treatment we received is the thoroughness of the program. The child having four days in an isolated situation and the training of the parents by good professionals that are well trained.

7. Are there any additional comments you would like to make about the program? Be critical.

    We feel the follow-up and help we have received since we left the program is excellent. They have come to visit Kathy's school to be sure the right program for Kathy was continued.

8. Please compare the relative contributions by the child's mother and father to the program's outcome.

    Both of us cooperated and were willing to do as you instructed. I feel without the parents' participation in the program the children would come home and revert back to their same problems.

9. Please describe briefly your overall opinion of the Intervention Program you were involved in at UCLA. Were you in general satisfied with the treatment your family received? Is this the kind of family Intervention Program that you would recommend to other families with similar needs to your own?

    We were so pleased to be a part of this program because we can now live with Kathy and be happy and feel good about our relationship with her. We are looking forward to the future instead of dreading it. We were very satisfied with the treatment we received from everyone concerned. We not only recommend this program to any parents with similar problems in their family, but all our friends who have seen what it has done for our family are recommending it to their friends.

Comment. In the KC family the general success of the treatment reflected the combined effects of many complex interventions, applied by a number of professional therapists. The primary variables appeared to be (1) the effective deceleration and skill-building hospital programs; (2) the mother's rapid development of home maintenance interventions; and (3) the mother's major attitude change, from extreme pessimism prior to treatment to a realistic and optimistic expectance of Kathy's behavior during the follow-up period.

This case is important because it illustrates the flexible use of the available intervention procedures and facilities in a way that was maximally helpful for the family. By the flo-chart model, the sequence followed was (1) baseline and direct child intervention (deceleration procedures); (2) a variety of basic discrimination training procedures including maintenance training; and (3) parent counseling. The emphasis in the KC family, as in all families in systematic parent training, was on the selection of intervention procedures as needed to accomplish a specific subgoal of treatment with minimal professional time and effort. Thus the "cost" of treatment in the KC case was relatively great due to hospitalization (four months of inpatient care, and over twenty hours of direct parent training), but was nonetheless minimized by the planned integration of effective interventions.

The interpretation of "successful" treatment in the KC family is cautiously made. There was a relative paucity of independent data supporting Mrs. C's uniformly positive reports of Kathy's follow-up home adjustment. Since there were no prehospital or public HCP records, the therapist had to rely on the mother's records and informal verbal and written reports. However, there was sufficient information to at least *estimate* Kathy's treatment response and one-year maintenance of progress which supported the joint application of intensive, individual treatment and systematic parent training for problems such as initially observed in Kathy's behavior.

SUMMARY

It was emphasized earlier in the chapter that the four cases included here illustrate the flexible and individualized use of the flo-chart model of systematic parent training. However, these cases also illustrate the important features which characterize all carefully applied intervention programs.

First, although each treatment program was in some ways unique, each of the family intervention sequences could be understood and conceptualized within the systematic framework of the flo-chart model. It is probably not necessary to be able to plan in advance the required interventions although, as is discussed in Issue No. 4, Chapter 15, in some cases this is possible. The only require-

ments for an intervention system which can allow a minimization of professional time and effort without diminishing the effectiveness of treatment are that the procedures be sufficiently *broad* to deal with the majority of problems and sufficiently *specific* to allow detailed behavioral assessment for accountability purposes. In this chapter each family's course of treatment differed in the particular intervention sequence used; and the therapist's choice of interventions was determined by the relative intensity of treatments required by the family at each assessment point.

Second, in each case the overriding emphasis was on *acceleration* procedures using positive reinforcement which could build positive parent-child interaction and optimize the child's socialization and self-management abilities. The punishment and negative reinforcement procedures used were at times temporarily necessary, *but were only the means to a common goal:* namely, the encouragement of family models of effective development and problem solving that were based on *nonpunitive and positive interaction.*

Third, one of the major effective "ingredients" in each family's success was the parents' response to the therapist's *homework* assignments. The clinic time spent with each family was limited in each case, except possibly in Case No. 4 where inpatient treatment was required. The primary value of the family's contact time with the therapist was *to allow the parents' acquisition of new or improved behaviors that could be applied to their daily life at home,* and thus to restructure their children's most meaningful environment. Parents in child treatment centers differ in the intensity and complexity of homework they require and in their responsiveness to their daily application of the therapist's suggestions. However, the treatment outcome probably depends to a large extent on the therapist's skill in getting positive interactions *started in the clinic and practiced at home* until they are integrated into the family's unique life style.

FIFTEEN / ISSUES IN SYSTEMATIC PARENT TRAINING

This chapter on issues in systematic parent training is included to point out some of the broader problems, considerations and principles that underlie this approach to child and family treatment. The correct use of the procedures in this manual requires a potentially significant restructuring of the way interventions are provided and assessed in child mental health treatment facilities. It is thus important to elaborate some of the concerns which the authors and other practitioners of this treatment modality have experienced.

OVERVIEW OF THE BASIC ISSUES

First, the difficult problem of defining "deviance" with respect to the complexities of unsatisfactory family interaction is considered within dimensions that have conceptual and practical relevance for the intervention agent. Second, the "philosophy" of systematic parent training, if there is one, is presented in terms of the desirable clinical or humanistic *end goals* of systematic parent training, but within a framework that allows procedural accessibility to the conceptual goals. Third, a scheme for assessing outcome criteria is described, and the *sine qua non* of maintenance of intervention progress is emphasized. Fourth, important individual differences in parents are discussed to show that both success and failure in systematic parent training is the joint responsibility of the parents *and* the therapist. Finally, a discussion of important future issues in systematic parent training is presented, including the need for research directed toward enhancing treatment efficiency through prediction, prevention, and broader application.

ISSUE NO.1: THE ASSESSMENT OF DEVIANT PARENT-CHILD BEHAVIOR

There are many prevailing definitions of "deviant behavior." In systematic parent training it is important to conceptualize deviant behavior and deviant interaction in a way that immediately allows the therapist to know what to do about it, and also to feel that the designated behavior represents a meaningful dimension of the family process. Some of the operational-conceptual considerations of deviance which can be useful to the parent training therapist are discussed in this Issue.

The Interactional Context of Deviance. The deviant behavior of one member of the family should be assessed in terms of the environmental context in which it occurs, as well as in terms of its unique characteristics. Thus the child's deviant behavior should first be viewed as *one aspect of a more general family problem.* The usual clinic referral involves a family who brings their "disturbed" or "disturbing" child for help. Often parents (and professionals) go to great lengths to show that the child *is* deviant, or *has* some problem. However, this phenomenon of labeling should not detract from the central issue: *no one family member can have disturbing behavior that is independent of the problems of the other family members.* Thus a primary treatment target, or the *locus* of deviance, is the *interactional context* of the disturbing behavior which means that, in the case of children, their parents and often their siblings must be included in the treatment program. The interactional focus of deviance in families does not always mean that each member contributes equally to the disturbing interactions. In systematic parent training it is assumed that the *parents* have primary responsibility for determining whether or not their children optimize their potential to function effectively at any particular time. Thus parental characteristics receive considerable emphasis throughout this manual.

An additional implication of the emphasis on the interactional locus of deviance is that *the relevant aspects of deviant behavior* occur in the present, and can be observed, documented, and treated *without extensive reference or knowledge of the past.* In systematic parent training historical factors are not ignored since they provide important information about the development of individual learning styles and repertoires of family members. However, disturbing behavior is important because of its *present aversive consequences* in the family. The functional analysis of the observable cues and consequences of the behaviors which produce negative interaction is usually sufficient to develop effective and efficient interventions, even though the problems may stem from the disturbances that arose much earlier in the family member's development.

The Relativity of Deviance. The therapist's individual assessment of a child's disrupting behavior is based upon temporal-developmental, intensity-frequency, and functional-social considerations. Each of these factors determines the *relative significance* of the child's reported and observed problems. First, temporal-developmental factors relate the child's behavior to his chronological and, more importantly, to his mental age. Also, temporal factors concern the therapist's judgment about the extent to which the disrupting behaviors will have negative consequences in the future *if untreated.* Thus the definition of deviant behavior includes *predictive* and *preventive* functions since the recommendation for parent training may be partly based on the presence of problems that the therapist assumes will become more significant as the child grows older.

Second, intensity and frequency factors, like temporal-developmental factors, are also relative to nonspecific norms since the extent of deviance is estimated *by the degree to which the environment is disturbed by the behavior.* Most problem behaviors affect the environment because of their cumulative consequences and are very *frequent,* but they are not judged intense when observed in isolation. Common examples in this book are noncompliance and negative verbal interaction. Other behaviors acquire significance because of their *intensity,* and have serious consequences for many people in only a few occurrences or even in single occurrences. Examples cited are aggressive and destructive behaviors. By first documenting the subtle, high-frequency antecedents of high intensity behavior, the procedures in this manual are applicable to many intense behavioral disruptions as well as the more common high-rate problems of childhood.

Third, functional-social factors provide a rationale for determining the child's relative deviance that avoids the *labeling* of

his disturbance with traditional diagnostic categories. In one sense, the purpose of the screening procedures described in this manual is an attempt to differentiate the child's physical or mental *handicaps* and poor socialization skills. For example, the child may "have" a physical handicap, learning disorder, mental retardation, chronic hyperactivity and poor attention span, or seriously uneven development of adaptive skills. Any of these problems may provide an upper limit on the child's long-range development, just as all people have limitations. However, it is often useful to distinguish between the child's "handicap" and his *social problems,* which may be increased by his long-standing difficulties but which can be improved by effective intervention programs. Also, by specifying the child's adjustment problem, regardless of his clinical diagnosis, the therapist's and parents' intervention tasks can be better (and more optimistically) planned. It is assumed that the child's socialization skills, or lack of them, represent *a learned style of adapting to the environment within the limits of whatever handicap he possesses.* Thus whether the child's "adaptive style" is *deviant* or *effective* is directly determined by the environmental influences which shape his behavior rather than by internal factors or any particular diagnostic disorder. According to this formulation "deviance" becomes the child's relative failure to optimize his potential to function effectively according to prevailing family and social standards. More importantly, the task of systematic parent training is to *optimize the child's social functioning regardless of his hypothesized or documented handicap.*

Thus it is argued here that many children have some genetic, constitutional or developmental anomaly that limits their potential to be productive and self-sufficient members of society. The therapist's role becomes one of helping the parents to understand that their child's disrupting behavior does not necessarily represent such a limitation, but rather is part of a responsive, changeable repertoire that can be improved with effective child management and development practices.

The Parents' Labeling of Deviance. The parents' act of labeling their child's behavior as deviant is determined by their *current perceptual* and *attitudinal* standards and expectancies. This rather obvious point is made to emphasize the amount of preparation the therapist must make both before treatment and in the communication of suggestions to the parents. Prior to the interventions the thorough assessment of child-family deviance must include some understanding of these factors, both for their own sake, and to insure that the interventions provided are relevant to the family's stated and professionally determined needs.

There are many historical antecedents for parents' current perceptions and attitudes, including individual cultural and personality differences. It is a truism in mental health treatment that when the attitudes of the people treated (in this case, the parents' attitudes about their children) are congruent or at least not rigidly different from those of the therapist, the treatment is more effective. The challenge in systematic parent training occurs when the therapist encounters parents whose background or personality is such that they are able to meet strong personal needs by maintaining counterproductive, negative ideas and feelings about their children. As was seen in many of the cases presented in this manual, the parents' negative attitudes and expectancies often constitute a treatment focus as well as, *or instead of,* the child's labeled "deviance." The importance of the parents' attitudes as an intervention variable was discussed in Chapter 12 and 13 (Parent Counseling), and is further explored in Issue No. 4 in this chapter.

Also, as commonly thought, and recently supported experimentally by Bates (1973), the parents' attitudes can be influenced *by the child's behavior.* Thus it is likely in some cases that an otherwise "normal" or "adequate" parent may become a "deviant" parent by overresponding to a constitutionally difficult child, who influences the parents' expectancies and behavior to further exacerbate his problems, and so on. The child's labeled "disrupted behavior" is in these cases *directly* determined by the parents' negative contingencies and expectancies, and *indirectly* by the child's own predisposition for high-rate behavior that many parents might find aversive. Also, these cases illustrate how the child's constitutional "handicap" can interact with his adaptive abilities.

ISSUE NO. 2: THE DETERMINATION OF GOALS IN SYSTEMATIC PARENT TRAINING

Throughout this manual, the emphasis has been on the specification of goals so that each suggestion by the therapist has a clear rationale and standard for assessing its effects. These *short-term* treatment goals all relate to the desired behavior change which allows the family functioning to become more positive and effective; *long-term* goals relate to the maintenance of the attained progress in follow-up.

Both the short- and long-term intervention goals share the characteristic of being *specific* and *observable.* However, there are other *conceptual* and *practical* goals in systematic parent training which, while more difficult to assess, provide important standards by which the therapist makes decisions in the weekly application of the interventions. These general goals were formulated as a result of the author's study of families that were intervention "successes," and by the examination of parent-child interaction in nonclinic families. Thus *the major conceptual and practical criteria for success in systematic parent training are based on the characteristics of well-functioning families.*

Conceptual Goals. There are three characteristics observed in well-functioning families that constitute the general goals of parent training. The parent-child interaction in these families is, for the most part, *consistent, contingent,* and *positive.*

Consistency. As discussed in Chapters 7 and 12, intra- and interparental consistency are very complex phenomena involving parental attitudes, response sets, expectancies and, not least, the marital relationship itself. Consistency implies *general agreement* between parents in the discrimination of appropriate and inappropriate family members' behaviors and their behavioral consequences, as well as the unique family goals. It implies *stability* of the individual parent's response patterns specific to given interaction sequences among family members. Finally, consistency implies a *predictability* of important parental behaviors, which is assumed to be a necessary condition for the development of stable behavior repertoires in children.

Contingency. The second goal, *contingency of appropriate parental attention,* supplements consistency in the generation and maintenance of predictable parent-child interaction. Contingency implies the presence of *a functional relationship* between two events; the behavior of one family member is influenced by regular consequences applied by another person. Contingencies operate with or without a person's awareness and, with the exception of certain extreme personality disturbances, regularly applied behavioral consequences (and their intrapersonal representation, as in "guilt" or "hope") maintain much human behavior.

Since all behavioral interaction systems are assumed to already be organized according to usually unspecified schedules of reinforcement, the goal in systematic parent training is to develop *appropriate, explicit* conditions for behavioral consequences. The arrangement of conditions in which positive and negative reinforcements and punishments are effectively dispensed is thus basic to successful parent training programs. Following successful intervention and follow-up, the prevailing treatment contingencies become less explicit and labeled, although family members continue to behave according to the new rules within the family's "natural" style of living.

Positivity. The third goal of family intervention gives substance and direction to the first two. It is the generation and maintenance of behavioral interaction by *positive* reinforcement. Since many referred families are shown to have their interaction controlled by negative reinforcement, an important intervention goal is the transition *from negative to positive control of family interaction.* One of the immediate practical implications of this goal is the relative emphasis on behavioral management by positive consequences rather than negative reinforcement, extinction or punishment consequences. Thus the majority of intervention programs would focus on the acceleration of desirable target behaviors by positive reinforcement, especially emphasizing the development of those behaviors that are *incompatible* with the disrupting behaviors.

The rationale for this goal of positive contingencies in family intervention programs has both empirical and humanistic determinants. Empirically, as noted above, it can be shown that successfully treated families and "effective" families are characterized by a higher rate of positive consequences for appropriate behavior and less negative interaction than families with behaviorally disturbing children (Wahl et al., 1974; Amundson, Miller and Auerbach, 1974; Lobitz, 1973). Humanistically, it is the author's bias that family intervention programs which utilize negative reinforcement and punishment programs are themselves models of problem solving via negative interaction for children and thus should be used with reservation and caution. Thus if the therapist wants the family to engage in more positive interaction, the treatment presented to the parents should be based primarily upon positive reinforcement, even if interim punishment procedures are necessary.

The problems which attend the use of punishment procedures were described in Chapter 10. These problems are restated here because of the tendency of many family intervention agents and parents to give direct deceleration plans priority in training programs and thus to become "trapped by the short-term pay-offs of negative reinforcement" (Patterson, 1974).

It is assumed, then, that if these "ideal" qualities of consistency, contingency and positivity are already characterizing a given family's interaction, they will not be referred for treatment; and if after intervention these qualities are learned and maintained, they will not require further treatment.

Practical Goals. Together with these conceptual goals which underlie the therapist's long- and short-term treatment planning, there are *practical* decisions that must also be made in the parent training program.

First, there is the issue of *how much* of the family problem should be treated. The therapist's choices, in the extreme, are basically to work on individual problems or to provide interventions for the entire family interaction system. In systematic parent training the general guideline is to provide treatment for the components of the system which have been determined to maintain the inappropriate, negative communications. In this sense systematic parent training represents a departure both from those behaviorally oriented programs which treat individual problems, *and* traditional family therapies which involve global family problems and issues. Individual problems are seen as reflections of disturbed daily interaction that cannot be effectively improved without attending to the interactional context in which they occur. In the HCP, as described in Chapter 8, the charts do not contain five or six items so that more individual problems can be treated at the same time, but so that a significantly disturbing period of the day can be improved *as a whole.* Thus while the period can only be improved by focusing on each component behavior as it occurs, the specific aspects of the intervention should be seen as a mechanical means for improving family interactions and relationships.

Second, and closely related to the above issue, the therapist must decide how much emphasis will be placed upon the parents' complaints as opposed to the therapist's determination of intervention targets. In systematic parent training, as in many other therapies, both the parents' and therapists' views are important, but ultimately the therapist must decide what to treat. For example, while the ongoing treatment sessions and instruments like the "Parent's Assessment of Therapy" (see Chapter 14) are essential to determine that the parents' needs are met during and after the interventions, the therapist should be aware that the "compliance structure" (see Chapter 7) is often basic to the treatment of families with disturbing children, whether or not the parents initially complain about noncompliance.

Also, while the parents have a large input to all phases of the intervention program, the therapist's commitment is to the *whole family,* which means that at times what is best for the child's treatment is not always congruent with the parents' stated needs. Common examples occur with parents who want their child treated, not for the child's health, but because the problems are interfering with their life style; or parents who, in a diversionary tactic of their own, bring the child in for treatment when their marital conflicts constitute the basic problem.

Third, the therapist in almost every case is presented with the task of resolving an ongoing family "crisis" in the sense that an immediate problem is interfering with the family functioning to some degree. As such, the decision must be made whether to resolve the problems directly and terminate treatment, or to try in some way to restructure the family interaction so that the family develops *collateral, generalization skills* which reduce the probability of future problems. The specific issue is whether or not systematic parent training, or any therapy, provides the parents with a *child rearing technology and philosophy* as well as a resolution of their presenting complaints. Systematic parent training contains both elements: it is primarily an *intervention strategy* that, when well applied, provides the parents with *preventive skills.* Therefore, the least result of successful treatment is relief from current family and parent-child stress, and if the parents develop consistency, contingency, and positivity as guidelines for daily living, they will possess the tools of maintenance as well.

ISSUE NO. 3: THE DETERMINATION OF INTERVENTION OUTCOME AND THE MAINTENANCE PROBLEM

It was noted in the previous issue that when parent training is successful, the parents not only reduce the presenting problems but also develop general parenting skills which function to *maintain* their progress and thus *prevent* many serious problems that might otherwise arise in the future. Each intervention in systematic parent training includes *maintenance training* for these generalization and prevention purposes. Then, at the end of the overall intervention program, maintenance issues are discussed with the parents, emphasizing that (a) the concepts and procedures in social learning concepts and basic discrimination training can help the parents deal with most problems which arise in the future; (b) the HCP and interim punishment procedures can be applied for specific accelera-

tion or deceleration changes when required; and (c) the therapist remains available for parent counseling if needed.

However, despite the therapist's (and, occasionally, the parents') best efforts, many families fail to maintain their attained intervention progress. Issue No. 4 is concerned with individual differences in families and intervention agents that may contribute to the inadequate response of some families, both in treatment and in follow-up. In the present Issue the concern is with the therapist's conceptual and procedural analysis and categorization of the family's long-term response to treatment.

There are two major criteria that can facilitate the therapist's categorization of a family's response "type" in the follow-up assessment. First, the therapist should assess the relative number of *specific intervention goals attained,* including preintervention and later additional goals. For example, "75% maintenance of six HCP items for six months," or "little or no hitting for six months," or even "an acceptable level of compliance observed by both parents for six months" might constitute achievement of intervention goals.

The second criterion concerns the relative degree of professional time and effort required to achieve the therapist's and family's intervention goals. Thus while some more difficult or older children require complex, lengthy programs, the major factor of concern here is the amount of professional time and effort required to achieve autonomous *parental* maintenance of desirable behavior.

Using these conceptual and empirical guidelines, it is possible to delineate four major treatment and outcome response types in systematic parent training. Figure 15 (p. 152) schematically shows the overall or most significant intervention responses of each of the four types.

The curved lines represent the idealized desirable behavior acquisition curve as assessed by the cumulative records of intervention progress, usually made at the time formal interventions are completed. The straight lines show what happens to the achieved progress after a period without intervention during the follow-up assessment.

Type 1. The striking features of this small segment of the clinic population (estimated at 15% in families treated with systematic parent training at the Neuropsychiatric Institute, UCLA) are the rapid response to the therapist's suggestions, the significant demonstration of parental initiative in utilizing the interventions, and the autonomous maintenance of intervention progress during the post-

Figure 15 Four Hypothetical Treatment and Outcome Response Types in Systematic Parent Training

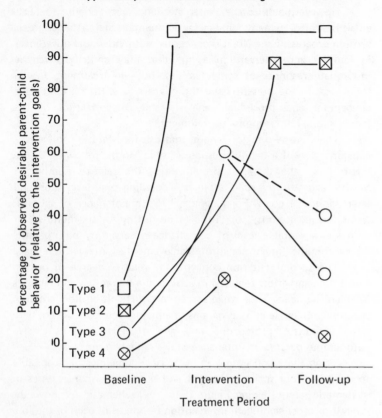

treatment period. The JM case (Case No. 1, Chapter 14), in which the parents made extremely prompt, effective and lasting changes in the family interaction, illustrates the reduced professional time and effort requirements in the Type 1 family. Also, the KC family (Case No. 4, Chapter 14) made an overall Type 1 response, based on the findings that Kathy and her mother responded almost immediately to every intervention used even though the initial problems were judged to be severe. Thus while the overall professional time required was great due to the need for hospitalization, the rapid and lasting effectiveness of the mother's and child's response was unambiguous and uninterrupted.

As both the JM and KC cases demonstrate, the parent training time required in Type 1 is about twenty hours or less. In some cases, as the flo-chart on page 10 shows, the treatment can be successful after Interventions I and II have been applied so that the time required may be less than ten or twelve hours.

Type 2. In the second type of treatment and outcome response the *end result* is observably the same as in Type 1, although minor complications and parental doubts about the improvements may at times persist. The hallmark in Type 2 is the occurrence at several points in the treatment of interference factors that require the therapist to provide either extensive repetition of parent training procedures (Interventions I-IV) or to utilize other, more complex procedures such as concomitant parent counseling (see Chapters 12 and 13), marital therapy, or individual treatment for one or both parents.

A large percentage of cases seen in many child clinic settings fall into Type 2 (45% from samples at UCLA), and usually the therapist's parent training time exceeds twenty hours. Often the full repertoire of systematic parent training procedures is required to achieve and maintain successful treatment. Perhaps for that reason therapists often judge the Type 2 families to be both challenging and rewarding because their hard work "pays off" in the end. Figure 15 shows the observed treatment course in the Type 2 families as reflected in the therapist's records. The curve shows the typically delayed but successful goal attainments, although the therapist's "extra" efforts may at times be directed toward maintenance issues when the family makes a good initial response.

In Chapter 14, both Case No. 2 (the GW family) and No. 3 (the TF family) illustrate the increased parent training time required and the long-term positive results. In both cases the mothers doubted their own abilities, even in follow-up, *despite their excellent progress*. The case of Tommy F (No. 3) also shows the importance of the father's role in supporting the mother's often difficult experience in applying the home interventions. Case No. 4 could be included here on the basis of the total therapist efforts required, and this case also illustrates the overlap between Types 1 and 2.

Types 1 and 2, then, comprise the majority of cases (60% in several UCLA samples) usually seen in child clinics, and while complex treatments may at times be required, they have the common, long-term positive results. However, the professional time and effort required to achieve and maintain success in these families may vary considerably in different clinics.

Type 3. The Type 3 response to intervention is, in a large sense, the focus of this Issue since its defining characteristic is the *maintenance* *problem.* While Types 1 and 2 require various efforts, the maintenance of progress is almost always accomplished. However, in Type 3, as the hypothetical curve in Figure 15 shows, the gains achieved during the intervention are poorly maintained after treatment. Also, the progress made is usually less than that observed in Types 1 and 2 because of the parents' erratic response to the therapist's suggestions. Greater than 25% of the families seen in the clinic may be in the Type 3 category. The dashed line in Figure 15 is added to show how some of the treatment gains in this group can be maintained by long-term maintenance support contingencies. Several available support procedures which can be modestly fruitful follow.

1. Early detection of the likelihood of poor posttreatment maintenance so that specific environmental supports can be planned in advance. The best available predictor of Type 3 is probably the parental response during the regular interventions. Thus, if there are interruptions in the treatment progress caused by the parents' failure to follow the therapist's suggestions which are serious enough to require parent counseling, the therapist should probably assume that more intensive efforts and structure will be necessary in the postintervention *maintenance training* sessions. This suggestion would apply to Type 2 families as well as those in Type 3.

2. Individual training of the parent(s), where the focus is on improved discrimination of environmental and personal response-produced *cues.* Even marginally motivated parents can learn to recognize external and internal stimuli that produce counterproductive parental and family responses, and then learn to use these cues to inhibit the behavior. They can also identify cues which can serve as self-initiated *prompts* to perform responses which engender positive interactions. For example, as was discussed in Chapter 7, parents can acquire the skill of "covert labeling," in which they recognize stimuli that usually elicit negative or excessive responses, and inhibit the response by literally "thinking before responding" with the aid of a cognitive label or cue. Also, many difficult parents can be trained to think of their children's behavior in *strict categories* so that there are concrete, salient, perceptual cues for responding with positive attention. Thus the parent's conditioned thought "I like that response" or observation of "five minutes of nonnegative interaction with sibling" can become cues to deliver praise. Bandura (1969), Cautela (1969), and

Mahoney and Thoresen (1974) have discussed a number of procedures for the stabilization of behavioral improvements through the development of these kinds of "self-regulatory" and "self-control" procedures. These parental self-regulatory procedures can also be applied in many cases to the referred child so that he or she may also develop *self*-praising or inhibitory habits.

3. Applying *external* supportive procedures, such as long-term public HCP and home "rules"; training siblings in the home to prompt the parent's response, or to provide the contingencies themselves; and utilizing paraprofessional volunteers, neighbors, and previous parent training "graduates" who can provide support and even advice about maintaining intervention achievements. In some communities weekly informal church or business meetings can provide the opportunity for parents to share experiences and ideas which can help them continue their progress, and even to solve new problems using their collective parent training skills. The therapist should of course be available to these paraprofessional "maintenance agents" as well as to the parents when needed.

Using these procedures, the therapist can begin to improve the durability of effective systematic parent training for Type 3 families. The clinical and research endeavor to improve the success rate of an agency by developing techniques which induce Type 3 families to function like those in Type 2 is one of considerable importance in every treatment agency.

Type 4. The final major response type in systematic parent training is observed in families whose parents and children make little or no response to the interventions even with considerable professional time and effort, or those whose behavior becomes worse. In several UCLA samples, about 10 to 15% of the families are in this category. The assessment of outcome in both Types 3 and 4 is often difficult to evaluate since the negative nature of the parents' response is such that few records are kept or brought in for analysis; most of the available information on Type 4 families comes from research studies where intensive efforts are made to observe the families with minimal demands on the parents to cooperate. In the usual clinic experience many Type 4 families terminate prior to establishing a treatment record, and may resist most of the therapist's attempts to alter the family system, although the parents may persist in demanding relief from a disturbing child. Therapists who have worked with Type 4 families often note that systematic parent training is inappropriate as the initial treatment modality, and more intensive marital and individual therapies are indicated, either singularly or concomitant with highly structured and contingent parent training procedures.

In order to maintain the gains in the Type 4 family, all the suggestions and available procedures used for Type 3 families should be applied with an even greater degree of monitoring and structuring of the maintenance training procedures.

The maintenance of intervention progress is a major issue in systematic parent training since *the entire determination of successful or unsuccessful treatment depends upon careful follow-up analysis of family functioning.* With the regular collection of follow-up data, *accountability* in parent training programs will no longer be based upon demonstrations of treatment-induced change, but rather upon long-term maintenance when the therapist's role has ended or at least has become minimal.

To accomplish this new criterion of accountability, the therapist should obtain the specific, relevant follow-up information by reinstating the baseline measures and carefully comparing the pre- and posttreatment records whenever possible. Also, therapists should develop systems of outcome criteria for their own treatment populations such as those presented in this Issue so that replication, validation, and prediction studies are possible. The ultimate value for the community of mental health procedures such as systematic parent training will depend upon these public demonstrations of interventions that are not only efficient but have enduring effectiveness.

ISSUE NO. 4: INDIVIDUAL DIFFERENCES IN SYSTEMATIC PARENT TRAINING

The original impetus for this manual was the observed need to systematize the available parent training procedures so that each family coming into the clinic with a problem child could receive treatment that was maximally tailored to their particular needs. However, it was apparent that the realization of such a sophisticated goal would depend first upon the development of objective outcome criteria.

In the previous Issue it was argued that four relatively independent outcome types could be operationalized according to the observed behavior change in the family and the professional time and effort necessary to produce the change. Assuming that the avail-able data warrants such a four-way outcome system, it then becomes important to attempt to isolate the "active ingredients" in systematic parent training which contribute to or determine the outcome types of families following intervention. The possible sources of variance contributing to treatment outcome are many and complex. In Chapter 3 the primary desirable clinic, therapist and family characteristics were briefly described, and it was suggested that each of these variables is important in the family's treatment response. The clinic must explicitly support directive family treatments such as systematic parent training; therapists must be sensitive, competent clinicians who can be assertive in applying the available intervention technologies; and at least one parent must be responsive to the therapist's suggestions. In this Issue several important factors are discussed, with the emphasis on the individual characteristics of the parents.

Individual Differences in Parents. The flo-chart on page 10, and its application to the cases in Chapter 14, illustrates the individualized use of the available interventions based on the therapist's weekly judgment of the child's or parents' relative progress. Families with responsive parents require relatively little professional time and effort to begin follow-up, while other families require repeated flo-chart procedures at considerable expense before a satisfactory level of desirable family interaction is achieved.

In Issue No. 3, a major defining criterion of a family response type was presented as the parents' response to the therapist's suggestions, which presumably determined the degree of desirable behavior change achieved. In short, it was assumed that when the parents cooperate with the therapist, the correct application of the flo-chart model is sufficient at least to generate a Type 1, 2 or 3 response; and if they have congruent attitudes with the therapist and are committed to self-regulated maintenance of progress, they can also make a Type 1 or 2 "success" response.

This hypothesized close relationship between the parents' individual responsiveness to the therapist's suggestions and the treatment outcome has considerable potential importance in the development of the intervention system presented in this manual and warrants careful examination.

Components of Parental Responsiveness. There are a number of personality and other individual factors which influence how parents respond to parent training as well as to other demands in their daily life. Two individual characteristics which will be discussed here are parental attitudes and parental initiative.

Parental Attitudes. The importance of parental attitudes in systematic parent training has been repeatedly emphasized in this manual. Attitudes have been discussed as important in child rearing styles, recognizing and labeling child deviance, and as an interfering or facilitating factor in the intervention programs. In this Issue the focus is on parental attitudes as a major determinant of the parents' individual response pattern to the therapist's suggestions. Parental attitudes as a factor influencing treatment outcome is relevant in terms of the valence and flexibility of the attitudes. *Valence* concerns the relative degree of the parents' verbalized optimism or pessimism as well as other observations and indications of their ability to influence the child prior to, during and after intervention. The *flexibility* of the attitudes reflects the degree of the therapist's influence required to alter the attitudes.

To a large extent valence and flexibility of the parents' attitudes determine and are determined by the course of treatment in systematic parent training. It is not uncommon prior to treatment to see a parent or parents who have negative attitudes about their child and perhaps the clinic, the therapist, and perhaps themselves as well, but who alter their attitudes during treatment. Also, while parental attitudes with negative valence are especially important if they are also inflexible, *extreme* parental pessimism is significant, due to the professional efforts required, even when it can be changed. Likewise, some parents show few indications of pessimism or negative attitudes in their descriptions of the referred child, but prove to be almost completely rigid about their interpretation of and response to their child's behavior. A problem with the flexibility dimension of attitudes is that, unlike the valence dimension, the therapist usually only becomes aware of the parents' rigid attitudes after considerable intervention efforts have already been made.

If professional time and efforts increase when rigid, negative attitudes exist, it is also important to note that positive and flexible attitudes about treatment and their children *facilitate* the parents' acquisition and implementation of home intervention procedures. In most of the cases seen in clinics, extreme rigid and negative attitudes do not preclude successful treatment, but they do play an important role in the family's individual response characteristics. Each of the cases presented in Chapter 14 illustrates in different ways the role of parental attitudes.

In Case No. 1, Mrs. M was extremely concerned and pessimistic about John's potential, based on his very poor and erratic adjustment, but she readily modified her views following John's demonstrated adequate behavior. By follow-up she was openly optimistic about her son's future. In Case No. 2, Mrs. W responded rapidly to the therapist's suggestions and gradually became more optimistic about George, but faced a serious struggle with her relatives and future husband concerning their relatively rigid attitudes about child rearing, which were at odds with the goals of systematic parent training. Her perseverance and initiative in modifying their views were seen as a major element in the maintenance of George's behavior. In Cases No. 3 and No. 4, Mrs. F and Mrs. C both verbalized very negative preintervention attitudes about their children and their own ability to change or improve the home problems. Mrs. F, like Mrs. M in Case No. 1, was initially convinced that her son was "brain damaged" but, unlike Mrs. M, she clung to that view even after treatment. In her case, however, she was flexible and positive enough about her overall ability to influence Tommy, with the support of her husband, to achieve nearly all of the intervention goals. Mrs. C (Case No. 4), as noted in Issue No. 3, showed characteristics of both outcome Types 1 and 2, but was impressive in her rapid, total and lasting attitude change about Kathy.

All parents have some kind of *theory of their child,* made up of attitudes, feelings, behavioral expectancies and evaluation guidelines which determines, to a significant degree, how they respond in daily family interaction. It appears to matter less that attitudes are negative in valence than inflexible and unresponsive. Parental attitudes interact dynamically with the child's attitudes and with the behavior they observe in others and in themselves.

Parental Initiative. Parental initiative, for the purposes of this manual, is defined as any behavior initiated by the parents, without the specific direction of the therapist, that is consistent with the family's intervention goals. Of all the observable characteristics of Type 1 and 2 families that are present *during the interventions,* parental initiative in implementing and amplifying the therapist's suggestions is the most striking and common. It is striking because of the reinforcing effect on the therapist when the parents are observed to function appropriately and independently in ways that the therapist likes and, in many cases, can learn from. The observation of parental initiative reminds the therapist that it is parents, not therapists or interventions, who are the innovators in effective child care and development. The development of a program for the treatment of disturbing interaction is largely based on the therapist's observations of effective family functioning, and thus on the parents' initiatives in family problem solving.

The determination of parental initiative in any given family can only be made after observing the parent over a period of time. However, as was emphasized in each intervention in this manual, parents always have opportunities to take the therapist's suggestions and go forward on their own. Once it is observed that the parents' independent judgments and behaviors repeatedly approximate those of the therapist, this finding should become an explicit issue of each training session. The therapist should specify and acknowledge each instance of the parents' appropriate autonomous behavior. With these families "maintenance training" can begin almost immediately in the treatment since the therapist can begin to depend on the parents' competent responsiveness to his suggestions as soon as it is established that the parents possess basic skills. Thus the treatment response is accelerated and at the same time the therapist can function in the preferred role of family consultant rather than intervention agent.

Parental initiative is of course a complex quality and is observed in different degrees in different parents and even within the same parent over time. However, therapists continue to observe that parents who exhibit initiative do better in their home application than those who require constant, explicit direction by the therapist. In the cases in Chapter 14, referred to also in the preceding discussion about attitudes, it was noted that in each family, except possibly Case No. 3, the parents' initiative was an important variable.

In Case No. 1, Mrs. M personally and correctly applied the HCP to problems other than those in the therapist's immediate treatment plan, and made a number of other useful innovations. In Case No. 2, Mrs. W showed initiative both in presenting the intervention plan to her resistant family, and in educating the therapist about the importance, in many cases, of maintaining public HCP charts. In Case No. 4, Mrs. C's initiative was evident in her excellent application of home interventions when Kathy came home from the hospital each weekend, and especially in the follow-up assessment when her home records were far more complete and informative than the therapists requested.

Case No. 3 also indicates the importance of initiative, although by its conspicuous absence. Mrs. F was so tense and worried throughout the treatment that she was overly dependent on the therapists for direction, indicating that *initiative behaviors require a degree of child-directed commitment by the parent* which is not inhibited by negative emotional arousal.

Both parental initiative and positive, flexible attitudes, then, are highly desirable individual characteristics of parents that can facilitate their response to treatment and thus reduce the professional time and efforts required. However, this discussion is not meant to be exhaustive, and there are undoubtedly other important individual differences in parents, children, therapists, and treatment settings that contribute immeasurably to the treatment and outcome responses of different families.

Various methods and modalities for influencing parental behavior directly and indirectly have been discussed in this manual. As has been noted, the alteration of qualitative, personality-related characteristics such as attitudes and initiative often involve the parents' implicit *motivation* and *sense of commitment* toward changing themselves and their families. Thus the issue for the intervention agent often becomes one of understanding and dealing with the parents' "internalization" of the procedures, principles and commitments necessary for them to function effectively without the necessity of the situational contingencies suggested in this manual. In clinical settings it is commonly argued that psychoanalytically oriented and other long-term, complex therapies are required to change complex but essential qualities such as the parents' motivation, attitudes, and internalization of the therapist's values in resistant individuals. However, the nature of such intensive and lengthy treatments is such that (a) little empirical evidence is gathered to support (or not support) their use, and (b) many clinics do not have the resources or the time to apply them for the population seeking help.

Future efforts to develop the technology necessary to improve parental motivation and commitment directly within a reasonable period may succeed in providing a means for helping parents who do not possess the facilitating attitudes and initiatives discussed here. However, until such technology is available, the parent training therapist must continue to emphasize the importance of interventions based upon effectiveness, efficiency, and accountability.

ISSUE NO. 5: FUTURE ISSUES IN SYSTEMATIC PARENT TRAINING

Previous Issues in this chapter have concerned ongoing considerations and emphases which help to provide a foundation for the principles and procedures discussed in this manual. This Issue briefly presents possibilities for further enhancement of the efficient application of systematic parent training.

The Development of a Prediction Model. Early in this manual it was emphasized that, at the current state of development in systematic parent training, the *criterion model* for applying the interventions should be used. Each family begins at the first stage of the flo-chart procedures and continues until some resolution of the presenting problems is reached, or until the family terminates treatment. At present this method is the recommended one because it cautiously and completely allows the therapist to treat the parent-child problems using currently established procedures. However, following the development of tentative outcome criterion Types, in which individual families are grouped according to common outcome responses, it becomes a feasible *research goal* to attempt to identify the *preintervention correlates* of a given family's outcome response Type for prediction purposes. Accurate preintervention prediction of outcome would allow increased *effectiveness* and *efficiency* of parent training procedures since those procedures with a relatively high probability of success would be applied *first* in a family's treatment. In this way the family could better utilize the particular intervention sequence chosen and, by deferring low pay-off interventions, the required professional time and effort and family expense would be reduced. For example, many parents who previously labored through the early interventions and finally were able to respond to concomitant parent counseling or individual treatment should probably have received the intense treatments first. Other families appear to make adequate responses during treatment but regress in follow-up (Type 3), putting the therapist again in the role of "repairman" rather than "prevention consultant." Still other families appear, following many screening procedures, to require intensive treatment initially, or to suffer from clinic policies which require each family to undergo extensive evaluation and treatment. In these cases accurate prediction of a Type 1 or even a Type 2 response would allow the family to receive less intensive interventions, such as Interventions I through III, without extensive diagnostic or treatment procedures.

An accurate prediction model would allow efficient treatment at its fullest since both *excessive* and *inadequate* professional efforts would be reduced. An immediate effect of improved efficiency would be the increased accessibility of parent training for families in the community. The clinic or treatment agency staff would be able to better allot their time so that in many cases Type 1 and 2 families could be treated in *groups,* with increased utilization of paraprofessional staff, while the professional staff would be available for the intensive efforts required in many Type 3 and Type 4 families.

There are many methodological and ethical problems in the development and application of pretreatment prediction information, and research in this area is only in the beginning stages (Miller and Gottlieb, 1974). Methodological problems concern the difficult empirical task of isolating critical preintervention correlates of a family's outcome response Type, and the necessity for cross-validation evidence supporting the predictions, at least within the population treated. Ethical issues relate to the problems of faulty prediction, and the need to use the predictor *to estimate the efforts required to help individual families* rather than to make decisions about which families to treat or not to treat. However, as noted, there are many potential benefits of appropriately applied, accurate prediction procedures for community intervention agents and agencies, and this area warrants increased attention.

The Utilization of Nonprofessionals in Systematic Parent Training. The primary rationale for developing para- and nonprofessional individuals to assist intervention agents in parent training programs is clear: there are not enough professionals to go around. In many of the intervention procedures discussed in this manual, nonprofessionals have been alluded to as potential resources for facilitating the application of treatment. Research on the present and potential effectiveness of these resources should be an important priority in agencies which provide parent training programs. Currently, nonprofessionals can serve an important role by performing the following kinds of specific functions:

1. Providing transportation assistance and even babysitting service for many families who would not otherwise be able to attend the training sessions.

2. Providing assistance in the screening procedures by organizing and planning family appointment details, administering and scoring questionnaire forms, preparing and organizing the family's individual case file, and keeping records of events and professional time utilized.

3. Helping to collect and summarize baseline information by learning clinic and home observation skills; providing useful anecdotal material and informal notes in observation sessions when the therapist is absent; making graphs and charts for the therapist's and family's use.

4. Functioning as observers and recorders of the process and transactions of the parents' individual or group sessions.

5. Facilitating the parents' complete and successful utilization of the therapist's *homework* assignments. Often difficult family problems require daily contact in the initial stages of home intervention, e.g., in the form of telephone conversations in which prompts are given to the parents and daily parent records are reported.

6. Actually providing direct therapy assistance in rare cases where the volunteer or nonprofessional is a successful parent training "graduate" or other well-trained individual who can serve as a kind of "maintenance consultant" for other families, under the professional therapist's supervision. These assistants can provide supportive and corrective inputs to many families experiencing the daily problems of maintaining treatment progress and, if the parents and "consultant" happen to be neighbors, it is likely that the assistance provided would be more direct and relevant than that from many therapists. Likewise, in rare cases certain nonprofessionals are capable of dealing with *brief parent counseling* issues in regular clinic sessions.

It will be increasingly important for the future development of parent training programs to research and develop the fullest use of community resources, many of which, to date, are unrealized and even unknown. It has been estimated that fewer than 25% of the families seeking help for adjustment disturbances come to mental health professionals and agencies (Rosenblum, 1970). The other 75% either seek relief from available community resources or seek no relief. By further developing the role of nonprofessional assistants, and by carrying the available technology of parent training and family development *to the available resources,* still larger segments of the community will profit from treatment.

The Need for Prevention Research. Much has been written about the prevention of emotional and behavioral problems, and it has been often noted in this manual that successful parent training is successful in part because it provides *general parenting skills* which can attenuate the expected problems of family and child development. As available treatments become more systematic and outcome-oriented, it is important to begin subjecting them to the ultimate test of accountability, effectiveness and efficiency; that is, demonstrating that communities applying the available technology show reduced incidences of serious child adjustment disorders.

As an experimental project, for example, several similar, stable communities could be chosen and baseline data collected on the current incidence and nature of reported child and family disturbances. Then, treatment programs based upon systematic parent training procedures could be instituted in randomly chosen community child guidance centers. As separate or combined variables, the schools in the community could institute courses (for credit) in the high schools for instruction in social learning principles and pre-family counseling, and even provide more direct and intensive parent planning for those people electing to enhance their parent skills. Also, the community clinic or school personnel could arrange "effective parenting workshops" for groups of parents of nursery, day-care, and elementary school children. Then careful quantitative and qualitative follow-up studies could be made at five- and ten-year intervals, and the results compared with the neighboring "control" communities that would presumably have continued to use relatively nonsystematic procedures without emphasizing preventive educational projects. With the proper methodological and project design cautions, the results of such prevention studies would provide an estimate of the *efficacy* of at least one prevention model. Other models, separate and in combination with the social learning programs, could provide additional valuable information.

Prevention has too long been an informal standard for mental health programs. As treatments become systematic, so should prevention programs. In this way the ultimate value of an intervention model can relate to the long-term increased happiness and productivity of families in the community as a whole.

SIXTEEN / CONCLUSION

In this manual the attempt has been made to describe interventions which can facilitate the clinician's practice of child therapy in a sufficiently organized manner to allow the systematic application and assessment of the procedures in various treatment settings. Although systematic parent training is a complex and often difficult enterprise, there are four basic assumptions upon which this approach rests and which can be usefully restated here:

1. Reasonably well-adjusted and happy families in the community are characterized by, among other attributes, the presence of interactions that are largely consistent, contingent and positive.

2. With these characteristics of effective family functioning as training goals, the systematic application of the available technology of parent training can provide effective and efficient treatment for many families with disturbing children.

3. Most parents are positively reinforced by improvements in their children and in their family's interactions, and work to produce and maintain intervention progress.

4. Without the parents' cooperation and commitment to positive family change, the professional time and effort requirements for successful training increase.

There are important limitations of systematic parent training, and it has been noted that this treatment approach is not for all families and children. Disturbing children need relationships as well as programs; and when parent training cannot or does not improve the parent-child interactions necessary for the child's development of social and relationship skills, problems may continue or new problems may arise and require additional treatments. Thus while this manual has placed relative emphasis on the *mechanical* aspects of parent-child interaction, the therapist should not ignore the *relation-ship* variables in parent training. Specifically, the therapist should attend to the interpersonal *and* educational properties of the treatment, especially when the parents fail to "cooperate" and accept the therapist's values. Likewise, the parents should be trained not only to improve their children's behavior, but also to promote their children's individualized and personal development.

It is a problem with current parent training methodologies that children, who are the ultimate focus of the treatment, are given little opportunity for making inputs into the programs that directly affect them. In future programs, it will perhaps be shown that children can have a more active role at an earlier age than currently emphasized.

Another problem with parent training occurs on the upper chronological side of child development: namely, the lack of emphasis in manuals like this on the treatment of *adolescent* problems. Younger children have the advantage of fewer, more stable environmental dispensers of their critical reinforcers who can be positively influenced by intervention technologies such as those described here. Older children and adolescents, on the other hand, have their behavior stimulated and reinforced by less accessible internal (complex fantasies and maturational phenomena) and external (peer) factors. It is probably true that for older children active involvement in the treatment, and the therapist's relationship-building skills are *especially* important.

An additional limitation of this manual is unavoidable due to the nature of the medium. An attempt has been made to describe the conceptual details of systematic parent training as well as the means for applying the procedures. However, it is a major shortcoming that the full excitement and challenge of parent training could not be presented here. These *media* variables are easily as important as the *content* of the interventions, and yet it must be left to the reader to "turn on" to parent training and *translate* these procedures into effective clinical practice.

BIBLIOGRAPHY

Amundson, M. J., Miller, W. H., and Auerbach, D. The effects of automated videotape feedback training on mother-child interaction in the home. Unpublished doctoral dissertation, University of California, Los Angeles, 1974.

Bandura, A. *Principles of behavior modification.* New York: Holt, Rinehart and Winston, 1969.

Bates, J. The effects of a child's imitation vs. non-imitation on adults' verbal and nonverbal positivity. Unpublished doctoral dissertation, University of California, Los Angeles, 1973.

Becker, W. *Parents are teachers: A child management program.* Champaign, IL: Research Press, 1971.

Behrens, E. M. Individual vs. group training of parents in behavior modification techniques. Unpublished master's thesis, University of Utah, 1970.

Binet, E. and Anthony, J. *The Binet-Anthony Family Relations Test.* London: National Foundation for Educational Research in England and Wales, 1965.

Berkowitz, B. P. and Graziano, A. M. Training parents as behavior therapists: A review. *Behaviour Research and Therapy,* 1972, *10,* (4), 297-317.

Bernal, M. E. Behavioral feedback in the modification of brat behaviors. *Journal of Nervous and Mental Disease,* 1969, *48,* (4), 375-385.

Bernal, M. E. Training parents in child management. In R. Bradfield (Ed.), *Behavioral modification of learning disabilities.* San Rafael, CA: Academic Therapy Publications, 1971.

Bernal, M. E. *Training social agents in behavior modification,* unpublished paper, 1974.

Bernstein, D. A. and Borkovec, T. D. *Progressive relaxation training: A manual for the helping professions.* Champaign, IL: Research Press, 1973.

Buckley, N. and Walker, H. *Modifying classroom behavior: A manual of procedure for classroom teachers.* Champaign, IL: Research Press, 1970.

Cautela, J. Behavior therapy and self-control: Techniques and implications. In C. Franks (Ed.), *Behavior therapy: Appraisal and status.* New York: McGraw-Hill, 1969.

Crandall, V. C., Good, S., and Crandall, U. J. The reinforcement effects of adult reaction and non-reactions on children's achievement expectations: A replication. *Child Development,* 1964, *35,* 485-497.

Creak, E. M. Childhood psychosis: A review of 100 cases. *British Journal of Psychiatry,* 1963, *109,* 84-89.

Davids, A., Ryant, R., and Salvatore, P. D. Effectiveness of residential treatment for psychotic and other disturbed children. *American Journal of Orthopsychiatry,* 1968, *38,* 469-475.

Dische, S. Management of enuresis. *British Medical Journal,* 1971, *2,* 33-36.

Eaton, L. and Menolascino, F. J. Psychotic reactions of childhood. *American Journal of Orthopsychiatry,* 1967, *38,* 469-475.

Eisenberg, L. and Gruenberg, E. M. The current status of secondary prevention in child psychiatry. *American Journal of Orthopsychiatry,* 1961, *31,* 355-367.

Ferster, C. B. and Simons, J. Behavior therapy with children. *The Psychological Record,* 1966, *16,* 65-71.

Fisher, D. People helping people. Paper delivered at the Fifth Annual Southern California Conference on Behavior Modification. Los Angeles, October 25-26, 1973.

Galloway, C. and Galloway, K. Parent groups with a focus on precise behavior management. *IMRID Paper and Reports, Vol. 2.* Nashville: George Peabody College, J. F. Kennedy Center, 1971.

Gelfand, D. M. and Hartmann, D. P. Behavior therapy with children: A review and evaluation of research methodology. *Psychological Bulletin,* 1968, *69,* (3), 205-215.

Gendlin, E. T. and Rychak, J. F. Psychotherapeutic processes. *Annual Review of Psychology,* 1970, *21,* 148-189.

Gottschalk, L. A., Mayerson, P. and Gottlieb, A. Prediction and evaluation of outcome in an emergency brief psychotherapy clinic. *The Journal of Nervous and Mental Disease,* 1967, *144,* (2), 77-96.

Guilbert, P. and Miller, W. H. The use of behavior therapy with an hyperactive child. In *Behavior Therapy: Praktische und theoretische Aspekte.* European Association for Behaviour Therapy and Modification, First Meeting, 1971, Munich. Munich: Urban and Schwarzenberg, 1973.

Hathaway, S. R. and McKinley, J. C. *The Minnesota Multiphasic Personality Inventory.* New York: The Psychological Corporation, 1943.

Hawkins, R. P., Peterson, R. F., Schweid, E. and Bijou, S. W. Behavior therapy in the home: Amelioration of problem parent-child relations with the parent in a therapeutic role. *Journal of Experimental Child Psychology,* 1966, *4,* 99-107.

Hirsch, I. S. Training mothers in groups as reinforcement therapists for their own children. *Dissertation Abstracts,* 1968, *28,* (11-B), 4756.

Hirsch, I. S. and Walder, L. Training mothers in groups as reinforcement therapists for their own children. *Proceedings of the 77th Annual Convention of the American Psychological Association,* 1969, *4,* (2), 561-562.

Homme, L. et al. *How to use contingency contracting in the classroom.* Champaign, IL: Research Press, 1970.

Hood-Williams, J. The results of psychotherapy with children. A re-evaluation. *Journal of Consulting Psychology,* 1960, *24,* (1), 84-88.

Howard, O. F. Teaching a class of parents as reinforcement therapists to treat their own children. Paper presented at the Annual Meeting of the Southeastern Psychological Association, Louisville, Kentucky, 1970.

Humphreys, J. Behavioral therapy with children: An experimental evaluation. Unpublished doctoral dissertation, University of London, 1966. (Cited in S. Rachman, *Effects of psychotherapy.* New York: Pergamon Press, 1971.)

Johnson, S. A. A comparison of mother versus child groups and traditional versus behavior modification procedures in the "treatment" of disobedient children. *Dissertation Abstracts,* 1970, *31,* (5-B), 2989.

Kelman, H. C. Attitudes are alive and well and gainfully employed in the sphere of action. *American Psychologist,* May 1974, *5,* (29), 310-324.

Levitt, E. E. Results of psychotherapy with children: An evaluation. *Journal of Consulting Psychology,* 1957, *21,* 189-196.

Levitt, E. E. Psychotherapy with children: A further evaluation. *Behaviour Research and Therapy,* 1963, *1,* (1) 45-51.

Liberman, R. P., King, L. W., DeRisi, W. and McCann, M. *Personal effectiveness: Guiding people to assert themselves and improve their social skills.* Champaign, IL: Research Press, 1975.

Lieberman, S. The effects of changes in roles on the attitudes of role occupants. *Human Relations,* 1956, *9,* 385-402.

Link, W. E. Psychotherapy outcome in the treatment of hyperaggressive boys: A comparison of behavioristic and traditional therapy techniques. *Dissertation Abstracts,* 1968, *29,* (6-B), 2205.

Lobitz, G. Normal versus deviant children: A multimethod comparison. Unpublished doctoral dissertation, University of Oregon, Eugene, 1973.

Locke, H. J. and Wallace, K. M. Short marital-adjustment and prediction tests: Their reliability and validity. *Journal of Marriage and Family Living,* 1959, *21,* 251-255.

Luborsky, L., Chandler, M., Auerbach, A., Cohen, J., and Bachrach, H. M. Factors influencing the outcome of psychotherapy: A review of quantitative research. *Psychological Bulletin,* 1971, *75,* (3), 145-185.

Mahoney, M. J. and Thoresen, C. E. *Self-Control: Power to the person.* Monterey, CA: Brooks, Cole, 1974.

Miller, W. H. and Gottlieb, F. Predicting behavioral treatment outcome in disturbed children: A preliminary report on the responsivity index of parents (RIP). *Behavior Therapy,* 1974, *5,* (2), 210-214.

O'Leary, D. K., O'Leary, S., and Becker, W. C. Modification of a deviant sibling interaction pattern in the home. *Behaviour Research and Therapy,* 1967, *5,* 113-120.

Patterson, G.R. Behavioral techniques based upon social learning: An additional base for developing behavior modification technologies. In C. M. Franks (Ed.), *Behavior therapy: Appraisal and status.* New York: McGraw-Hill, 1969.

Patterson, G. R. *Families: Applications of social learning to family life.* Champaign, IL: Research Press, 1971.

Patterson, G. R. Changing behaviors in the process of parenting. Paper presented at the Sixth Banff International Conference on Behavior Modification, Banff, Alberta, April, 1974.

Patterson, G. R. Follow-up evaluations of a program for parents retraining their aggressive boys. Paper presented for Jewish General Hospital and McGill University. Third Annual Symposium, Montreal, Canada, November, 1972.

Patterson, G. R. and Cobb, J. A. A dyadic analysis of "aggressive" behaviors: An additional step toward a theory of aggression. In J. P. Hill (Ed.), *Proceedings of the Fifth Minnesota Symposia on Child Psychology. Vol. V.* Minneapolis: University of Minnesota, 1971.

Patterson, G. R., Cobb, J. A. and Ray, R. S. A social engineering technology for retraining the families of aggressive boys. In H. E. Adams and I. P. Unikel (Eds.), *Issues and trends in behavior therapy.* Springfield, IL: C. C. Thomas, 1973.

Patterson, G. R. and Fagot, B. I. Selective responsiveness to social and deviant behavior in children. *The Psychological Record,* 1967, *17,* 369-378.

Patterson, G. R. and Gullion, E. *Living with children: New methods for parents and teachers.* Champaign, IL: Research Press, 1968.

Patterson, G. R., Ray, R. S. and Shaw, D. A. Direct intervention in families of deviant children. *Oregon Research Institute Research Bulletin,* 1969, *8,* No. 9.

Pawlicki, R. Behavior therapy research with children: A critical review. *Canadian Journal of Behavioral Science,* 1970, *2,* (3), 163-173.

Peine, H. A. Effects of training models on the modification of parent behavior. *Dissertation Abstracts,* 1971, *32,* (3-A), 1341.

Rachman, S. *Effects of psychotherapy.* New York: Pergamon Press, 1971.

Raush, H. Interaction sequences. *Journal of Personality and Social Psychology,* 1965, *2,* 487-499.

Rimm, D. C. and Masters, J. C. *Behavior therapy: Techniques and empirical findings.* New York: Academic Press, 1974.

Rondell, F. and Michaels, R. *The adopted child.* New York: Crown Publishers, Inc., 1965.

Rose, S. D. A behavioral approach to the group treatment of parents. *Social Work,* 1969, *14,* (3), 21-29.

Rose, S. D. *Treating children in groups.* San Francisco: Jossey-Bass, 1973.

Rosenblum, G. Can children's services flourish in a comprehensive community mental health center program? In S. Chess and A. Thomas (Eds.), *Annual progress in child psychiatry and child development.* New York: Brunner-Mazel, 1970.

Rosenthal, D. and Frank, J. D. Psychotherapy and the placebo effect. *Psychological Bulletin,* 1956, *53,* (4), 294-302.

Ryback, D., and Staats, A. W. Parents as behavior therapy technicians in treating reading deficits (dyslexia). *Journal of Behavior Therapy and Experimental Psychiatry,* 1970, *1,* (2), 109-119.

Scott, P. M., Burton, R., and Yarrow, M. R. Social reinforcement under natural conditions. *Child Development,* 1967, *38,* 53-63.

Shaw, D. A. Family maintenance schedules for deviant behavior. Unpublished doctoral dissertation, University of Oregon, 1971.

Sines, J. O., Pauker, J. D., Sines, L. K., and Owen, D. R. Identification of clinically relevant dimensions of children's behavior. *Journal of Consulting and Clinical Psychology,* 1969, *33,* (6), 728-734.

Stuart, R. Operant-interpersonal treatment for marital discord. *Journal of Consulting and Clinical Psychology,* 1969, *3,* (6), 675-682.

Stuart, R. and Lederer, W. *How to make a bad marriage good and a good marriage better.* New York: W. W. Norton and Co. In press.

Ullmann, L. P. and Krasner, L. (Eds.). *Case studies in behavior modification.* New York: Holt, Rinehart and Winston, 1965.

Wahl, G., Johnson, S., Johansson, S. and Martin, S. An operant analysis of child-family interaction. *Behavior Therapy,* 1974, *5,* (1), 64-78.

Walker, H. I. Placebo versus social learning effects in parent training procedures designed to alter the behaviors of aggressive boys. Unpublished doctoral dissertation, University of Oregon, 1971.

Werry, J. S. and Wollersheim, J. P. Behavior therapy with children: A broad overview. *Journal of the American Academy of Psychiatry,* 1967, *6,* 346-370.

Whaley, D. L. and Malott, R. W. *Elementary principles of behavior.* New York: Appleton-Century-Crofts, 1971.

White, G., Nielsen, G., and Johnson, S. Time out duration and the suppression of deviant behavior in children. *Journal of Applied Behavior Analysis,* 1972, *5,* (2), 111-120.

Wills, T. A., Weiss, R. L., and Patterson, G. R. A behavioral analysis of the determinants of marital satisfaction. *Journal of Consulting and Clinical Psychology,* 1974, *42,* (6), 802-811.

Wiltz, N. A. Modification of behaviors of deviant boys through parent participation in a group technique. Unpublished doctoral dissertation, University of Oregon, 1969.

Wiltz, N. A. and Patterson, G. R. An evaluation of parent training procedures designed to alter inappropriate aggressive behavior of boys. *Behavior Therapy,* 1974, *5,* (2), 215-221.

Wolpe, J. *Psychotherapy by reciprocal inhibition.* Stanford, CA: Stanford University Press, 1958.